REVOLUTION
IN THE MAILBOX

REVOLUTION
IN THE MAILBOX

HOW DIRECT MAIL FUNDRAISING IS CHANGING THE FACE OF AMERICAN
SOCIETY—AND HOW YOUR ORGANIZATION CAN BENEFIT

MAL WARWICK

STRATHMOOR
PRESS

100 STRATHMOOR DRIVE • BERKELEY, CA 94705

Printed in the United States of America

ISBN 0-9624891-0-7

Strathmoor Press
100 Strathmoor Dr.
Berkley, CA 94705

Read This Book . . .

. . . if you serve in a leadership role in a nonprofit organization as executive director, development director, controller, financial manager, marketing director or as a member of the board of trustees.

. . . if you're contemplating a fundraising, development or membership-building program for your organization.

. . . if you contribute money or time to a public interest group or a charity.

. . . if you're managing a political campaign, or running for public office.

. . . if you're involved in public relations or advertising for nonprofit organizations or political campaigns.

. . . if you've taken an interest in the activities of a public interest organization or a political campaign as a reporter, news producer, consultant or student.

. . . or if you simply want to understand better what direct mail fundraising is all about.

In memory of

John George
Florence McDonald
Don Rothenberg

whose life-long dedication to the public interest
is a continuing source of inspiration

Contents

1. The Strange New World of Direct Mail Fundraising

2. Starting Out

3. Anatomy of a Direct Mail Fundraising Package

4. Settling In for the Long Haul

List of Illustrations

The Components of Direct Mail Fundraising Packages

Packages Mailed in One Public Interest Campaign

Packages Mailed for Jesse Jackson in One Month

Acknowledgments

It's all Ron Dellums' fault.

I got into the direct mail business ten years ago to help Congressman Ron Dellums launch a nationwide fundraising campaign. His 1980 reelection race was expected to be difficult. It wasn't. Dellums is now serving his tenth term and chairing both the Congressional Black Caucus and two legislative committees. He won hands down that year, and so did I. Because he had insisted I personally supervise the direct mail consultants we'd hired, I got a taste of direct mail fundraising at its very best — and I was hooked for life.

Since those exhilarating days in the fall of 1979, when I was often forced to stay up until the early hours of the morning to count all the checks rolling into the Dellums campaign, I've worked with hundreds of nonprofit organizations and political committees. My coworkers and I have mailed uncounted millions of letters and raised many tens of millions of dollars to promote the public interest. In the process, I've come to know hundreds of supremely talented individuals who have committed years of their lives to make the world a better place — a list of people far too long to reproduce here. They, my clients, ultimately deserve any credit I may get for writing this book. I've learned far more from them than they from me.

Several of my friends in the public interest community read the manuscript of this book at various stages in its development and offered helpful criticism, sometimes lengthy and detailed. I took all their advice seriously and made many changes they suggested, but not all. I'm particularly grateful for the insightful comments and notes I received from Fred Krupp (Environmental Defense Fund), Rick Smith (the Support Center), John Berger (Restoring the Earth), Jeanne Friedman (Sempervirens Fund), Donna Fletcher (the Museum Society, formerly with the Sierra Club), David Lawson (Information Prospector) and Nick Allen (Neighbor to Neighbor). Neither they nor their organizations (which I mention only to help identify them) are responsible in any way for the contents of this book.

I am very grateful to two clients in particular for their direct contributions to this project. Sylvia Siegel, founder and former Executive Director of TURN (Toward Utility Rate Normalization), and Audrie Krause, TURN's current Executive Director, graciously gave their permission for me to reproduce the direct mail fundraising packages reproduced in Chapter 6. I am deeply indebted to the Rev. Jesse L. Jackson. The fundraising packages comprising Chapter 7, which were mailed on behalf of his 1988 presidential campaign, represent some of my coworkers' and my best efforts in ten years of direct mail fundraising; I am pleased to be able to reproduce them here. The Jackson campaign afforded us many opportunities for innovation, and the successful results played a large role in moving me to write this book.

I'm also greatly indebted to my 150 friends and colleagues in Mal Warwick & Associates, The Progressive Group and our affiliated companies. They're an extraordinarily gifted and dedicated bunch of people, and I am privileged to work by their side. For their assistance on this book, they deserve triple credit. Not only did they teach me most of what I know about lists, production, statistical analysis, design and copywriting. They also covered for me over the past six months when I stole away from the office to write. Moreover, many individual employees of Mal Warwick & Associates and The Progressive Group helped me in major ways in writing this book. Some deserve special mention here.

Without the help of Stephen Hitchcock, Executive Vice President of Mal Warwick & Associates, I could not have written *Revolution in the Mailbox*. His continuing encouragement and support, his awesome managerial ability and critical editorial eye came to the rescue on more occasions than I can possibly recall. Steve's comments on two early drafts of the manuscript and on a later draft of the book's final chapter helped steer me away from dire embarrassment. The wisdom Steve has gained in twenty years as a professional fundraiser has found its way into nearly every chapter of this book. I've borrowed liberally from him, sometimes consciously, sometimes not. In particular, Steve is largely responsible for my comments about donors' needs and motives, for one of the several approaches cited to analyze donors' value over time, and for the Reading List.

Royce Kelley, Senior Consultant at both Mal Warwick & Associates and our political fundraising affiliate, Changing America, put his matchlessly analytical mind to work in reading two early versions of the manuscript, and again in reviewing a near-final draft. At the outset, Royce extricated the project from hopeless muddle and showed me how to reorganize the material into a far more logical and readable order. He was also of great help on the illustrations, some of which he produced. You will find this book much more useful because Royce put so much time into it.

My good friends at The Progressive Group, co-founder and President Joseph H. White, Jr. and Vice President Kelly Mahoney, contributed substantially. They didn't just provide detailed criticism about the draft sections on telephone fundraising. Making use of their broad experience in fundraising and strategic planning, both Joe and Kelly offered insightful, page-by-page suggestions on the first draft of the full manuscript. Their imprint is visible throughout. Joe also generously took the time during a particularly hectic period to gather together the illustrations for the sections on telephone fundraising.

My resourceful assistant, Eric Oliver, has suffered considerable abuse because of my many absences to work on this project and because writing makes me cranky. Nonetheless, he gracefully served as my research assistant on the book, digging out and checking facts, compiling the draft of the Glossary, assembling the List of Illustrations and constructing the Index. When, several times, I needed two- or three-hundred-page versions of the manuscript printed out, photocopied and distributed for review, it was Eric who did the work. There was a lot of it, and I'm grateful to him.

I'm very thankful to Julie Levak, Senior Consultant at Mal Warwick & Associates (MWA), for her help in clarifying the distinction I've drawn between strategy and tactics and for several other significant suggestions. Julie's incisive comments about recycling were particularly helpful in writing Chapter 1, and her contributions to Chapter 9 were considerable. Julie also brought her extensive knowledge of direct mail fundraising and her fine sense of design to bear in assembling the materials which appear as illustrations in Chapter 3.

Other coworkers made important contributions, too. MWA Client Consultant Deborah Agre, MWA's Vice President for Marketing, Bill Rehm, MWA Board members Martin Rabkin and Karen Paget, and our consulting accountant, Paul Hammond, all reviewed the manuscript and made useful comments. Deborah Agre's comments about strategy and tactics and Marty Rabkin's remarks about political fundraising were especially important.

In the later stages of this project, two people's contributions stood out.

My editor, Nancy Adess, helped enormously. She salvaged many otherwise meaningless paragraphs by cleaning up my garbled grammar and punctuation and straightening out my syntax. (Ten years of writing direct mail fundraising letters is not the best practice for writing a book!) Nancy performed her editorial wizardry with great good grace and in record time. However, her contributions were not limited to copyediting. As editor of a magazine on fundraising and of other books in the field, and as the former executive director of a national nonprofit public interest organization, Nancy was able to address the substance of the material as well as the form. Her broad experience came in especially handy as she guided me through the maze of fundraising ethics in Chapter 1.

My publisher, Wallace Rutherford III, pulled together the disparate strands of a project that was threatening to get totally out of hand and made it possible for this book to appear in print before the 20th Century drew to a close. Apart from performing the many tasks that typically confront people who publish books — making arrangements with designers, typesetters, printers, binders, reviewers and the many other organizations and individuals who play important roles in producing and distributing a book — Wally executed many of the charts and diagrams appearing in this book. He also laughed at my jokes.

For all the many important contributions that others have made to this book, none of them bears any responsibility for its contents. I've borrowed a great many ideas, but the words and images on these pages were all mine except where I've indicated otherwise. Now they're yours, too — and welcome to them!

Your Contribution Will Be Appreciated

Once you've read this book, I want to hear from you.

I want to know if you take issue with something in these pages. If your experience with direct mail fundraising has taught you a lesson I haven't learned, I want you to tell me about it. The same goes if you have illuminating facts at your fingertips, or fascinating stories about direct mail fundraising, or important arguments I've ignored.

Please use the handy reply form that Strathmoor Press has inserted between the pages of this book. Or write me at Mal Warwick & Associates, Inc., 2550 Ninth Street, Suite 103, Berkeley, California 94710.

I'll do my best to answer you. And some day, perhaps, I may immortalize your contribution in a revised edition of *Revolution in the Mailbox*.

Thank you for your support.

Introduction

In the years following World War II, the Easter Seal Society and a few other big American charities began making extensive use of the mails to meet their increasingly ambitious fundraising goals. With little cash outlay, they mailed millions of inexpensive fundraising letters and consistently reaped huge profits.

So successful were these early mass-mail fundraising efforts that some charities simply banked the proceeds without bothering to record the contributors' names and addresses. It was cheaper to send out virtually the same appeal again the next year to the same millions of addresses.

That was nearly half a century ago. A great deal has happened since: a more than twenty-fold increase in charitable contributions, the advent of ZIP codes and mainframe computers, fundraising scandals on network news, flexible personal computers, 800% inflation in nonprofit postal rates, and a comparable rise in printing costs — and, above all, *competition* in the form of appeals mailed by thousands upon thousands of public interest groups both large and small.

In 1988, the U.S. Postal Service distributed more than 13 *billion* pieces of mail for nonprofit organizations — most of them appeals for funds. Direct mail fundraising accounts for a major share of the support given many of our country's biggest charities, and it has come to loom large on the political landscape as well.

This proliferation of mail has created a challenge for nonprofit organizations and political campaigns to make profits through direct mail. To help meet this challenge, hundreds of consulting firms have come into existence, offering a staggering variety of approaches and levels of skill. Now, more than forty years into its history, direct mail fundraising has gotten *complicated*.

The pages ahead are my attempt to explain some of the complications.

I've written this book in response to years of seeing desperate and bewildered looks on the faces of clients, employees and friends. These looks are often justified: not only are there those in the industry who go out of their way to mystify the process, but there are things about direct mail fundraising that are confusing; in fact, some are downright illogical. I hope the following pages help demystify this crazy business and cast a little light on some of its counter-intuitive aspects.

While excellent books have been written about direct mail, and even about direct mail fundraising in particular, all but a few (noted in the Reading List) are either highly technical discussions laden with statistical formulas and bearing a disturbing resemblance to college textbooks, or much more superficial treatments chock full of tips about writing good fundraising letters. This book is neither. It presents a point of view that I might as well state clearly at the outset:

> ***Successful direct mail fundraising has little to do with statistics or with letter-writing. It's a long-term process that requires intelligent planning and careful, consistent management.***

To succeed in direct mail fundraising over the long term, it's essential to *distinguish between strategy and tactics*. As in any other field, you can win the battle and lose the war. In this book, I hope to help illuminate the difference.

In military usage, the distinction between a nation's strategy and tactics is straightforward:

❏ *Strategy* is the manner in which a nation seeks to ensure its security in peacetime as well as war, employing large-scale, long-range planning and development to make the best possible use of *all* its resources.

❏ *Tactics* are the choices made concerning the use and deployment of military forces in actual combat.

Since few appreciate this bold distinction, the word "strategy" is often confused with tactics. In this discussion, I mean to draw the line just as sharply as do the Joint Chiefs of Staff.

The *strategy* employed by a public interest organization includes decisions about its leadership and policy priorities as well as resource development — not a plan but a vision. To set strategy is not to engage in "long-term planning" to determine how existing resources may be put to the best possible use. Setting strategy means dreaming about what you want your organization to accomplish. How to marshall the resources to reach that goal is an operational question — a matter of *tactics*. Those tactics may include a direct mail fundraising program designed to help get you where you want to go, just as they may also include lobbying, public relations, establishing fees for services, or merchandising.

I'm uncomfortable with this bellicose metaphor. I'd prefer to describe direct mail fundraising in terms of streams and rivers — or seeds that grow into trees, which cluster into groves and then over time become forests. "Strategy" and "tactics" smack of the nasty things I've spent many of my waking hours helping our clients stop. But I

know of no other terms that help to draw so clear a distinction between decisions that are really important and those that aren't.

■ ■ ■ ■ ■

For the sake of simplicity in these pages, I assume that you're the
executive director or chair of the board's fundraising committee of a
nonprofit organization, or that you're a candidate or manager in a
political campaign. I also assume you know next to nothing about
fundraising.

In the examples I cite, I refer consistently to "public interest
groups." I mean that term to include a great many nonprofit organizations dedicated to cultural, educational and charitable goals as well as
environmental, civil rights, social justice, women's and other advocacy
organizations.

Most of my professional experience has been with groups or candidates advocating changes in public policy, as the illustrations will
make abundantly clear. However, I believe that what works well for a
consumer group may also do the trick for a university, museum or
hospital. Moreover, while a political campaign may use the principles
of direct mail in ways different from those common in the nonprofit
world, they're the same principles. Many of the techniques of direct
mail fundraising are broadly transferable. From conversations with
friends who raise money by mail in Canada and Australia, I know that
the same fundamental approach works elsewhere in the English-
speaking world.

■ ■ ■ ■ ■

This book won't show you how to write, design and mail an
appeal for funds. Nor will it tell you how to think or plan or manage
your organization. It will help you understand what direct mail can do
for you. Its purpose is to explain and illustrate direct mail fundraising
in context, as the means by which many public interest groups have
grown, increased their influence and ensured their long-term financial
stability.

At the outset, in Chapter 1, I explain how you can use direct mail
to pursue your *strategic* goals. I give you a sense of what you can

expect from direct mail and whether it may — or may not — be right for your organization.

In Chapter 2, I address the principal *tactical* issues that will arise when you launch your direct mail fundraising program: what makes direct mail work or fail, what sort of letter to write, what other items you might include, who should sign it, to whom you should mail it, and when. In Chapter 3, I deal piece by piece with each of the elements included in many fundraising packages, addressing common questions and misconceptions.

I return to strategic considerations in Chapter 4, reviewing the *long-term* requirements and advantages of investment in direct mail. This will give you a picture of what you need to do to sustain a successful direct mail fundraising program. Next, in Chapter 5, I spell out for you some of the many ways you can work to maximize your returns from your direct mail fundraising program.

Against that necessary background, I take you inside two large-scale direct mail fundraising programs, so you can see what form these principles can take in the real world. First, in Chapter 6, I examine each of the many components in one complex — and successful — direct mail fundraising campaign for a nonprofit organization. Then, in Chapter 7, I take a slice-of-life approach to describe one month's direct mail fundraising work for Jesse Jackson's 1988 Presidential campaign. In both chapters, you'll be able to read the actual packages we produced and mailed.

In the book's final chapters, I return once again to the strategic perspective that I believe is the *only* justification for undertaking a professional program of direct mail fundraising in the first place. Chapter 8 suggests guidelines for working with a consultant to put all these lessons into practice. Finally, Chapter 9 puts the whole field into national and historical perspective. I take a look at the impact of direct mail fundraising on American politics, review the dramatic changes that have occurred in direct mail during the past twenty years and cite many of the new techniques and new technologies now being put to use in direct mail fundraising. In concluding, I offer a few speculative remarks about what the future of fundraising may hold.

■ ■ ■ ■ ■

Chances are, direct mail is one of the most effective tools your organization can use to prepare for the next century. But you can do so only by a creative, no-holds-barred, entrepreneurial approach to direct mail, making use of the newest insights and the latest technologies to gain maximum advantage for your organization.

I look on direct mail fundraising as a *business*, and you should, too; it's an entrepreneurial tool that can be used in a great many ways, for good or ill. Viewed narrowly as letter-writing or an occasional fund appeal, direct mail is unlikely to serve you well as the year 2000 draws near. But if you can make it serve the needs of your overall fundraising plan, it can help lay the foundation for your organization's continuing success well into the 21st Century.

Not all the terms used in this book — or the methods described — are universally accepted among direct mail fundraisers. My colleagues and I in Mal Warwick & Associates, Inc. (Berkeley, Calif.) cherish a view of ourselves as creative, and we've actually won awards and a lot of public attention in support of that view. While all of us in the business follow the same basic rules — and it's standard practice to copy successful techniques from each other — the *particular* approach to direct mail fundraising laid out in these pages is ours alone. Direct mail practitioners in other firms may not even recognize some of the terminology used here.

Much the same goes for my much briefer references to telephone fundraising. I'm also involved in that industry, as co-founder and board chair of The Progressive Group, Inc. (Northampton, Mass.) The language I use and the examples I cite relating to telephone fundraising are from the experience I've gained through The Progressive Group.

I am also founder and President of Response Management Technologies, Inc. (Berkeley, Calif.), which processes gifts and provides "list maintenance" and data processing services to many public interest groups. Doubtless, my role in Response Management not only gives me a deeper understanding of the issues involving "back-end" services (discussed in Chapter 5) but also helps account for my bias favoring specialized service bureaus over in-house donor management programs.

To learn from people with biases different from mine, and for a fuller understanding of direct marketing in general and direct mail fundraising in particular, I suggest the books and periodicals cited in the Reading List.

Some of the examples cited here are obviously hypothetical, while others are real. Every real-life case study described here is derived from the experience of Mal Warwick & Associates, Inc., and so are all of the direct mail packages pictured in the illustrations. Wherever I refer to "us" or "we," that's who I mean.

To avoid distractions and make the subject of direct mail fundraising as accessible as possible, I've chosen not to use footnotes either to note parenthetical points or to cite references for facts or quotes. My graduate school instructors may be very disappointed, but I operate under the assumption that if something's important enough to include in a book, it ought to be in the text, not in a footnote.

Some of what follows may not be popular in the fundraising community. So be it. *My* reason for getting into this business in the first place was to change the world. A lot has happened in the ten years since I stopped licking stamps and bought my first computer. As a group, direct mail fundraising consultants have played a major role in many of those events. We've helped public interest organizations meet urgent human needs, shape public opinion and expand the boundaries of our culture. Direct mail has had profound impact on American politics and society. But I think the world *still* needs changing.

Berkeley, California
September 1989

The Strange New World
of Direct Mail Fundraising

1

The Strategic Uses of Direct Mail

For many nonprofit organizations and political campaigns, direct mail fundraising is a question of life or death. Often, it is *strategically* important simply because so much money is involved.

No one really knows how much American charities raise in a year, but the best available estimate for the year 1988 is that the figure topped $104 billion. This doesn't include more than 19.5 billion hours of volunteer time contributed by 80 million Americans, which added an estimated value of $150 billion. It's particularly difficult to determine how much of that money was contributed in response to appeals sent by mail. But after studying the figures and the techniques by which they were gathered, Arnold Fishman (as he reported in *The Guide to Mail Order Sales*) was convinced that direct mail fundraising yielded more than $40 billion in 1988.

Forty *billion* dollars.

That's nearly one percent of the Gross National Product of the United States, or one out of every one hundred dollars generated by the largest economy in the world — a *big* business by anyone's standards. Direct mail fundraising is a business that very few public interest groups can afford to ignore or misunderstand.

While direct mail has become increasingly competitive, expensive and difficult in recent years, other sources of charitable and public interest funding have also become more difficult to tap:

❐ Grants from the federal government were sharply curtailed by the Reagan administration, and a massive budget deficit offers little hope that future administrations will be much more generous to nonprofits.

❐ At best, foundations have always been reluctant to fund programs in perpetuity. Despite recent efforts to persuade foundation executives to grant funds for general support, most still want only to provide leadership gifts for pilot or demonstration projects. And seed grants for fundraising programs are the exception, not the rule.

❐ Corporate giving rises and falls with frequent changes in tax laws and trends in corporate finance. The mergers and acquisitions characteristic of the 1980s have reduced many corporate philanthropic budgets.

❐ Mushrooming sales of products and services by nonprofit enterprises have attracted unwelcome attention by the Internal Revenue

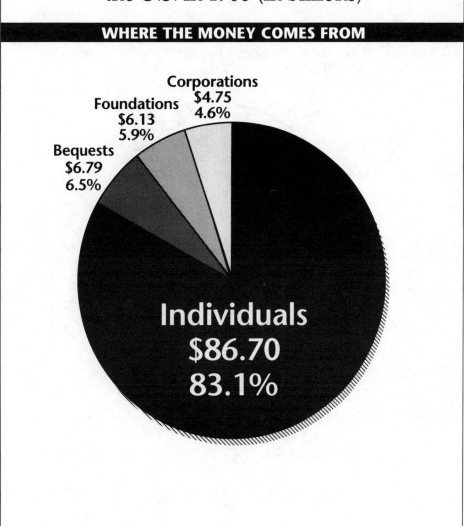

Charitable Contributions in the U.S. in 1988 (in billions)

WHERE THE MONEY COMES FROM

Corporations
$4.75
4.6%

Foundations
$6.13
5.9%

Bequests
$6.79
6.5%

Individuals
$86.70
83.1%

ILLUSTRATION 1: Individuals give five of every six charitable dollars

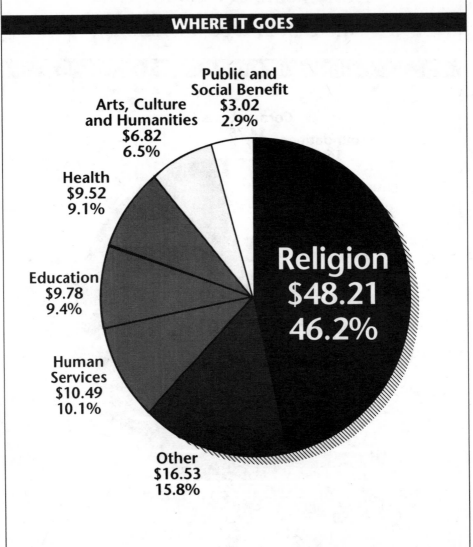

Charitable Contributions in the U.S. in 1988 (in billions)

WHERE IT GOES

Public and
Social Benefit
$3.02
2.9%

Arts, Culture
and Humanities
$6.82
6.5%

Health
$9.52
9.1%

Education
$9.78
9.4%

Human
Services
$10.49
10.1%

Other
$16.53
15.8%

Religion
$48.21
46.2%

ILLUSTRATION 2: *Nearly half of all charitable dollars go to religion*

Illustrations 1 and 2 reprinted with permission from *Giving USA, The Annual Report on Philanthropy for the Year 1989,* New York: American Association of Fund-Raising Counsel Trust for Philanthropy, 1989.

Service and Congress, and statutory changes threaten this rich source of financial support for many organizations.

By comparison, direct mail may be an extremely attractive option for your organization. It's the most widely employed technique to seek financial support from large numbers of *individuals*. Of an estimated $104 billion donated by Americans in 1988, more than $87 billion came from individuals. Corporations contributed less than $5 billion, and foundations only a little over $6 billion. Even the remaining $6 billion in bequests originated from individuals; they were simply no longer alive.

Because of its ability to target, reach and motivate individual people in large numbers, direct mail has come to occupy a significant place in our society and culture. Direct mail helps account for the vigor and broad scope of the so-called "Third Sector" or "Independent Sector" — that proliferation of seemingly countless voluntary associations in America about which De Tocqueville commented with such wonder more than 150 years ago.

There is no other country in which private citizens, working together in voluntary nongovernmental organizations, play such a vital role. U.S. public interest groups meet urgent human needs, train our young, enrich our culture and help shape our public policy. They are one of the principal mechanisms in the larger system of checks and balances that guarantees the stability of American democracy.

The Internal Revenue Service reports that 117,183 nonprofit, tax-exempt organizations filed tax returns in 1988 showing income of $25,000 or more — but that's only part of the picture. It's estimated there are as many as *one million* nonprofit organizations in the United States that are dedicated to educational, charitable or cultural work. Thousands more are engaged in political or public policy campaigns. For the majority of these groups, direct mail fundraising is an indispensable tool.

Chances are your organization is already involved in direct mail fundraising. Even if you don't use direct mail to recruit or "acquire" donors, members or subscribers, direct mail is probably an essential component of your overall development program. You may just call it something else.

Membership renewal notices, "annual appeals," newsletters, "special appeals," "action alerts," annual reports, "house mailings," "Letters from the Executive Director," "emergency appeals," subscription renewal notices — all these and many more possible forms of communication between you and your supporters play vital roles on the larger stage of your development program. It makes no difference at all whether you *call* them "direct mail."

Direct mail communications can help — or hinder — not only your fundraising efforts but all the work you do. Too many "emergency appeals" may undermine your credibility. Delays in sending dues renewal notices may cause your membership to shrink. Conflicting messages may confuse your clients or constituents. Failure to keep your supporters up to date through a newsletter may mean their response to your annual appeal will be poor. Multiple mailings of the same letter can anger even an ardent supporter. To ensure that all these communications devices play a constructive role, it's important to take a close look at them *as a whole* in the context of your relationship with your constituency — and to consider how they all fit into your organization's strategy.

One thing is certain: your supporters will *expect* something in the mail from you. Mailing brings organizational credibility. Voters often tell campaign volunteers, "I'll just wait till I see something in the mail before I make up my mind." Your donors or members may be waiting, too.

Direct mail fundraising isn't just about money. It's often used to cultivate and recruit volunteers or prospects for fundraising dinners or other events. Direct mail is widely used for grassroots lobbying or other forms of political action by public policy groups and political campaigns. Schools, colleges, hospitals and cultural institutions make wide use of direct mail to promote their community programs.

Direct mail is a flexible tool that you can use to serve any one of a great number of organizational strategies. If direct mail fundraising works for your organization, it can take you down five divergent paths:

❑ *Growth* — by helping you build a bigger membership or list of contributors (called a "donor base")

❑ *Involvement* — by persuading your supporters to become actively involved

❑ *Efficiency* — by maximizing the net revenue you derive from your mailings, and thus raising funds at the lowest possible cost per dollar raised

❑ *Stability* — by reaching and maintaining an optimum level of direct mail fundraising activity

❑ *Visibility* — by publicizing your work among a particular constituency or the public in general

Later in this chapter, we'll take a look at several hypothetical case studies to explore some of these strategic paths and their tactical implications — that is, the specific forms of activity these contrasting approaches require. I hope that in that context the difference between strategy and tactics will become clearer. First, however, let's get down to the basics of direct mail fundraising so that we can establish a common basis of understanding the issues.

What You Can Expect from Direct Mail

Direct mail is a difficult and expensive way to raise money. It requires capital investment, marketing skill, patience and managerial agility.

Still, despite increased costs and ever fiercer competition for funds, direct mail fundraising remains the most effective way to build and cultivate a broad financial base. Over time, a properly managed direct mail fundraising program may be able to provide you with predictable, continuing support, year after year — and yield big dividends for your other fundraising programs as well.

But getting started in direct mail isn't easy. It's even harder if you have exaggerated or otherwise distorted expectations. I suggest the following as the first principle of direct mail fundraising:

> *Most of the time, almost no one will respond to your appeals for funds by mail. The only reason direct mail fundraising works is that someone who does send you a first gift is very likely to send another when asked.*

Direct mail fundraising is built on slim margins. Many mailings are regarded as very successful if just *one* in one hundred prospects responds with a gift. Of those who do respond, *ten* in one hundred may send their second gifts in response to a subsequent appeal.

The trick, then, is to identify your best prospective donors, to persuade the largest possible number of them to become first-time donors, to educate and motivate those newly acquired donors to give again and again, and to gain the maximum value from your committed donors by providing them with opportunities to support your organization ever more actively and generously.

Nowadays, for most organizations, acquiring new donors through the mail probably means *losing money* at least on the initial effort.

Public interest organizations have to expect to lose fifteen to thirty percent of their investment in mass-mail "prospecting" or "donor acquisition" programs carried out over time. That loss is sometimes even greater in the initial test mailing, which generally requires an up-front investment in creative and management services.

Despite the initial loss, this investment will help build your list of donors. However, it may be difficult for you to see all the way to the other end of that particular tunnel. I often feel that counseling clients to expand their prospecting efforts in the face of mounting losses is a lot like telling a child, "eat your vegetables." Prospecting is sometimes hard to swallow.

If you do, however, you'll see your list grow steadily over time and yield continuing dividends. Your newly acquired donors will, on average, remain donors for about two and one-half years. In that time, they'll typically make two or three additional gifts, averaging up to one and one-quarter times the size of their initial contributions. Many will increase the frequency with which they give; they may also increase the size of their gifts. A very few will stay with you for life, loyally contributing year after year — and even go on giving after they die, by remembering you in their wills.

Perhaps most significant, among these newly acquired donors will be some individuals willing to contribute — or help raise — major gifts. For some organizations, a major gift can be as little as $100; for others, it may be $1 million or more. But the principle is the same: direct mail can help you identify, recruit, cultivate and educate that small, vital group of prospective major donors who are capable of making a very big difference for your organization. There's no way to predict how many such donors will surface, but for many nonprofit organizations the gifts from these major donors eventually provide fifty percent — and ultimately perhaps ninety percent or more — of total annual income.

But it takes a lot of hard work to achieve this enormous potential. A successful direct mail fundraising program requires a carefully or-chestrated schedule of additional mailings as well as telephone contact. Believe it or not, extensive research and testing have demonstrated that direct mail donors (a) really do like receiving mailings, (b) enjoy giving to lots of organizations, and (c) make repeated gifts to the groups that interest them the most.

That means your most active donors should receive six or more fund appeals per year from your organization. Some groups mail twelve, sixteen or even twenty solicitations per year while also con-ducting telephone appeals and staging public events and other fundraising efforts. In the final months before an election, at the end of the calendar year, just before a vote in Congress, or at some arbitrary program deadline, mail and telephone solicitations every seven to twelve *days* are not uncommon.

It's not difficult to understand why we mail so frequently. Most donors — especially direct mail donors — make contributions from *current* discretionary income. At any given time, they're likely to have only small amounts to spare. For all but the very rich or the very frugal, that's life in America today. Even those generous donors whose gifts to you may total more than $100 per year may be more comfortable sending several $50 checks than one much larger donation. They may even *think* of themselves as "$50 donors" and reflexively send checks in that amount to several organizations each month that inspire them to give — perhaps even without regard to whether they've recently given to any of them. Most direct mail donors write checks to charity when they're paying their bills on a weekly or monthly basis. Few people have large, fixed pools of money into which they dip for the funds to make small contributions. Even if they plan and schedule their charitable giving, they're likely to get the funds from their current income stream.

Few donors are aware how frequently they're solicited by mail. Again and again, surveys show that direct mail donors underestimate how many appeals they've received from a given organization. And while you may think that a majority is likely to complain about oversolicitation, most survey respondents say the frequency of appeals from organizations they support is "too little" or "just about right." Complaints much more commonly arise from individuals who *don't* support your organization.

Nonetheless, in a well-run direct mail fundraising program, you'll mail most of your appeals to only *some* of your donors. The key is to pick those who are most likely to respond, and to plan the most effective possible sequence and combination of solicitations.

Kind Strangers and Loving Friends

There are distinctly different types of mailings to meet different fundraising needs. In the broadest terms, mailings are intended either to *acquire* new donors, members or subscribers, or to *resolicit* previous donors for additional support. Between them is all the difference in the world.

It's the difference between the love of friends and the casual kindness of strangers.

"Donor Acquisition"

"Donor acquisition" or "prospect" mailings — sometimes also called "cold mail" — are designed to persuade each potential donor to take the big step of giving you a first gift. While there are occasional and notable exceptions, acquisition mailings tend to be relatively inexpensive ($0.20 to $0.70 each) and are often produced in large quantities (50,000 to 1 million letters or more) and mailed relatively infrequently (perhaps two to six times per year). Acceptable "response rates" — the percentage of those who send gifts — are typically in the range of one-half to two and one-half percent.

Acquisition mailings almost always cost more money than the total of contributions received; in other words, they don't often break even. Their success or failure is generally evaluated in terms of *"donor acquisition cost,"* that is, the difference between the cost of the mailing and the amount it generated in contributions, divided by the number of donors acquired.

For example, if a $50,000 mailing generates proceeds of $40,000 and 2,500 new memberships, the acquisition cost is $4 per member ($50,000 less $40,000, or $10,000, divided by 2,500).

	PURPOSE	TYPICAL COST PER PIECE	TYPICAL QUANTITY PER MAILING	TYPICAL RESPONSE RATE
Donor Acquisition Mailings	build donor base	$0.20 — 0.70	50,000 — 1,000,000	0.5% — 2.5%
Resolicitation Mailings	net profit	$0.40 — 5.00	3,000 — 300,000	6% — 12%

ILLUSTRATION 3: *Donor acquisition and donor resolicitation mailings are normally different*

The key is to calculate a donor's *value over time* — and keep the acquisition cost as far below it as your organizational strategy may dictate. (We'll go into that arithmetic in Chapter 5.)

The logic of this process is derived from the world of commercial direct mail. Based on the behavior of past subscribers, *Newsweek* knows how likely you are to renew your first-year subscription and thus they know to the fraction of a cent how much additional revenue they can expect from you. L.L. Bean can guess to the penny how much additional merchandise you'll buy. Both *Newsweek* and L.L. Bean are willing to *pay* to persuade you to purchase a subscription or a woolen shirt. They're counting on the fact that sizable percentages of first-time customers will buy more of their goods. Those percentages are sizable enough that *Newsweek* and L. L. Bean will probably pay a lot *more* in direct mail costs than the revenue they receive from you. But don't shed any tears for them. Neither company is in any danger of going belly-up, because they make their profit in repeat sales that more than compensate them for the loss of acquiring new customers. Many large direct mail-based public interest organizations shrewdly apply similar rules in their donor acquisition programs.

For some organizations — sometimes for valid reasons, sometimes not — *no* net loss in prospecting is acceptable. For others, the acceptable acquisition cost may range anywhere from $1 or $2 per donor to $25 or more.

To achieve maximum economies of scale and help minimize your acquisition cost, you'll usually do best to develop *one* general donor acquisition package and remail it indefinitely in the largest possible quantities, so long as the package continues to produce acceptable results. While you'll be well advised to test alternative approaches at every opportunity, this standard, or "control," package will become the backbone of your donor acquisition program. Ideally, the control package is an "evergreen" appeal, theoretically good for all time. (For example, the control package for the *Wall Street Journal's* subscription promotion efforts in 1989 was reportedly first mailed in 1972. Just as examples abound in the world of commercial advertising of familiar, long-running campaigns, there are many other examples of durable direct mail control packages in fundraising for nonprofits.) Some large programs have several control packages, each targeting a different market, but the principle of standardization is much the same.

"Donor Resolicitation"

By contrast, *"donor resolicitation"* or *"donor renewal"* mailings — often called "special appeals," "house appeals" or "house mailings" — have time value and are usually written afresh for each appeal. In an

First-year Quantities for Typical Start-up Program

MONTH	DONOR ACQUISITION MAILINGS	DONOR RESOLICITATION MAILINGS
January	50,000	
February		
March		1,000
April	100,000	
May		
June		3,000
July		
August	150,000	
September		5,000
October		
November		6,000
December	300,000	
TOTAL QUANTITY	**600,000**	**15,000**

ILLUSTRATION 4: Starting a direct mail fundraising program usually means launching a two-track effort

Overall Plan for a Representative Membership Renewal Series

EFFORT NUMBER	WEEKS BEFORE OR AFTER MEMBERSHIP LAPSES	ARGUMENT	TYPICAL RESPONSE RATE
1	12 weeks before	Renew early	25-30%
2	8 weeks before	Time to renew	12-15%
3	4 weeks before	Friendly reminder	6-8%
4	1 week before	Did you forget?	4-6%
5	4 weeks after	Last newsletter just mailed	2-3%
6	8 weeks after	What's the problem?	1-3%
7	12 weeks after	Telephone reminder	10-15%
TOTAL	24-WEEK CYCLE		60-80%

ILLUSTRATION 5: Persuading members to renew takes persistence

aggressive direct mail fundraising program revolving around a donor list of 250,000 individuals, this might mean designing and writing as many as two or three *dozen* resolicitation packages per year. To achieve optimal impact, you're likely to invest more in renewal mailings ($0.40 to $5.00 each) and mail them selectively in smaller quantities, depending on the size of your donor list (3,000 to 300,000 letters). Response rates may range from three percent to thirty percent or more, but are typically between six percent and twelve percent when sent to active, current donors.

The annual "membership renewal" letter is a special type of resolicitation used by organizations with formal membership structures. If yours is a membership group, you'll probably mail a *series* of inexpensive renewal letters — as many as six or eight — with each member receiving as many letters as necessary to force the issue. In a typical renewal series that is spaced out over six to ten months, perhaps sixty percent of the membership will sign up for another year — roughly half of them in response to the very first effort, and a quarter in response to the second. The final effort in the series is calculated to recapture reluctant members at a cost at least as low as that of direct mail prospecting (the "acquisition cost").

But this renewal series is *not* the organization's only source of membership contributions. Well-managed membership groups *also* mail special appeals to their members — often no fewer than are mailed by groups without a formal membership structure.

While an aggressive fundraising program may include a donor resolicitation every month, it's unlikely that a large number of the donors on the "file" (computerese for "list") will receive every appeal. Through "segmentation" we carefully select subgroups of donors for each package and each mailing, in order to achieve optimal impact and increase the program's cost-effectiveness. (We'll discuss segmentation in detail in Chapter 5.) *(See Illustration 6 on page 23.)*

We normally evaluate the success of renewal mailings in terms of *net revenue*. While there are different yardsticks to measure the net, we usually look at the ratio of revenue to cost, which tends to range between two-to-one and ten-to-one in all but the very largest programs. (In other words, the cost of a dollar raised will range from $0.10 to $0.50.) The ratio is likely to vary greatly with the segmentation chosen, since some subgroups tend to be far more responsive than others. *(See Illustration 7 on page 24.)*

In short, then, the challenge you'll face as you set out to launch a direct mail fundraising program is to acquire as many new donors as possible at a donor acquisition cost that is consistent with your strategy — and to analyze, cultivate and resolicit your donor file so you'll derive the maximum benefit for your organization.

The approach you take to direct mail fundraising has to fit *your* organization's needs. Just as a Jaguar isn't the "best" car for someone whose greatest need is for high fuel mileage, someone's formula-driven approach to direct mail isn't necessarily right for your organization.

Strategy and Tactics in Direct Mail

Now that we share a common vocabulary and framework of understanding about direct mail fundraising, let's take a look at how direct mail may be used as a *strategic* tool.

Through strategic planning, a public interest group can identify its goals and priorities. Ideally, the organization's staff leadership and

Monthly Schedule for a Representative Three-Track Direct Mail Fundraising Program

MONTH	MEMBERSHIP RENEWAL EFFORT NUMBER*	SPECIAL APPEAL NUMBER	DONOR ACQUISITION MAILING NUMBER
January		1	1
February			
March		2	
April	1		
May	2	3	2
June	3		
July	4	4	
August	5		3
September	6	5	
October	7		4
November		6	
December			
TOTAL NUMBER	7	6	4

Assumes annual membership renewal series unrelated to individual members' anniversary dates.

ILLUSTRATION 6: *A fully developed fundraising program means many mailings every year*

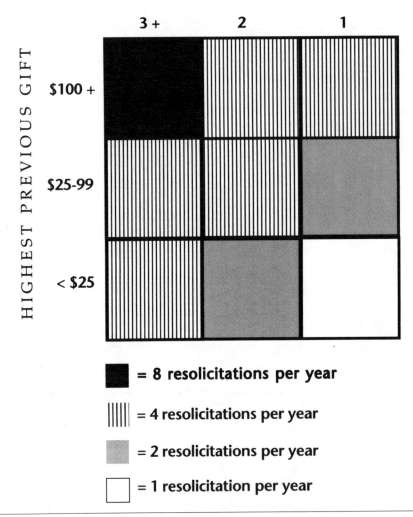

STYLIZED SCHEMATIC REPRESENTATION OF AN ANNUAL DIRECT MAIL SEGMENTATION PLAN.

NUMBER PREVIOUS GIFTS

ILLUSTRATION 7: Some donors receive many more mailings than others do

board will undertake a formal process, producing a written document that spells out its strategy and identifies the tactics to be used over a period of at least three years.

Despite the admonitions of outside consultants and bothersome board members, most nonprofit organizations don't adopt formal strategic plans. Nonetheless, even the most informal and inarticulate group needs to be clear about its long-term goals and know the difference between today and tomorrow. If you don't understand why you're in business and how you'll marshal available resources to serve your organization's ends, you've got much bigger problems than can be solved by starting a direct mail fundraising program.

Once your priorities are clear, however, you can use direct mail fundraising to help you achieve *growth, involvement, efficiency, stability* or *visibility* — whichever one your strategy requires. Within the tactical context of your direct mail fundraising program, all five of these goals may be important, and several of them indispensable — but as *strategies*, they may be mutually exclusive. To understand the tradeoffs and conflicts among them as you plan your direct mail fundraising program, consider four hypothetical case studies.

Case Study One: Strategy Dictates Tactics

Your strategic goal as executive director of a newly launched public policy organization is to reverse national policy on one highly controversial issue within five years. The issue isn't so explosive as abortion rights or flag-burning; let's say you want to lower the cost of auto insurance. Lacking other means, the *strategy* you've elected to bring this about is to mobilize public opinion and lobby the U.S. Congress for changes in the law.

Your $500,000 budget is met by a few venturesome foundations and fewer than 500 individual donors. Clearly, you lack the funding you need to mount the massive public relations campaign that might turn the tide in your favor. But you do have enough money to launch an aggressive direct mail donor acquisition program. If initial response is good, you might build a broad grassroots base for change within five years — and *ultimately* generate the funds to support a professional media campaign that will change attitudes among the general public and in the Congress.

This strategy dictates a likely set of *tactics*:

❐ a first-year investment of $150,000 or more in direct mail, with additional investment in the second year;

❏   a grassroots lobbying campaign that asks prospective as well as proven donors to become actively involved by signing petitions, mailing postcards to Congress, and the like (not to the exclusion of direct organizing and lobbying efforts but to supplement them);

❏   distinctive themes, logos, colors and slogans consistently employed on all materials used in the five-year campaign;

❏   an active outreach effort to involve your donors in educating and recruiting additional supporters.

While mailing millions of letters all across the country will enhance your visibility, it's no substitute for the public exposure which a well-executed advertising and public relations effort might obtain for you on nationwide television. However, without a sizable base and enough of a track record to gain the attention of skeptical reporters, your chances of free media coverage are slim. A massive direct mail base-building program is the fastest way to get there. Moreover, once you're there, the heightened public interest generated by national media coverage will boost your direct mail returns, perhaps dramatically.

To gain the maximum benefit from this approach, you'll reinvest all the proceeds of your direct mail program in additional and larger mailings for at least the first three years. Yes, this means that for three years every nickel of every direct mail contribution to your organization will be spent on mailing additional letters. These letters are the principal tool in service of your strategy, because they educate the public, involve thousands of people in active support of your cause, make you visible all across the country, and generate pressure directly on Congress.

If survey research and initial direct mail testing demonstrate substantial support for your goal of lowering auto insurance rates, this set of tactics will give you a real shot at achieving your strategic goal. But none of these tactics — not even the multi-million dollar prospecting program which is the centerpiece of the campaign — will be effective in isolation from the others. For example, without strong donor involvement and grassroots lobbying devices, the donor acquisition program will not support your *strategy* of bringing about a change in the law. All these tactics need to be seen in the larger context of organizational strategy — and executed as a whole.

To make the strategy work, you'll also have to *plan* the effort with great care. At the outset, numerical projections will be speculative and only marginally useful. But once results are in from successful initial tests, you'll be able to make meaningful projections. You'll be able to see — and plan — your five-year direct mail program as a continuous process, with growth targets established for each quarter-year along the way and a gradually quickening rhythm of activity in the final years that helps you reach your public policy goal.

Strategy often dictates tactics. In this case, a substantial initial investment in direct mail, aggressive donor acquisition and reinvestment for rapid growth, and a multi-faceted program of donor involvement are all simply *tactical* tools to use in support of your strategy.

Case Study Two: Tactics Don't Always Work

You're the executive director of an agency that provides vital human services for a population of one million. The city where your principal office is located takes pride in its progressive tradition of providing for its least fortunate members. Your clients are disadvantaged teenagers. The *strategy* set by your board of trustees is to stabilize the agency's finances by broadening and diversifying your financial base.

Currently, your $1 million budget derives from fees for service, government and foundation funding, and the generous support of a handful of major donors, several of whom sit on the board. The agency has good media contacts and has managed to acquire a highly favorable reputation with the general public. While neither you nor your clients is front-page news, there's lots of drama and human interest in your work. You're convinced that direct mail will work well for you.

However, because some of your larger grants are to be phased out soon, your budget may shrink by as much as $500,000 over the next three years. You hope that a direct mail fundraising program will enable you to make up the loss, thus contributing ten percent of your annual budget within three years. Over the longer term, you hope it will yield a great deal more through collateral fundraising efforts such as planned giving, bequests and other major donor programs. One of your funders has agreed to underwrite the effort to launch a direct mail program.

Among the *tactics* you've chosen to execute this diversification strategy are a public relations campaign to raise your agency's profile and an aggressive donor acquisition program. You hope to build an active direct mail base of some 30,000 names within three years, because you've been told that a fundraising program on that scale will generate net revenues of $500,000 per year.

That approach won't work. There simply aren't enough people living within the region you serve to sustain a direct mail program of such broad scope. Let's take a look at the numbers:

❑   Because of donor "attrition" during the three-year period (through death, illness, address changes or changing priorities), you'll have to acquire a total of perhaps 40,000 donors all together.

❑   To acquire 40,000 donors, you'll probably need to mail 4 million prospect letters. Even with substantial reinforcement from a well-focused public relations campaign, a direct mail response rate of one percent would be quite respectable.

❑   In other words, you'll have to mail as many as 1 million letters in the first year and 1.5 million in each of the following two years. There are only 1 million people living in your region — and relatively few of them can be considered good prospects. (Later, after we've discussed mailing lists, you'll understand this statement better.)

To carry out this strategy, your agency will need to become a household word locally. In neighborhoods where your best prospects live, you'll need to persuade virtually every household to contribute to your work. This may be practical for a zoo or a museum with a creative community involvement program and lots of tangible membership benefits, but it's not in the cards for a social service agency.

Here, more realistically, are your options:

❑   Settle for a much smaller donor base, and a much more modest contribution to your operating budget. Direct mail probably *will* work for your agency. It just won't live up to unrealistic expectations.

❑   Forego profits entirely for three years — or even longer — as you reinvest them in donor acquisition and continuing public relations efforts. Even so, you may need to wait a lot longer than three years before the program begins to make a significant contribution to your budget.

❑   Consider whether the implications of your work warrant mailing outside your region, perhaps even nationally.

❑   Look for other ways to supplement or substitute for direct mail donor acquisition. A broad-based program of neighborhood fundraising events may be feasible. So might a multi-media campaign to generate "inquiries" about your services from individuals who write or call in response to your offer to tell them "how you can help." Direct mail appeals may succeed with these "qualified prospects" who have demonstrated interest in your work.

However, despite your best efforts, it's possible that direct mail will never generate net revenues of $500,000 per year for you.

Strategy may dictate tactics — but the tactics must be realistic.

Case Study Three: Tactics Affect Strategy

The challenge you face as chief executive officer of a nationwide advocacy group is to maintain your large membership base — essential for your ongoing lobbying campaign — while increasing your operating budget by at least twenty percent annually over the next four years. The environmental issues your group addresses are of increasing concern to the general public, and your board is confident that there is lots of room for you to grow. The *strategy* you've successfully pursued for three years already is to publish and promote by direct mail a lush, four-color monthly magazine which is available to members only.

Repeated testing has shown that, by highlighting this attractive membership benefit, you can mail 5 million prospect letters per year and acquire 40,000 new members at breakeven with entry-level dues

Volume and Income Projections for Hypothetical Organization Cited in Accompanying Text

DUES LEVEL	VOLUME MAILABLE AT BREAKEVEN	NUMBER NEW MEMBERS	MAGAZINE AND MEMBER SERVICE COSTS	SPECIAL APPEAL INCOME	OTHER INCOME FROM NEW MEMBERS	NET INCOME FROM NEW MEMBERS
$12	5,000,000	40,000	$400,000	$120,000	$280,000	0
$15	4,000,000	35,000	$375,000	$157,500	$280,000	$62,500
$18	3,000,000	30,000	$350,000	$189,000	$270,000	$109,000
$20	2,500,000	25,000	$325,000	$218,750	$250,000	$143,750
$25	1,500,000	15,000	$300,000	$180,000	$165,000	$45,000

ILLUSTRATION 8: Financial realities help determine optimal dues and membership size

set at $12 — but there's a catch. It costs you another $10 per year to print and mail the magazine to each member, and the typical $12 member doesn't respond well to appeals for additional gifts. The upshot is that your membership program as a whole isn't operating at much better than breakeven; it's netting just enough to cover publication, distribution and overhead costs — with no significant net income to fund that twenty percent budgetary growth that is essential to your strategy.

One *tactical* solution to this dilemma is to raise your membership dues — in effect, your subscription price — to $15, $18, $20 or $25 (with testing to determine the optimal level). While the cost of fulfilling each individual magazine subscription will rise as circulation falls (because of reduced economies of scale), in all likelihood you'll be able to find a level of prospecting at which you can continue to acquire new members at breakeven while taking those added costs into account.

If you *reduce* your prospecting volume, you'll acquire fewer new members, so your membership base will shrink. But the shrinkage may be limited if you don't encounter great resistance to the higher dues level. And you'll be attracting members who will almost certainly respond better to your requests for more generous gifts. Because repeated testing shows that donors who send larger gifts also contribute more frequently and tend to be more loyal, those who pay dues of $20 or $25 per year are much more likely to be responsive to "special appeals." You can then finance the desired budgetary growth from these appeals and from a beefed-up major gifts program. It's also possible that with lower prospecting volume and fewer members you'll be able to cut costs in your fulfillment and membership departments, achieving the same effect as revenue growth.

But there are flaws in this tactical approach. You'll be operating with a smaller base, which runs the risk of undercutting your lobbying campaign. You may also be forced to lay off staff. Either of these considerations may rule out cutbacks in your prospecting efforts.

Thus, the tactics required to execute a sound strategy may dictate other changes in the way you run your organization. Some of these — such as a membership base that shrinks too much, or major changes in staffing requirements — may have unintended and unfortunate consequences. Careful planning will help minimize the problems. But only a clear sense of strategic priorities will allow you to make decisions that are right for your organization.

Case Study Four: Time is a Strategic Tool

You're managing the front-running campaign for governor in a prosperous industrial state with a population of ten million. Your candidate, a popular member of Congress, has everything going for her except money. Though the campaign is solvent and you're unlikely to face significant opposition in the primary, it will be difficult to raise enough money to mount a television advertising campaign in the general election. You'll need at least $4 million to be competitive with the incumbent, whose campaign is awash in funds from Political Action Committees (PACs).

Your *strategy* to win the general election, now ten months away, is to build a massive donor base that will produce an army of volunteers for an old-fashioned grassroots voter registration and "Get-Out-the-Vote" campaign while funding the overall effort. Your state party organization is weak and its support for your candidate lukewarm because she represents unpopular policies and unwelcome change. Polls show she can build a majority coalition, but she'll need to do so virtually overnight — and from the ground up.

Direct mail is the principal means you've selected to execute this strategy. You hope to expand five-fold your candidate's existing 20,000-name donor list. With 100,000 donors, a $4 million media budget will be within reach. Such a large list will also enable you to recruit two or three volunteers in every precinct in the state. And the donor acquisition effort itself will carry your candidate's message into millions of households, laying the groundwork for the television and radio advertising campaign planned for the final weeks before the general election. You're prepared to invest as much as you need to make this strategy work.

There seems to be only one problem. The $250,000 your campaign has in the bank must remain there for at least three more weeks, until the next financial disclosure deadline has passed. If you remove the funds before then to launch a direct mail program, your campaign may look weak enough for primary opposition to surface. And you can't find direct mail vendors who are crazy enough to give you credit. In other words, you may lose almost one out of the ten remaining months before the election.

Under the circumstances, even with ten full months ahead, you face a daunting challenge. To acquire 80,000 new donors will mean mailing 4 million letters (if the response rate is two percent, a level that is relatively more common in political fundraising than in the nonprofit world). A populist campaign that sparks widespread enthusiasm and lots of media coverage *might* be able to mail this intensively. The importance of the election, and the candidate's broad appeal, may make it possible for you to prospect for donors on a modest scale outside the state, thus broadening your direct mail market. But time is a major limiting factor both in and out of state.

To conduct list and package testing and to read the results, you'll need at least a couple of months at the outset. And, unless your results are unrealistically strong, you'll need to wind up your prospecting program a minimum of one or two months before the election. (Irrationally, response in political donor acquisition efforts often drops off as Election Day draws near. And, unless you're making a profit from your prospecting program, the value of acquiring new donors will decline sharply as the number of resolicitation opportunities is reduced.) In other words, you've got about six months to mail *most* of those 4 million acquisition packages, or about 667,000 *per month*. Cutting one more month from the schedule will increase the monthly prospecting volume to 800,000.

Those numbers aren't impossibly high, but you're unlikely to be able to reach them in the time available. It would be unwise to build your election strategy on such unsteady ground. Direct mail fundraising makes sense for your campaign. It will contribute substantially to your media budget while playing an important role in increasing your visibility, spreading your message and recruiting volunteers. You just aren't likely to achieve as much as you're hoping.

There is a way to launch your effort more quickly than it might seem. With an urgent overnight appeal to the most generous of your candidate's donors, you can solicit gifts before the financial disclosure deadline. This appeal may generate the seed funds for a large-scale prospecting program while increasing your politically important bank balance. Presumably, you'll be able to negotiate payment terms that allow you to begin work on a large donor acquisition mailing while leaving the money in the bank for the next three weeks. But that still leaves you with overambitious expectations for the direct mail program as a whole.

(A bit of advice for the next campaign: start building your donor base two years earlier, so you'll be facing the active phase of the election campaign with a list of 50,000 donors — and a much more modest tactical challenge.)

■ ■ ■ ■ ■

The most productive way I've found to view direct mail fundraising in the strategic planning process is as a method of *problem-solving*. Once you've identified the problem — too few members to give you clout on Capitol Hill; too little money to meet your clients' needs; too much unpredictability in your finances — you can devise a solution using direct mail techniques.

The trick, of course, is to figure out what the problem is.

❏ In the first of these four case studies, the new public policy organization, is the central problem finding funds for a public relations campaign ... or is it controlling the cost of auto insurance?

❏ In the hypothetical case of the human service agency, what's more important: broadening the funding base in the long term . . . or supporting the budget in the short run?

❏ For the environmental advocacy group, is it a higher priority to maintain a large membership base ... or to maximize net income?

❏ In the example of the gubernatorial campaign, is direct mail most important for the financial contribution it can make to the campaign ... or for its broader political value?

The answers to these questions are not obvious. There are sound arguments for either side — or for still different points of view. But it's absolutely essential that these questions be resolved. Decisions need to be made one way or another. Muddled priorities are a prescription for failure.

Designing an effective direct mail fundraising program is, first of all, a matter of distinguishing strategy from tactics. And for the program to achieve its goals, that distinction must be clear to everyone involved in its management. The difference between strategy and tactics should never be forgotten.

Direct Mail Is Not for Everyone

These days, what passes for conventional wisdom in direct mail fundraising is that your initial acquisition test mailing will be successful if it breaks even — in other words, if it yields enough in direct, immediate contributions to cover the full cost of the mailing. From this conventional point of view, your successful program will then proceed with a series of progressively larger donor acquisition mailings, breaking even all along the way, as you build an ever-bigger list of proven donors *at no net cost*.

While this is an unfairly optimistic picture of the recent experience of most small and medium-sized public interest groups — and of a great many large ones, too — direct mail fundraising may be hugely successful for them, anyway, if they can acquire donors at an acceptable cost and then profitably resolicit them. Even the most modest test results may lay the foundation for a fundraising program of enormous scale.

But before we drift off into never-neverland with our eyeballs full of dollar signs, let's make sure we agree on something:

This test mailing you're launching is really a test.

Direct mail is a risky business. Maybe — just maybe — your test won't work.

Sometimes a direct mail fundraising program gets off to a slow start. It may take more than one test mailing to identify a successful marketing concept, or to find the right market. But for some organizations, the *cost* of direct mail fundraising may be out of proportion to its potential yield.

Remember, a direct mail donor prospecting program must deliver new donors at an advantageous acquisition cost. If it doesn't do that, you'd better head back to the drawing boards. Direct mail may not be right for you.

Quite apart from the possibility that your initial test mailing may be poorly conceived or badly executed, public response may be limited for one or more of the following reasons:

❐ There may not be a large enough number of people who agree that your organization fills an important need — or it may be difficult to find mailing lists on which their names and addresses appear.

❐ People may agree the work you're doing is important — but not *care* strongly enough to send money.

❐ The ever-fickle public may feel the need you're filling has passed — or simply that it isn't *urgent* enough to require immediate support.

Organizations that operate on a small scale may have an especially difficult time launching the type of large direct mail fundraising programs I'm describing in these pages: those with annual budgets of less than $300,000, or with constituencies of fewer than 2,000,000 people. While there are important exceptions, for the most part the market for a local public interest group in all but the largest metropolitan areas may simply be too small to apply these techniques. Professionally managed direct mail fundraising is built on economies of scale.

The limited size of your constituency or market is only one of several sound reasons *not* to embark on a program of direct mail fundraising. Direct mail may not be a good bet for you, and it may not even make sense for you to launch an initial test if any of the following conditions apply:

❐ If you lack the necessary *capital* to invest in a test mailing.

❐ If your finances are fragile and you can't bear the *risk* of an unsuccessful test.

❐ If the *issues* involved in your work aren't specific, compelling and of concern to a broad public.

❐ If you can't effectively distinguish your organization from others serving the same constituency by identifying something *dramatic* or unique about you or your work.

❐ If your mission and *strategy* are unclear, so that it would be difficult to package your programs for a wider public.

❐ If you're just starting out and lack the track record, name recognition or credentials to establish your *credibility*.

❐ If you have neither sufficient staff nor an outside firm to ensure that donors will get the *service* they need.

❐ If your organization isn't committed for the *long haul*.

Direct mail may also be wrong for your organization if you or other central figures such as key board members, staff or the candidate are unable to swallow the unconventional logic on which the whole system is based — a set of principles and mechanisms that prompt some people to think of direct mail as somehow "immoral."

Is Direct Mail Immoral?

One memorable afternoon not many years ago, in a walnut-paneled Wall Street board room, I sat at a massive conference table across from a prominent former Cabinet member, engaged in one of the more frustrating conversations of my direct mail career. I was visiting him with the founder of a public interest group that the man supported enthusiastically. We hoped he'd agree to become the honorary co-chair of an intensive donor acquisition campaign based on the results of an encouraging initial test mailing. After our lengthy presentation, here's the gist of what he said:

"Let me see if I understand this correctly. You want me to put my name on a letter asking people to send $25 checks to my favorite charity — *so you can send out more letters?"*

Some feel this question poses difficult ethical issues for public interest organizations. To address them, let's review a few of the basic realities of direct mail fundraising:

❐ A well-planned and creatively executed direct mail fundraising program will ultimately raise a good deal of money for an organization committed to direct mail as one component of a long-term development campaign. At the same time, the direct mail program will give thousands — perhaps hundreds of thousands — of people the opportunity to support a public interest group they might otherwise be unaware of.

❐ It's true that initial returns from a direct mail program will be plowed back into producing and mailing more fundraising letters. Over time, however, the funds reinvested in direct mail will be a small percentage of the money earned by the program — and the rest of the money will be available to pay for the activities the group was set up to accomplish. As the years go by, the initial investment in direct mail may come to seem minuscule by comparison with the dividends it produces.

❐ *Every* fundraising program costs money, and a certain percentage of the returns from every fundraising effort goes to cover its costs — whether it's a benefit event, a newsletter, a T-shirt or a direct service. Because a direct mail program may require a large initial investment, continuing reinvestment and a long-term commitment, it appears that the bulk of the proceeds are simply used to generate more letters. If this were true, no nonprofit would continue its direct mail program. Obviously, to be useful, direct mail fundraising must raise money to fund the organization's operations.

❐ Furthermore, consider that direct mail donor acquisition is the most cost-effective — and sometimes the *only* feasible way — for a nonprofit to build a broad financial base, expand its operations and ensure its long-term survival.

There are those who feel it isn't right to ask the public to give by mail unless the organization discloses fully how it will spend every penny raised through the mail. As I was told in that board room, "Those $25 checks aren't going to be used to meet anyone's human needs. They're going to pay for more letters! I say it's immoral unless we *tell* people that's what their contributions are going to be used for."

The underlying principle here seems to be that if a fundraising letter asks people to send money to "Save the Whales," the public has the right to assume that every dollar they send will go directly to that specific purpose. That's just silly. No office runs without overhead, and no nonprofit runs without fundraising. A portion of every dollar raised — in any manner — must go to pay rent, telephone bills, office staff, and, yes, even further fundraising. Why should direct mail be singled out for scrutiny? A direct mail fundraising program can't be reduced to a formula. Numbers can be misleading unless you're looking at the big picture, because the numbers change over time — sometimes very rapidly.

Singling out the costs of direct mail also tends to distort its wider effects. A direct mail fundraising program must be seen in context because it contributes in a great many ways to the overall effort. For example, gifts from major donors probably won't be counted in the proceeds of a direct mail fundraising program, even if the program first made them aware of the organization's work. Thus, public disclosure about the *direct* costs and benefits of the direct mail fundraising program will obscure rather than illuminate the reality.

And there are some other important considerations when thinking about public disclosure issues:

❑ If costs and benefits are to be spelled out, it should be in the context of the organization's finances as a whole, rather than taking the direct mail program out of context. Existing law already provides for financial disclosure to the public, since charities' tax returns are available through the Internal Revenue Service and in many states their financial statements may be obtained through charities registration offices.

❑ Public disclosure of fundraising costs and proceeds is a very blunt weapon with which to attack the tiny minority of fraudulent charities and consultants. Invariably, overlapping boards of directors, sweetheart contracts or demonstrably fraudulent claims in the fundraising programs of these organizations will provide a much easier route to the heart of the matter.

❑ Freedom of speech is another applicable principle here. In fact, the U.S. Supreme Court has rejected on the basis of First Amendment rights the most stringent disclosure and reporting requirements legislated by the states. This freedom, in turn, encourages innovation — which may be the public interest sector's greatest contribution to American society.

With all this said, let me make absolutely clear that I believe direct mail must always tell the truth. No reputable direct mail consulting firm will work for any organization they feel isn't delivering on its promises. Ultimately, I'm convinced, donors will *respond* more generously to the truth than to exaggerated or distorted claims.

Now let's take a look at an entirely different argument used to question the ethics of direct mail fundraising. It crops up in cocktail party conversations from time to time, and in donors' letters to some environmental organizations:

"You people are cutting down millions of trees to send out God-knows-how-many letters nobody wants to receive. You should be ashamed of yourselves!"

I confess I do not feel an overwhelming sense of shame in the face of this argument, but it does warrant a response. Quite apart from the fact that there are much worthier targets of ecological zeal — chiefly, lumber companies who devastate the land by clear-cutting forests — there are several reasons why the argument is off the mark:

❑ Direct mail is used by public interest groups because it's cost-effective — that is, it consumes fewer resources than alternative methods of fundraising and communications. Many nonprofit organizations could not exist without large-scale direct mail fundraising programs. Others would need to curtail programs serving millions of Americans.

❑ There are just two ways for most organizations to communicate with their supporters: using paper, or using electronic means. Television, radio, fax and the telephone may all have roles to play in a fundraising or donor communications program, but they're no substitute for letters. Until we become a paperless society, public interest groups will have to go on using the mails to do their jobs. After all, no one's proposing to abolish the U. S. Postal Service to save trees.

❑ Direct mail fundraising packages account for a *very* small portion of the paper output of the United States economy. I can't prove it, but my doodling on the back of an envelope suggests that the *New York Times* and the *Los Angeles Times* together use more paper than all the country's direct mail fundraisers combined.

❑ Many direct mail fundraising specialists (myself included) are actively seeking ways to increase the use of recycled paper. But recycled paper averages three percent more expensive than paper made from new wood pulp – and even that small percentage can make a significant difference in a direct mail fundraising program that operates on the margin. My firm and others work with printers and paper manufacturers to seek solutions to this and other difficult problems.

Now, let's examine the question of what is ethical and proper in fundraising by examining more closely the question about financial disclosure raised in that Wall Street boardroom confrontation. This will help us see some of the broader issues and understand better some of the strategic implications of embarking upon a large-scale direct mail program.

Fundraising Ratios and Other Deceptions

Conventional wisdom holds that the best way to measure your organization's efficiency is to look at the percentage of your income spent on overhead and fundraising. The popular press, the charitable "watchdog" agencies and our own ingrown instincts all tell us this is the right way to determine whether you're doing a good job of running your nonprofit organization. As the argument goes, if you spend more than ten or twenty cents to raise a dollar — a "fundraising ratio" of ten to twenty percent — then there must be something wrong with you.

Well, that's bunk.

The fundraising ratio is a meaningful measurement for America's biggest charities: the Red Cross, the Salvation Army, UNICEF, Goodwill Industries, CARE, the American Cancer Society. All these groups are decades old, command instant name recognition, and have large development departments with the talent and the resources to use every conceivable means to raise money and can make the most of every dollar spent on fundraising. Each of them raises more than $300 million per year. But applying the same simplistic criteria to young public interest groups with budgets a hundredth or a thousandth the size usually makes no sense at all.

In exceptional cases, where fraud or flagrant mismanagement is suspected, an extremely high fundraising ratio *may* be an early warning signal. An organization which is spending ninety-five cents to raise every dollar after three or four years of extensive direct mail promotion is clearly not worthy of donors' support. A closer look may reveal that the organization is promising a miraculous cancer cure and working out of a third-floor walkup and a post office box, and that the organization's founder and $90,000-a-year executive director is the brother-in-law and former employee of its direct mail consultant. But, while fraudulent charities have existed since a charitable impulse moved some far-sighted noble to give away the first shekel, they are uncommon today. It's a tragic mistake to hobble thousands of sincere and effective public interest organizations with rules designed to inhibit a few bad actors. Moreover, where fraud is likely, an unusually high fundraising ratio is probably just one of many grave and obvious problems.

If charitable donors were to limit their gifts to the handful of the nation's nearly one million nonprofit tax-exempt organizations that meet these conventional criteria for nonprofit performance, charities would be few and far between. Groups springing up to meet new needs — or simply to keep the old agencies honest — would die as quickly as they were born. Because only an organization with a truly secure funding base can fulfill these extravagant regulatory fantasies.

When a few phone calls and a lunch meeting with a wealthy donor can produce a multi-million-dollar gift or bequest, fundraising costs are minimal when expressed as a percentage of the proceeds. Much the same goes for an organization with a large, loyal following of donors who can be counted on to renew their support year after year. In either case, the fundraising ratio is likely to be low.

But a small, less well-established group — or one just starting out to address a newly emerging need — is unlikely to be in a position to achieve the same results with such little effort. It may take several years of repeat giving and continuous cultivation before you can *count* on getting gifts from a donor.

Fundraising is hard work — and for *most* nonprofits, it's expensive, especially at the beginning.

Partly because so many so-called "authorities" keep beating the drum for the most restrictive definitions of acceptable fundraising practices, relatively few donors will give more than token sums to any but the best-established, blue-ribbon charities. To smaller and newer organizations, gifts are typically much less generous. And obtaining them can take a great deal of time and money. People tend not to trust what they don't know.

To show the contrast, let's look at two hypothetical nonprofit organizations:

(A) Founded thirty years ago, Charity "A" has an annual budget of $12 million, which it obtains in the following manner:

Trustees and major donors	$4,000,000
Bequests and planned giving programs	2,000,000
Income from endowment (established 15 years ago)	2,000,000
Foundation and corporate support	2,000,000
Direct mail and telephone fundraising (from 30,000 donors)	1,000,000
Sale and licensing of products and services	1,000,000
Total Income Budget	**$12,000,000**

(B) Founded three years ago, Organization "B" has a $2 million budget which it meets as follows:

Foundation support	$900,000
Direct mail and telephone fundraising (from 20,000 donors)	600,000
Trustees and major donors	400,000
Sale of products and services	100,000
Total Income Budget	**$2,000,000**

It's entirely possible that Charity "A" and Organization "B" could each be spending $1 million per year on fundraising and overhead. For "A," this represents one-twelfth of its budget, or *eight cents* on the dollar. For "B," $1 million is half its revenue, or *fifty cents* on the dollar — more than six times as high a fundraising cost as that of "A." Does that make "A" six times "better" than "B"?

Not on your life!

Leave aside for the moment the possibility that the $11 million which "A" has left over to spend directly on its programs might just be going down the drain on misguided or irrelevant projects, getting socked away in fatter and fatter "reserve" funds, or even keeping a passel of unimaginative people at work in featherbedding jobs. After all, "B" could just as easily have misbegotten priorities or incompetent staff. Let's just look a little closer at the *income* side of the ledger. The contrast is dramatic:

- ❏ "B's" work with major donors is just beginning. It's had few opportunities to identify or cultivate major donors or to establish a program of planned giving and bequests, much less an endowment fund. These are "A's" *principal* sources of financial support, but they took years to develop.

- ❏ Nearly half of "B's" $2 million budget is contributed by foundations. For "A," which receives grants worth more than twice as much, foundation and corporate support is only one-sixth of its total funding. Most foundations — and particularly corporate philanthropies, which may have stockholders to worry about — favor name-brand charities. Money attracts money.

- ❏ With its name less well established and its merchandizing program in its infancy, "B's" income from licensing and sale of products is only a tenth as great as "A's." Name recognition usually takes time to establish, and familiarity sells products as well as programs.

The real measure of a nonprofit organization's effectiveness is the cost of the *results* it gains. By that yardstick, many nonprofits with enviable fundraising ratios are singularly ineffective when compared to some of the scrappy, innovative, grassroots organizations with which I'm familiar — ventures which rarely are able to raise a dollar for less than thirty-five or forty cents.

Another big contrast between Charity "A" and Organization "B" lies in their direct mail and telephone fundraising programs:

- ❏ For "A," raising money from 30,000 direct mail donors, a great many of them of long standing, is a very profitable proposition. To replace those five or six thousand lost by attrition each year requires little new investment in donor acquisition. The full cost of "A's" direct mail program may be no more than $250,000. An overall revenue-to-cost ratio of four- or even six-to-one is not at all unlikely in a mature program of this sort.

- ❏ "B's" fast-growth direct mail strategy looks a lot different. In its second year of aggressive donor acquisition, "B" might even be spending on direct mail *more* than the $600,000 it's raising.

- ❏ "A's" direct mail program obviously emphasizes the cultivation and *resolicitation* of loyal, long-term donors. For "B," direct mail and telemarketing are tools to meet a different — and more costly — challenge: to identify and *recruit new donors*.

How does Organization "B" get to be like Charity "A?"
By doing precisely what it's now doing, methodically
building and cultivating its donor base year after year
after year.

As you can see clearly in this example, direct mail is only *one* of a great many fundraising tools that public interest organizations can employ in the service of their strategies to make the world a better place. In fact, for all but a handful of nonprofits and political campaigns, a large-scale direct mail program makes little sense in the absence of other fundraising efforts, especially on the high end of the donor scale. For example, "B's" expensive, fast-growth strategy will really start paying off only when its development program includes major gift opportunities such as "A's."

Nonprofit organizations spring into existence to fill unmet needs, to challenge old concepts, and to espouse new ideas. It's no accident that many public interest groups have such a tough time raising funds; what they advocate is downright unpopular.

But even those organizations that meet universally acknowledged needs and altogether avoid controversy are likely to face an uphill battle getting their fundraising programs up to a level of efficiency that allows for a consistently low fundraising ratio and still provides for necessary growth.

To do so takes *time*. After people, issues and money, time is the fourth dimension of fundraising. It's often unseen and rarely appreciated. But no fundraising program may be fairly evaluated without a full understanding of this most precious of commodities. Time's great value will become much clearer as we look at direct mail fundraising in greater detail in the chapters ahead.

Starting Out 2

Let's be optimistic.

We'll assume that the chair of your board's finance committee hasn't vetoed your plan to explore direct mail fundraising. In fact, she's helped you persuade other board members and your senior staff that the great potential in direct mail is worth the risk and the investment — even if you have to wait for several years to enjoy the payoff. You've budgeted the funds for a test mailing, obtained promises from board members of substantial additional capital if the test is successful, and contracted with a consultant, who will work with you to develop the test package, acquire mailing lists, and manage the testing effort on your behalf.

Now, let's make sure we see eye to eye on some of the basic terms and premises of direct mail fundraising.

What Makes Direct Mail Work – or Fail

You, as the leader of your organization, are the most important ingredient in your direct mail program — not so much because of your management or marketing skills but because of the quality of your leadership. Over time, the perception people have of you and your work will account for at least half the credit (or blame) for the success or failure of your direct mail fundraising efforts.

Your organization's record and the credibility and power of your message; the ties of your work to issues of broad public concern; how much publicity you get, and how good it is — all these factors will help determine how well you do in the mails. But they're only half the story.

There are many other factors — ingredients you and your consultants can control — which will greatly influence the results of your efforts to raise money through direct mail. Together, these controllable factors are about equal in impact to the leadership, reputation and programmatic assets that you bring to the program. The half that's controllable can be broken down in the following way:

List selection — This is far and away the most important controllable ingredient of a successful direct mail fundraising program; call it a quarter of the pie, or about as much as all the other controllable elements combined. The most brilliant appeal for the most dynamic and well-managed organization in the world won't work at all if mailed to the wrong people. The lists selected for your initial donor acquisition test mailing must accurately reflect a cross-section of your potential constituency or "market." They should be lists that have been proven responsive to similar appeals. To make the right list choices for your mailing, someone will have to put in a great deal of time and effort. It's difficult to spend too much time selecting the lists.

The "offer" — How we structure the "pitch" — what we ask for, and what we tell people they're going to get in return for their support — is the most important creative element in our work. Call it five percent of the pie. Every package needs to be built around a "marketing concept" — a simple, straightforward connection between the "offer" and the "market" or intended audience. Before we write a single word of copy, we spend as much time as necessary to find the right marketing concept, and frame it with the right offer. The right decisions at this stage of development can make copywriting easy and stack the odds in favor of a successful outcome.

ILLUSTRATION 9: Many factors make a mailing work — or fail

Copywriting — The actual wording of a fundraising appeal is less important than it's cracked up to be. Typically, the copywriter is responsible for researching the project and the letter-signer, devising the marketing concept, framing the offer, and in many cases for making major design and format suggestions as well; if all this is what is meant by "copywriting," the job is absolutely crucial. But the copywriter's *words* themselves may not account for more than ten percent of an appeal's success or failure. Many people insist that the letter is the single most important element in a direct mail package, and we put a great deal of effort into creating compelling fundraising letters. But there's more to writing a fundraising package than just creating the letter. We devote great care to the creation of the outer envelope, response device, and all other package elements. Good direct mail copywriting ties together all these pieces with the marketing concept.

Format — The size, shape and color of the envelope, the character of the inserts, the appearance and accuracy of the recipient's name and address, and the extent (or lack) of "personalization" may all have significant bearing on the results. ("Personalization" is a regrettably inelegant term that signifies the addressee's own name, address or other known individual facts are printed somewhere in the package.) Making the right format choices — especially whether or not to personalize, and if so to what extent — accounts for about five percent of the total. All the components of a direct mail package must fit together smoothly into an effective, working whole. Above all, a direct mail package must be not only cost-effective but also *credible*: the form of the package needs to match its purpose. We use a very wide variety of formats because every fundraising campaign is unique and requires a unique competitive edge.

Design — Once the format is set, the designer's skill can have equal influence on the outcome, or five percent of the total. Bad design can obscure or undercut the best of offers. There are a great many specialized techniques in the direct mail design trade. After years of trial, error and heartache — typically including brochures too big and envelopes too small — direct mail designers become superbly skilled at putting these techniques to work for their clients.

Now that all that's straight, you're ready to start. What's the first thing to do now?

Think. Because you're going to need a big Idea.

Your Marketing Concept

The marketing concept is the Idea that pulls all the elements together — lists, offer and signer — and ties them up with a bow. Direct mail fundraising is a form of marketing, and obtaining each individual contribution is a matter of closing a sale. Your "sales" — the monetary lifeblood of your organization — may sharply rise or fall as you succeed or fail in conceptualizing a marketing proposition that motivates your members, donors or prospects. Keep this fundamental principle in mind:

> *Each of your mailings requires a unique marketing concept. Every mailing, and every marketing concept, must fit into an overall marketing strategy.*

If it makes you uncomfortable to use the language of marketing, you might try another way of looking at the matter. Think instead about meeting donors' needs and solving their problems. Then your marketing concept might be thought of as the short form of a contract between you and your donors.

Your donors have to get something in return from you. While their motives for contributing to your work may seem to be uncomplicated altruism, the act of giving money reflects deeply held values and beliefs and responds to inner drives: for acceptance, for belonging, for feeling useful and effective, and for propagating their values and beliefs. These and other powerful impulses create expectations that are dangerous to ignore. Your marketing concept needs to address some of these deep-seated needs in an explicit and meaningful way.

Ask yourself what satisfaction a donor will receive from making a contribution to your organization. It might derive from any — or many — of the following:

❏   "doing something" about a critical problem — if only to protest or to take a stand;

❏   associating with a famous and noteworthy person;

❏   getting back at the corrupt or the unjust;

❏   belonging — as a member, friend or supporter;

❏   speaking one's mind, or offering an opinion;

❏   gaining access to inside information;

❏   learning about a complex problem or issue;

❏ being protected from the destruction of cherished values and beliefs; preserving one's world view;

❏ gaining a personal connection to another individual who possesses an emotional, passionate involvement in some meaningful dimension of life;

❏ releasing emotional tension caused by a life-threatening situation, a critical emergency, or an ethical dilemma.

A marketing concept won't work unless it can be expressed in a single sentence (although that sentence may be godawful complicated). To give you a sense of what I mean, here are four examples:

❏ "As one who appreciates the finer things in life, you will cherish for many years to come each magnificent issue of our bimonthly magazine on the visual arts, which you'll receive free of charge as a Charter Member of the Museum with a contribution of $45, $75, $150 or more, and you'll have the satisfaction of knowing that your gift will help us to showcase the exciting new work of emerging artists in our region."

❏ "By displaying the free stickers I'm sending you, signing the enclosed Protest Petition, and sending a tax-deductible gift of $25, $50, $100 or more to the Coalition, you will join thousands of other animal-lovers in America who are committed to stopping once and for all the shameful and short-sighted murder of sea mammals."

❏ "As a former U.S. diplomat with firsthand experience in Third World hotspots, I am writing you and a few other distinguished Americans who have demonstrated a commitment to world peace, to ask you to join me as a Sponsor of the Institute's innovative new conflict-resolution program with a tax-deductible gift of $1000."

❏ "Your renewal gift of as little as $25 to help house America's homeless children will buy $50 or more worth of lumber and tools, because it will be matched dollar for dollar by an anonymous donor through the Center's highly successful Matching Gift Program — so you'll get double the satisfaction from your act of generosity."

Note that each of these marketing concepts makes clear *whom* we're writing, *what* we want from them, *why* we need money, and what we're *offering* in return. A fully developed marketing concept must include all four of these elements. (Please note, too, that I don't mean to suggest the overcooked prose in any of the above examples would actually appear as is in any fundraising package; they're simply summaries of marketing concepts.)

In each of the four examples above, the organization has clarified precisely what it wants from the donor — a particular sum of money, and possibly other things as well — and what the donor will receive in return (although that may be implied or intangible). The marketing concept makes the connection between the signer of the appeal and the recipient, in recognition of the reality that the relationship will satisfy not only your organization's needs but the donor's needs as well.

Decide at the outset what you've got to "sell" and who you think will "buy" it. What you offer may be largely, or even exclusively, intangible, but even intangible benefits must be made explicit.

This task is akin to the fundamental challenge faced by any dynamic enterprise, whether nonprofit or commercial: figuring out what business you're really in. That may not be at all obvious. It may take considerable research and careful thought. But it's important you get it right.

Consider the four organizations cited in the foregoing examples:

❐ In the eyes of the general public, and in budgetary terms, the Museum's principal activity — "the business it's in" — may actually be to publish a bimonthly magazine on the visual arts, despite the fact that the Museum's board may consider its mission to be to showcase young local artists. The marketing concept rightfully focuses on the magazine.

❐ The Coalition's lobbying campaign about the murder of sea mammals may require more funds and more staff time than the public education program which its strategic plan identifies as its primary mission. It may make more sense to say that the Coalition is in the business of influencing policymakers, not educating the general public. The Protest Petition highlighted in the marketing concept reflects this reality.

❐ The Institute's "innovative new conflict-resolution program," envisioned as the centerpiece of its long-term strategy, may be less significant than its effort to recruit hundreds of prominent American citizens as Sponsors. The Institute may actually be in the business of organizing, lobbying or public relations, not conflict resolution. It's appropriate that the marketing concept emphasize the many non-monetary contributions Sponsors make to the Institute.

❐ Because of its focus on the needs of homeless families, the housing construction program instituted by the Center may be less important than the social services provided by Center staff. Thus, the

Center's marketing concept legitimately focuses on children and on donors' satisfaction at helping other people.

Unlike some other forms of advertising, *direct mail fundraising is rarely subtle*. When it is, its subtlety is simply and economically expressed. You have about four seconds for the recipient to decide whether to open your appeal. Once she's opened it, you may have another minute or two to involve her in reading the letter and to begin answering her many skeptical questions. Unless you want to lose her from the outset, you'd better be prepared to hit her over the head with a simple, straightforward proposition that's clear from beginning to end. Your principal task is to *motivate* the recipients of your appeals to *act* in a particular way — to reach for their checkbooks, and right away. In such circumstances, subtlety rarely works.

Effective envelope "teaser" copy draws the recipient directly into the package in a straight line to the heart of the marketing concept. The very best direct mail packages reflect the marketing concept on every sheet of paper, from the outer envelope through the letter and supplementary enclosures to the "response device." Even the reply envelope won't escape unscathed if you think your concept all the way through from beginning to end. (In an emergency appeal, for example, you might print the name of the campaign or the word "RUSH" in the upper left-hand corner of the reply envelope.)

If the "end" is a check that arrives in the mail, the "beginning" is the market itself: that group of individuals to whom you're mailing your letter. No direct mail marketing concept will work unless it's firmly grounded in an understanding of the list or lists you use.

The Wonderful World of Lists

In the 1989 edition of the mailing list catalog used most widely in the direct mail industry, there are entries for more than 25,000 lists. The catalog itself is three and one-half inches thick.

Yes, you got that right: 25,000 different mailing lists! It's a *big* business.

Lists are created because organizations save the names of their members or supporters. Publications maintain lists of their subscribers. Government agencies keep records of licenseholders and taxpayers. Merchants and catalog merchandisers track their buyers. There are also companies in the business of compiling lists specifically for profit.

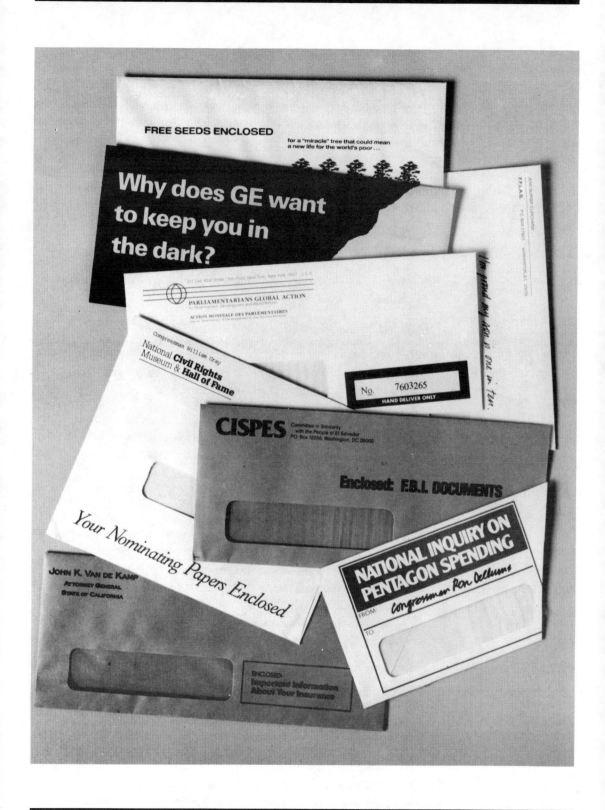

ILLUSTRATION 10: Envelope teasers provoke curiosity

Individual lists vary in size from a few hundred names to more than 80 million. All told, there are *tens of billions* of names and addresses appearing in these readily available mailing lists. Most of the more than 250 million living Americans appear dozens of times, and so do quite a few who are dead. Many of us are included as individuals on literally hundreds of lists.

Mailing lists are by no means all alike. There are numerous ways to categorize or describe them, but in the context of direct mail fundraising, it's useful to group them into seven general types:

(1) *Donors* — These people have contributed money, most likely in response to a direct mail fundraising appeal.

(2) *Members* — They've paid membership dues to an organization, probably by mail.

(3) *Subscribers* — These folks subscribe to a particular periodical. Many first did so in response to a direct mail subscription promotion.

(4) *Buyers* — They've bought books or other goods by mail, in most cases through a catalog they received in the mail.

(5) *Inquiries and sweepstakes entrants* — These are individuals who have responded to an ad or a direct mail package with a request for information or a response to a survey or sweepstakes. They sent in little if any money.

(6) *"Compiled lists"* — These are second-generation lists, produced by merging lists from different sources. For example, someone might compile a list of people who have joined or written letters of inquiry to many different organizations, perhaps dissimilar ones. Someone else's idea of a useful compiled list might be those individuals whose lifestyle or demographic characteristics — as revealed by such means as auto registrations or property tax rolls — fit a certain predetermined pattern. With rare exceptions, compiled lists do *not* consist of people whose principal shared characteristic is that they've contributed or spent money by mail.

(7) *"Good ideas"* — These are the people on your board chair's Rolodex, or a list of your friends or neighbors, or the thousands of individuals to whom you've been sending your newsletter because somebody five years ago was just *sure* they would take any opportunity to support you. (They haven't, and they probably won't.)

There are thousands of available lists in each one of the first six of these categories. In a few cases, they're available directly from the "list owner." Hundreds of "list brokerage" firms manage the others, representing the owners to negotiate and manage the arrangements under which outsiders use their lists. It's a big business, and list brokers tend to specialize — not just in such broad-brush areas as "fundraising" but in narrowly defined fields such as liberal or conservative political lists, Catholic lists or "New Age" lists. I don't hear very often about list brokers going out of business, so I assume they're doing well.

Through list brokers, you're able to gain access to the overwhelming majority of those 25,000 lists. Most are available on computer tapes in one or another of several standard formats that a direct mail service bureau is able to read. (Some lists are available only on mailing labels.)

> *The problem you face isn't getting hold of enough lists —*
> *it's figuring out which of them are likely to work for you.*

Very few will. Only a handful of lists will be sure bets to work for your initial direct mail fundraising appeal. These so-called "hot" lists — including your own active supporters and generous, recent donors to organizations engaged in very similar work — are sometimes hard to come by. "Warm" lists are a little easier to obtain. These are the files which, based on experience with similar appeals, we feel are *likely* to be responsive enough to be cost-effective. But most lists are "cold." Only testing can tell whether they'll respond cost-effectively, and in most cases testing is a long shot. The overwhelming majority of cold lists, as far as you're concerned, might as well be printed with invisible ink. They simply won't work for your donor acquisition campaign, and you might as well forget about trying.

Choosing the right prospect lists is a demanding and sophisticated task. As a group, millionaires aren't good donor prospects for a group seeking to aid the homeless; neither are people who are homeless. Just because the one group has money and the other has a direct interest in the issue is no guarantee that either will respond to the appeal.

You see, there's an ugly truth that applies even to your organization. Yes, yours is unquestionably the most exciting venture to come down the pike since the founding of the Smithsonian Institution. Even so, *very few people who are approached by mail will agree to support you.* That unpleasant fact — together with the limit on the money you're able to invest in direct mail donor acquisition — requires a very selective approach to the tens of thousands of available mailing lists.

To sift through all the possible lists for your initial prospect mailing we look at each list to evaluate the following elements:

❐ *Donor history* — The rule of thumb in our business is that "the people who give by mail are the people who give by mail." I've never heard a credible estimate of the percentage of the population that fits this category, but I suspect it's small — certainly a lot less than half, and probably less than a quarter of the American people. The best place to start looking for them is on *donor* lists.

❏ *"Mail-responsiveness"* — Generally, the best prospects are those who've developed the habit of using the postal system. That *doesn't* include everyone. Industry surveys suggest that only a little more than half of the American public will send money by mail for any reason whatsoever, other than to pay taxes, rent or utility bills, and a great many people won't even do that. The Direct Marketing Association recently estimated that only fifty-five percent of the American public are mail-responsive and can thus presumably be found on lists of donors, subscribers or catalog buyers. (Interestingly, the California Lottery Commission estimates that the same percentage of the adult population plays Lotto on a weekly basis.)

❏ *Recency* — One of the problems with most mailing lists is that they're not kept sufficiently up-to-date. In a society where one-fifth of the population moves every year, this can be a real problem. Generally speaking, only a mailing list that has been updated *within the past twelve months* is useful for fundraising purposes. A four- or five-year-old list may be worthless.

❏ *Accuracy* — A related problem for fundraisers is that the data entry on many publicly available mailing lists is atrocious. Some otherwise attractive lists may be poor prospects for your donor acquisition campaign simply because the list owner — or the computer service bureau that maintains the list — does such a consistently careless job. Among the most common and problematic errors are failure to record address changes and misspellings of names or addresses, both of which lead to high levels of undeliverable mail and to costly duplicate entries.

❏ *Affinity* — If your organization is building a children's hospital in Africa, donors to Save the Children or UNESCO might be a good bet for you to test in your donor acquisition campaign. The members of the National Rifle Association probably aren't. However, affinity is highly overrated and very limiting. The subscribers to a magazine specializing in international affairs could turn out to be your most responsive list of all. For one thing, that list may be far more accurate and up-to-date than most donor lists. Because it's so difficult to predict which lists will work, we do our best to find out which ones worked for similar appeals, thus taking the concept of affinity one step further.

The Marketplace of Lists

Most people seem to have the impression that mailing lists are bought and sold. In fact, this is only rarely the case. Lists are typically made available to direct mailers for *one-time use* only and may not be duplicated or re-used without explicit permission (which isn't often granted.)

Sometimes, lists are available on a *rental* basis. These days the going rate for most desirable donor and subscriber lists is in the range of a nickel to a dime per name ($50 to $100 per one thousand names). Some lists of "buyers" are even more costly. If you're forced to rely heavily on rentals, list costs may constitute one-sixth to one-third the entire cost of your donor acquisition mailing.

However, in many cases you'll be able to *exchange* lists and dramatically reduce this expenditure. Normally, exchanges are on a name-per-name basis. In other words, an exchange will obligate you to provide an equal number of equivalent names and addresses from your mailing list, usually weeks or months later. The cost of list exchanges is modest in comparison with list rentals.

The problem is, the owners of some lists which are available only on exchange may not be willing to trade with you. Unless you already have a sizable list of your own to prove your ability to reciprocate, you won't receive permission to use their lists.

If you're like most people I know, however, letting your organization's donor list out of your hands seems about as attractive as contracting a terminal illness. Here, then, is another reality you'll have to face at the outset: the business of direct mail fundraising is built in large part on (relatively) free commerce in lists, and those groups which lack desirable mailing lists or refuse to trade or rent their own are operating at a serious disadvantage.

There are three principal reasons some organizations advance to explain why they won't exchange or rent their lists. All lack substance.

First, it's said that once a list is in the marketplace, it's vulnerable to theft. This is simple to combat. Like everyone else in the business, we insert what are termed "seed names" in each list we trade or rent; these are dummy names and addresses known only to us and not to the mailer who's getting our list. When the list is actually used, we receive "seed packages" at these dummy addresses. If packages turn up when they weren't supposed to, we take action. It almost never happens, and practical remedies are available if and when it does.

A *second* objection often raised to justify withholding a donor list from the market is that it will allow other organizations to "steal" a group's donors by making a more powerful and effective appeal. This reflects an unfortunate but common misunderstanding about fundraising realities: no organization "owns" its donors. All but the tiniest minority of donors contribute to a great many organizations, and certainly not just one. This is especially true of direct mail donors. Under some circumstances — such as when the timing of an appeal is inconvenient — it might make good sense to deny permission to competitive organizations to use your list. But most of the time it makes no sense at all. The truth is, a directly competitive organization probably has half a dozen other ways to reach *your* donors with its appeal — through the periodicals they're likely to read or the areas where they live or the other groups to which they contribute. You might as well be neighborly about it and get something in return.

The *third* reason frequently given to deny outside access to an organization's donor list is that the list will be "worn out" by overuse if other groups mail their appeals to it. My intuition tells me that there's some truth to this, and like some of my equally cautious colleagues in the industry I normally recommend that outside use of a list be limited to a maximum of one mailing per week — and avoided altogether during certain critical times on the fundraising calendar. But I honestly can't say I've ever seen any *evidence*, convincing or otherwise, that heavy outside usage of a donor list makes any difference whatsoever. There are even those who contend that it's advantageous to allow others to appeal to your list, because it helps cultivate the habit of giving by mail!

Now let's plunge directly into planning your initial test mailing.

The Initial Test Mailing

As the very first step in a planned campaign to establish a broad financial base for your organization, we normally conduct a donor acquisition or prospect *test* mailing. While the scope of initial tests varies from as few as 2,000 letters to as many as half a million, we typically begin with a mailing of between 30,000 and 100,000 packages. Usually, a test mailing will involve from one to three different fundraising letters, each with its own marketing concept.

The character and contents of the packages we mail may vary considerably, but they all share at least one common feature: some mechanism to identify each resulting gift by its *source*. To study the results of the mailing, we have to distinguish among the returns from different lists and from different package versions (if more than one is mailed). Normally, this mechanism is a "Cheshire label" — a small rectangle of thin paper glued to the reply device or directly to the reply envelope — that serves double duty as a mailing label and as the bearer of a symbol or "keycode" identifying the package and the list that correspond to each response we receive.

For example, the keycode "620218" might signify a response to the 18th list and the second of two packages in mailing number 62. Coding mechanisms of this sort allow us to *test* in what the more presumptuous direct mail specialists call a "rigorous, scientific" manner.

The *goal* of the initial test mailing is to determine your organization's potential to sustain a cost-effective, broad-based, direct mail

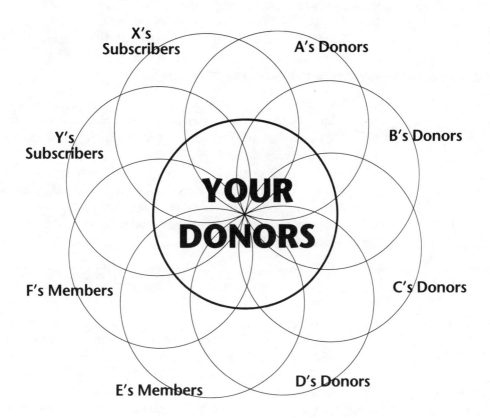

ILLUSTRATION 11: No organization commands its donors' exclusive loyalty

prospecting program through which you can build a substantial list of responsive donors. The specific *objectives* are typically as follows:

(1) to test at least six and perhaps as many as thirty lists from several different "markets" or constituencies for their potential to yield acceptable returns;

(2) to produce donations over the first few months that recover a substantial portion of the cost of the test;

(3) to generate hundreds of new donors, members or subscribers;

(4) and, *most important of all for the future of your direct mail fundraising program*, to produce at least one marketing concept and package design that will be the basis for subsequent resolicitation and prospecting mailings.

A typical initial test mailing at 1989 prices cost from $10,000 to $75,000 (including all production and mailing costs as well as the consultant's fees). The average cost of a 50,000-piece test of one package was $20,000 to $30,000. Major cost variables include the number of different "packages" employed, the number of letters mailed, the consultant's fees, the quality of printing, the postage rate and the technology used to print, address and process the mailing.

It's always difficult, at best, to estimate the returns from an initial test mailing, but it's rarely prudent to assume it will recover more than two-thirds of its cost. We've frequently conducted *profitable* test mailings, but I'm always loathe to predict that outcome from an initial test. When starting a direct mail fundraising program from scratch, the management and creative fees can constitute a substantial overhead and raise the unit cost of the initial mailing. What you spend on the test mailing constitutes an *investment* in the possibility of a long-term development program.

Ten to sixteen weeks normally elapse from the time you and your consultant agree to conduct an initial test mailing until the day it's in the mail. When bulk rate postage is used, the first returns are likely to arrive no sooner than ten days after the maildate, and it may be a total of three weeks before you receive *significant* returns. However, we usually prefer to wait for an additional three or four weeks of significant returns before drawing even preliminary conclusions about the effectiveness of the mailing, and to get a clear picture of the project — to draw conclusions about what lists might be included in a second, "continuation" mailing — we like to have a full eight to sixteen weeks of returns. In other words, a total of about five to eight months will elapse from the formal commitment to conduct a test mailing until the results are analyzed.

In some cases, the timetable for the initial test can be accelerated, and results made available much sooner, but that's not always advisable. Both creative development and list acquisition are complicated and time-consuming processes, often surprisingly so. Devising an effective marketing concept normally takes concentration and time. List brokers and computer service bureaus have timetables, procedures and priorities of their own; so do printers and "lettershops" (where the individual components of your mailing will be collated, inserted and packaged for the post office). It's risky to speed up the people who perform these vital services. Another of the ways corners can be cut — with uncertain effect — is to eliminate that step in the process which reduces the number of duplicate appeals.

What to Do About Duplicate Appeals

At the outset, you may be able to avoid the issue of duplicate appeals. With initial test mailings of fewer than 50,000 names — some say 100,000 — it's generally not recommended to take steps to reduce duplication. Sooner or later, though, the issue will catch up with you — because your donors (or your trustees) write or call to complain, or because it dawns on you how much money you're losing by printing and mailing duplicates. For some organizations, this becomes an emotional issue of major proportions. It's wise to think through in advance how you'll handle it.

Let's assume you and the chair of your board's fundraising committee have the same visceral reaction to duplicates as I do: you *despise* them. You may also be convinced that enough of your potential supporters will be annoyed by receiving duplicate appeals that in the long run it will even be worthwhile to pay a little extra for the test mailing to cut down the number of duplicates.

Using a computer technique called a "merge-purge," it's possible to combine all the names in your mailing into one merged list, and then to identify and isolate the duplicates (called "multi-buyers," "multi-donors" or "merge dupes") so you can save money on printing and postage. However, it's not quite that simple.

For one thing, merge-purge is a costly procedure, running anywhere from a few tenths of a cent per name to as much as one and a half cents (or about $3 per thousand to $15 per thousand). In most situations, a merge-purge will save you money, but not always. In a 50,000-piece test mailing, you're unlikely to pay more than $700 for a merge-purge, but the cost may mount to thousands of dollars in larger acquisition mailings.

A merge-purge often adds days, and usually a week or longer, to the time needed to prepare a mailing. Like the added cost, this is a price that needs to be analyzed.

Merge-purge is a broad concept that refers to a range of techniques and approaches. Some merge-purge programs are permissively "loose" — allowing lots of possible duplicates to get through, for fear of cutting down on the number of good names to mail — and some are "tight." The difference can be considerable. Merge-purge programs sometimes also offer many optional features: correcting bad ZIP codes, eliminating incomplete names and addresses, sorting names into order for postal "pre-sort" discounts, screening for surnames of particular ethnicity, affixing Congressional district or other geodemograhic information, and other possible enhancements. The list is long, and the implications for your direct mail program can be significant.

For an organization with a donor list of significant size, there is one overwhelming reason to conduct a merge-purge for every prospect mailing: it makes it possible to eliminate most (though not all) of your own donors. Not doing so may be very costly. Some of your contributors will become mightily annoyed by receiving duplicate appeals, especially appeals that don't recognize the fact they've already given you money. More important, however, your prospect letter probably doesn't ask for a big enough gift and will give your donors a way to get off the hook with smaller gifts than they would send in response to a resolicitation. The difference can be considerable.

If you actually read a merge-purge report, you'll lose forever any remaining illusion that your donors are exclusively your own. The report for your initial test mailing may show ten, twenty, thirty, or even forty percent or more overlap among the lists you're testing. The rate of duplication will vary greatly from one list to another, but you're likely to find that the very "best" lists — those that are most responsive to your appeals — are the ones that overlap the *most* with your own list (and with each other.) Those that overlap the least — and are thus most dissimilar — tend to be less responsive.

In a typical 50,000-piece test mailing, you may find you'll need a total of 56,000 names, or an additional twelve percent, to produce the correct number of mailing labels. Merging 56,000 names derived from, say, twelve different lists, the computer may identify approximately 47,000 as "unique" names. Most of the other 9,000 names duplicate some of the 47,000 unique names, and in some cases each other as well. Three thousand of the 9,000 merge-dupes match *just one* of the 47,000 names. These 3,000 will be formed into a list of their own; including the 47,000 unique names, this will make a total of 50,000 names "out of

Schematic Representation of Simple Merge Cited in Accompany Text

LIST	QUANTITY BEFORE MERGE-PURGE	UNIQUE NAMES AFTER MERGE-PURGE
1	5,000	3,800
2	5,000	3,900
3	5,000	4,000
4	5,000	4,100
5	5,000	4,200
6	5,000	4,300
7	5,000	4,500
8	5,000	4,600
9	4,000	3,100
10	4,000	3,300
11	4,000	3,500
12	4,000	3,700
Merge-Dupes		3,000
TOTAL	56,000	50,000

ILLUSTRATION 12: A merge-purge identifies and reduces duplicates

merge" on twelve original lists plus a list of merge-dupes. The other 6,000 names are either multiple duplicates (which appear on *three* or more lists) or bad addresses; in this case, all 6,000 names will be ignored.

The list of merge-dupes has a special function — one that helps to justify the cost and the time spent on the merge-purge. Since you've already paid for them at least twice (either in cash or in names to be exchanged), it's perfectly appropriate for you to *mail* to them twice. It's often profitable, since these are the names of those who are *most* likely to respond to your appeal. Some of these individuals are direct mail junkies who may contribute regularly to scores or even hundreds of organizations (and some are probably consultants like me who are reading everything the competition is sending out!). Chances are, you'll mail the merge-dupes three to six weeks following the main maildate of your test, and the list will likely perform at least as well as the average of the other twelve lists. Occasionally, it proves to be the *best* of them all.

In this hypothetical example of a 50,000-piece test mailing, the "merge factor" or "dupe rate" — the percentage of names identified as duplicates or bad addresses — was 16%. (That's 9,000 divided by 56,000.) In larger quantities, when you're mailing the full lists and not just small "test panels" of 5,000 names or so, that percentage will go *up*. (Don't ask me why. I'll blame it on statistics.)

In such cases, with high merge factors, the economics of merge-purge will be favorable for you. Your 50,000-piece test mailing will "save" you the cost of mailing to 6,000 multiple duplicates and bad addresses. If your cost in the mail is $350 per thousand, that's a savings of more than $2,000 — far more than you'll pay for the merge-purge. Of course, you might argue that you never had any intention of mailing to more than 50,000 individuals — but, the truth is, you're getting the *benefit* of mailing to 56,000. In much larger quantities — if the merge factor is still high — the advantage might be even greater, since merge-purge costs fall more rapidly than most other mailing costs as quantities increase.

The merge-purge is just one of those many details that can make or break your direct mail fundraising program. Another is the nettlesome issue of who will sign your letter.

Choose the Right Signer

For reasons that are not entirely clear to me, at least one-third of the initial test mailings we've helped to launch over the years have been delayed — sometimes for more than *a year* — while the executive director or the board chair chased after the supposedly "perfect" signatory.

It's not worth the wait.

In fact, you should immediately rule out the following three persons as prospective signers for your direct mail donor acquisition letter:

(1) that Hollywood star you cornered at somebody else's fundraiser, who told you then he'd really love to help you out;

(2) the famous novelist who went to college with the chair of your board and who could probably help punch up the letter a little bit, too (and maybe even write it herself); and

(3) that college professor who's a world-renowned expert in the issue your group is addressing and is well known to all forty-five people in his field.

That "famous" novelist, actor or expert *may* have the name recognition to get an envelope opened — but will anyone be convinced she knows what she's talking about? Is she genuinely involved in your issue, and preferably in *your* organization as a long-time board member or volunteer? Is her image such that she'll be taken seriously? What will she say if someone asks her a question about you on a TV talk show? And is she really widely known among the general public and not just to a narrow audience? Name recognition is easily overestimated, and it may not last.

For a successful direct mail fundraising program, the person who signs your appeal needs to be prepared for the long haul, too. Does she understand that if the letter works well, you need to mail it again and again to achieve economies of scale? Or will she inform you after you've printed her name on 250,000 envelopes for the next mailing that she's decided not to allow you to use her name anymore?

Now, how about copy approval? Is that Hollywood star of yours available to review the draft of the letter — or is he on location in Tashkent for the next four months and reachable only by camel train? Will his agent, manager or secretary actually show him your letter? Once the copy reaches him, will he declare dogmatically that he won't sign anything longer than one page? Will he insist on rewriting the letter because it doesn't fit his image to ask directly for money? Will he refuse to allow you to include any references to his own, relevant experiences because "that's too personal"? Will he sit indecisively on the text without responding to your phone calls, while the maildate for your test slips ever farther into the dim recesses of the future?

Lest these problems sound farfetched, I hereby affirm that I have encountered every single one of them at least once — and in some cases five or six times — within the past ten years. This experience has helped lead me to the conclusion that, as the executive director of your organization, *you* are probably the very best signatory for your donor acquisition letter.

After all, who can more *credibly* tell your story than you?

A famous name alone is no guarantee of good response for a direct mail appeal. Time and again, I've seen appeals signed by Hollywood stars or celebrated authors outclassed by comparable letters mailed over the signatures of unknown, unsung staff or board members.

While staff signatures don't seem to work as well in politics as they do for nonprofit groups — generally, it's essential that the *candidate* sign fundraising appeals — there are instances where the campaign manager or fundraising chair may be a stronger signatory than even the most famous political candidate.

In all cases, the key is *credibility*.

If someone else can tell your story more credibly than you — someone with good name recognition to boot — you may be well advised to take a back seat. If you do, just be sure the signatory you've selected has really bought into the process and won't cause more trouble than she's worth.

And lest you're tempted, out of insecurity, a need to compromise, or other motives, to *co-sign* your letter with a second person who will lend added authority to the appeal, keep this in mind:

A direct mail fundraising appeal is not a manifesto. It's a *one-to-one* communication — a letter from one person to another, written in the first person singular and addressed in the second person singular. Its success requires an emotional bond between the two. Only one person can sign a fundraising letter.

Whatever *individual* can write most convincingly and emotionally about your work is the best person to sign your appeal.

The Best Time to Mail Your Appeal

"The best time to mail your appeal is when you've got it printed and there's enough postage in your account."

When my first direct mail teacher gave that answer to an earnest question I'd asked about seasonal influences on direct mail fundraising, I didn't know whether to be puzzled or annoyed. Then came five or six years during which I watched appeals be delayed by red tape, procrastination, reluctant funders, screwups in the postal system and computer crashes as well as arguments about seasonality. Finally, several dozen clients later, I understood at last:

If you're waiting for the perfect time to mail, your letters may never make it to the mailbox. And if there's any key to success in direct mail fundraising, it's this: you have to mail, and mail, and mail some more.

Yes, there *are* seasonal influences on direct mail fundraising, just as there are on just about every other form of marketing. A seasonality study conducted by a leading list brokerage firm showed that in the period March 1988 through February 1989 an estimated twenty percent of all fundraising appeals went into the mails in November, while fourteen percent were mailed in August and nearly twelve percent in February. But those figures have changed greatly over time, according to the same study. Our own testing has shown January and August to be the most favorable months for prospecting, and increasingly so in recent years. Chances are, though, the patterns of seasonality will be different for *your* organization than they are for others. And unless you've got a huge budget for testing, you may never be able to afford the research needed to determine the seasonal patterns that bear on your particular direct mail program.

And besides: you can't possibly mail *only* during what you think is the "best time."

Some groups limit their prospecting efforts to one or two large mailings per year, presumably in the most favorable months; with sufficient capital, that may well be their very best donor acquisition strategy. Resolicitations, however, are another matter altogether: donor resolicitation is a year-round process. As much as forty percent of all the funds contributed by mail are donated within the final quarter of the calendar year. For most — not all — nonprofit organizations, November and December are the "best" times to seek renewal gifts. But the most successful year-end appeal won't come close to making up the revenue lost by failing to resolicit your donors during the other ten months of the year.

Keep in mind, too, that a month that's dead time for one group's fundraising program may be fruitful for another's. We've often found that mailing during months that are generally avoided by large, established charities produces better results for organizations that are less well known. Not everyone can compete with the Sierra Club or the Salvation Army — and you might be unwise to try.

Now, please join me in a look at the typical contents of a direct mail fundraising package — and at some of the issues commonly raised about them.

Anatomy of a Direct Mail Fundraising Package

3

In this chapter, I'll show you in pictures and words the individual components of a typical direct mail fundraising package.

Keep in mind as you examine each of the individual elements portrayed in this chapter that there is no "best" or "perfect" example of any one of them. Every element in a successful direct mail fundraising package is a part of a *whole* — unified by a marketing concept.

In Chapter 6, we'll take an inside look at *one* particular public interest direct mail campaign. There you'll have an opportunity to examine, page by page, the entire contents of seven fundraising packages that were written concurrently for one organization to appeal to a total of 295,000 individuals. Each of the seven packages was mailed to a different portion of the target audience.

In Chapter 7, I'll reproduce the contents of the seven fundraising packages mailed within a thirty-day period during the 1988 Jesse Jackson-for-President campaign.

Right now, though, let's take a quick look at what many fundraisers consider the most important element in a direct mail package: the outer envelope.

The Outer Envelope

Outer envelopes, otherwise called "carrier envelopes" or simply "carriers" or "outers," come in a bewildering profusion of shapes, sizes and colors. Occasionally, direct mail fundraising appeals are packaged without envelopes, in the form of self-mailing brochures or magazines or in such nontraditional formats as "card decks" (which are just about what they sound like they are). But most fundraisers keep coming back to the boring old technique of inserting letters in envelopes because, most of the time, it *works* better than other formats.

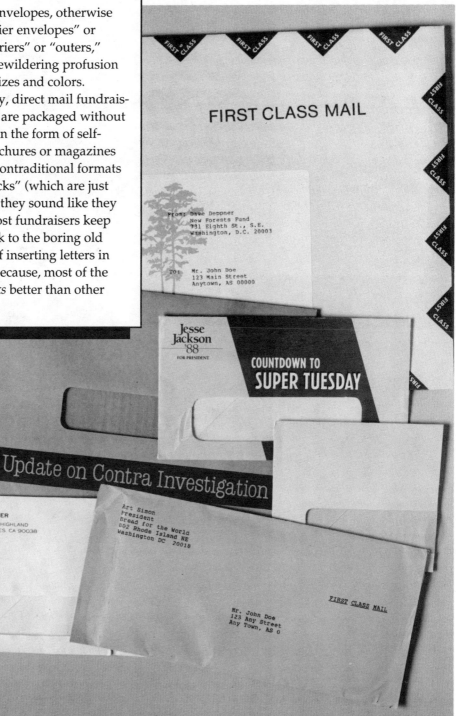

The Outer Envelope

Direct mail designers, copywriters and envelope manufacturers wrack their brains for ever new and more unusual wrappings, in relentless pursuit of the envelope to end all envelopes: one that *everyone* will open. But reality intrudes: through our research, we've learned that, despite all these clever machinations to capture their attention, what people really look at first is how their names and addresses are spelled!

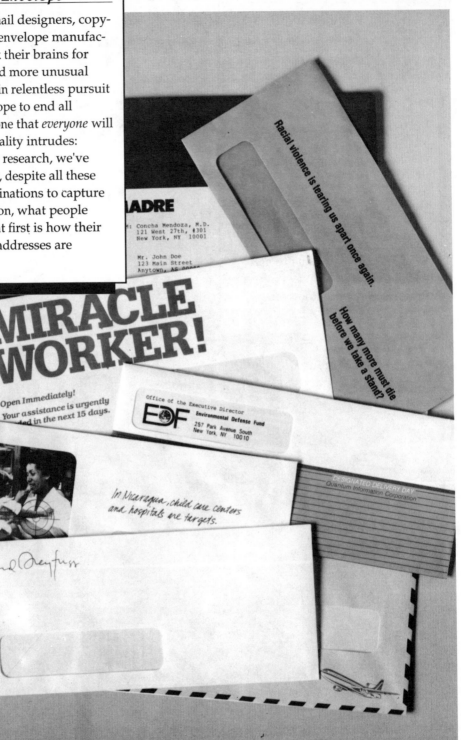

Postage

In its inscrutable wisdom, Congress requires the U.S. Postal Service to offer a wide variety of postal rates and delivery options. Although runaway inflation has reduced the advantage (and federal budget-cutting threatens to eliminate it entirely), comparatively low rates are still available to most nonprofit organizations. The very cheapest rate applies to huge mailings "pre-sorted" into bundles for individual letter-carriers, but discounts are also available on first class postage if you pre-sort. There are also several format options: stamps, metered postage, and pre-printed postal "indicia." Choosing among them is not a trivial matter, because any one may dramatically affect a mailing's results.

It's tempting to use the least expensive postage — but here's another one of those counter-intuitive aspects of direct mail: the opposite is often true. We make extensive use of first class postage — because it gets there faster and more reliably, because it's for-wardable, because it gets more envelopes opened, and, most of all, because research often shows that first class postage is more *cost-effective* than cheaper postal rates. Ultimately, you may get just what you pay for, even when you're buying it from the U. S. Postal Service.

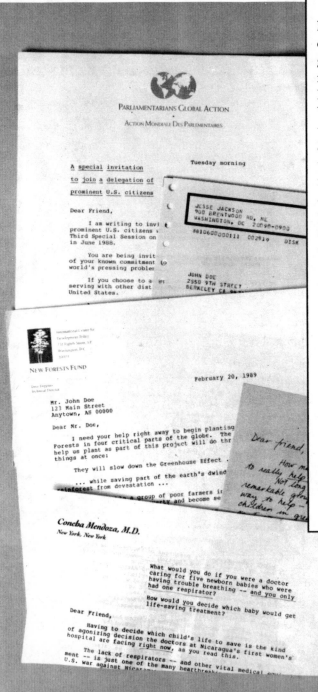

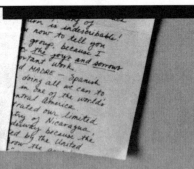

The Letter

If I've heard it once, I've heard it ten thousand times: "Why do you insist on sending out these godawful four-page letters? *I* never write such long letters, and I'm sure I'd never *read* them!" Well, let's review the facts: (1) By testing this proposition again and again, we know that, almost all the time, longer letters generate more donations than shorter ones; and (2) studies show that lots of people actually do read four-page fundraising letters — in fact, many people even *like* getting them. This continues to be true even now, after years of overflowing mailboxes, and even though *you* may automatically throw them into the trash. Ultimately, direct mail fundraising doesn't work on theory or intuition but on empirical fact.

Fundraising letters are almost as varied as the envelopes they're mailed in. But they're not much like business or personal letters, or even like advertising copy. Direct mail fundraising follows rules and rhythms of its own.

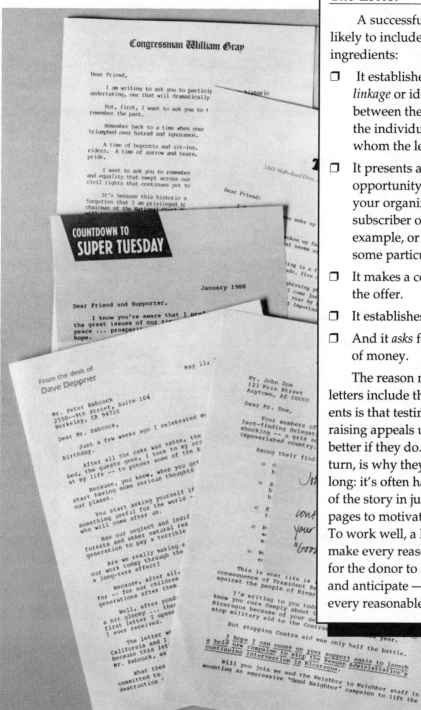

The Letter

A successful appeal letter is likely to include five essential ingredients:

❏ It establishes a one-on-one *linkage* or identification between the letter-signer and the individual person to whom the letter is addressed.

❏ It presents an *offer* of an opportunity to participate in your organization (as a subscriber or member, for example, or by supporting some particular program).

❏ It makes a compelling *case* for the offer.

❏ It establishes *urgency*.

❏ And it *asks* for a specific sum of money.

The reason most direct mail letters include these five ingredients is that testing proves fundraising appeals usually work better if they do. And that, in turn, is why they're typically long: it's often hard to tell enough of the story in just one or two pages to motivate a donor to *act*. To work well, a letter needs to make every reasonable argument for the donor to send money now, and anticipate — and satisfy — every reasonable objection.

The Reply Device

A detached, stand-alone "reply device" or "response device" or "form" (occasionally called a "donation coupon," though I don't favor the term) has repeatedly proven to be an indispensable element in fundraising packages, with only rare exceptions. For one thing, using a reply device is the most efficient way for you to obtain the donor's name and address, which normally appears on a label or direct imprint on the reply device. But there's an even more important reason we include these devices. Studies prove that donors are more likely to respond if they're given something to *do* other than just write and return a check. If nothing else, they give donors a chance to correct the spelling of their names and addresses. The reply device is the first thing most donors see when they open a fundraising package. Many donors set appeals aside, promising themselves they'll write checks later; they often keep reply devices but toss out the letters.

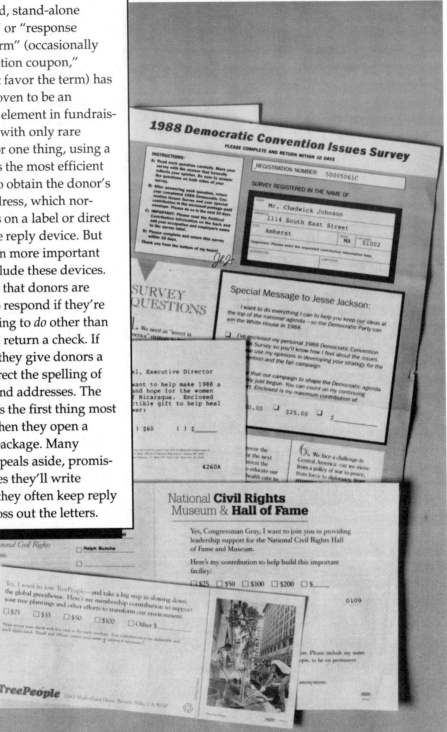

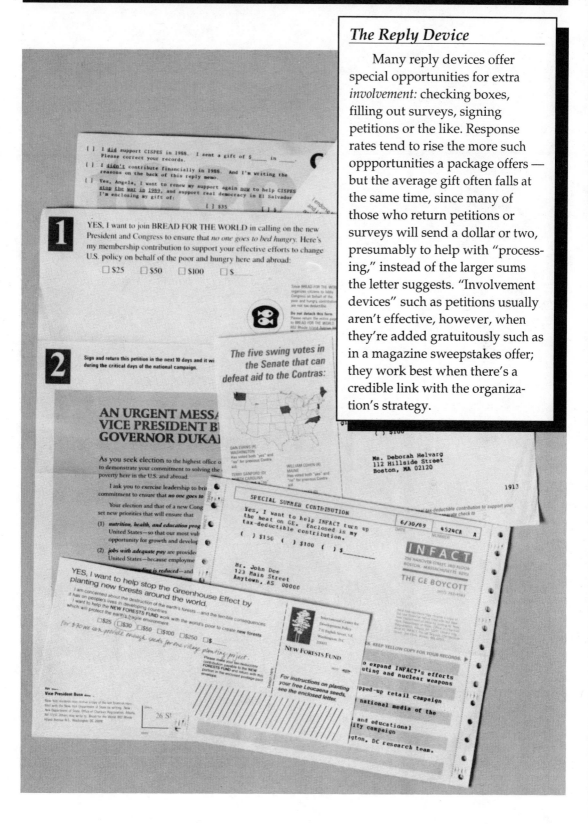

The Reply Device

Many reply devices offer special opportunities for extra *involvement:* checking boxes, filling out surveys, signing petitions or the like. Response rates tend to rise the more such opportunities a package offers — but the average gift often falls at the same time, since many of those who return petitions or surveys will send a dollar or two, presumably to help with "processing," instead of the larger sums the letter suggests. "Involvement devices" such as petitions usually aren't effective, however, when they're added gratuitously such as in a magazine sweepstakes offer; they work best when there's a credible link with the organization's strategy.

The Reply Envelope

Direct mail fundraising appeals work best when it's easy for a donor to respond. This almost always means they'll include a reply envelope — and most of the time it will be a "Business Reply Envelope" that the donor can mail postage-free without hunting for a stamp. (It will cost your organization $0.38 at current rates for the Postal Service to process each one.) But in many circumstances it makes sense to ask the donors to affix their own stamps: some organizations obtain higher response when they do. Other times, it's wise to put a "live stamp" — a real, live first class stamp — on the reply envelope. Only experience and testing can establish the appropriate approach for each mailing.

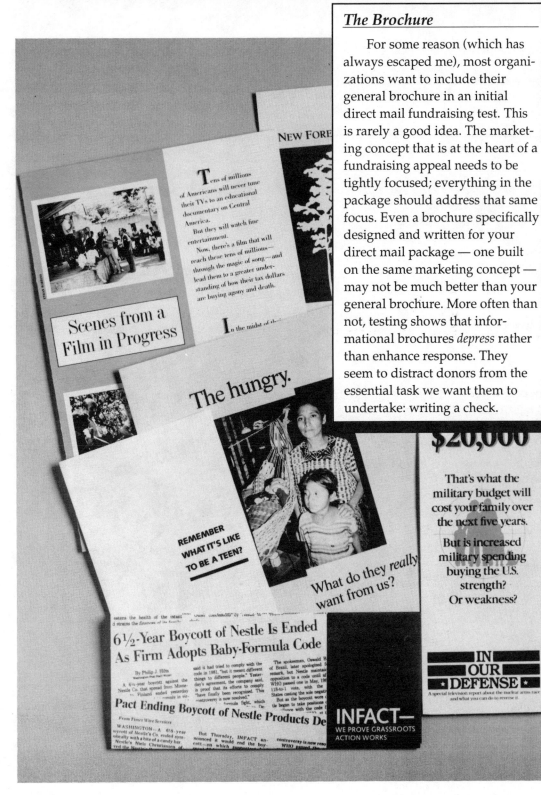

The Brochure

For some reason (which has always escaped me), most organizations want to include their general brochure in an initial direct mail fundraising test. This is rarely a good idea. The marketing concept that is at the heart of a fundraising appeal needs to be tightly focused; everything in the package should address that same focus. Even a brochure specifically designed and written for your direct mail package — one built on the same marketing concept — may not be much better than your general brochure. More often than not, testing shows that informational brochures *depress* rather than enhance response. They seem to distract donors from the essential task we want them to undertake: writing a check.

"Front-End Premiums"

Ask anyone in the advertising business to identify the most powerful word in the English language, and you're likely to be told it's "FREE." Wonder no more, then, why so many direct mail fundraising packages come with free stickers, decals, stamps, keychains, address labels, letter-openers, bumperstickers and other such items. These are so-called "front-end premiums" — as opposed to "back-end premiums," which are sent only in response to gifts from donors. The psychology established by these unsolicited free gifts is often not subtle: the operative mechanism is *guilt*, and it's no accident that many donors send in a dollar or two in re-sponse. But there may be better reasons for you to use front-end premiums; at their best, decals, stamps and such can also be effective "involvement devices" that give donors something to do, reinforce the marketing concept, heighten your organization's visibility, and even play a role in your public education program.

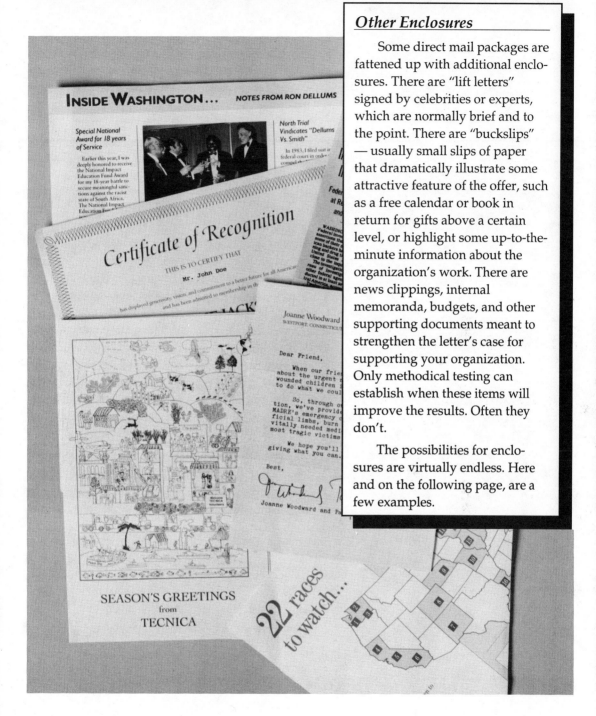

Other Enclosures

Some direct mail packages are fattened up with additional enclosures. There are "lift letters" signed by celebrities or experts, which are normally brief and to the point. There are "buckslips" — usually small slips of paper that dramatically illustrate some attractive feature of the offer, such as a free calendar or book in return for gifts above a certain level, or highlight some up-to-the-minute information about the organization's work. There are news clippings, internal memoranda, budgets, and other supporting documents meant to strengthen the letter's case for supporting your organization. Only methodical testing can establish when these items will improve the results. Often they don't.

The possibilities for enclosures are virtually endless. Here and on the following page, are a few examples.

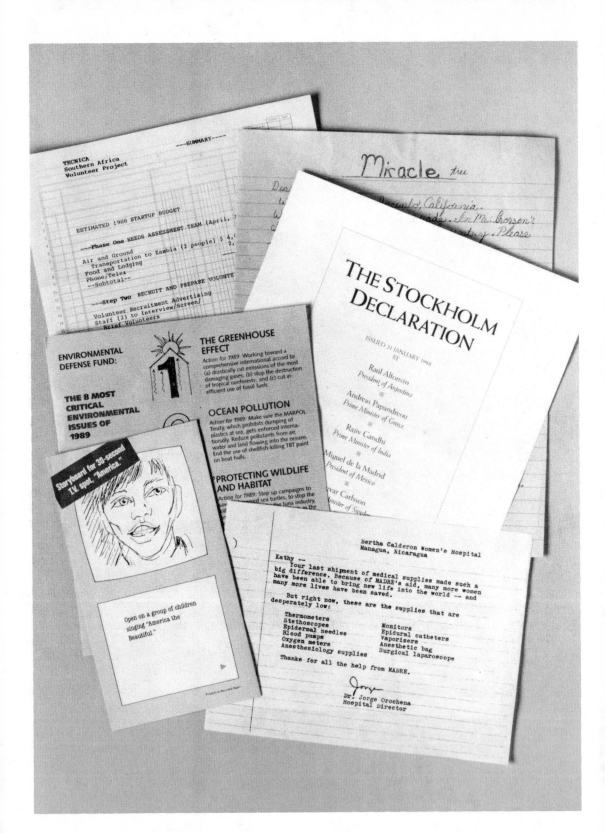

As you can see, putting together a direct mail fundraising package is not simply a matter of writing a letter and wrapping it up. In fact, the letter is often the *last* element I write. Rather, the entire package must reflect a clearly thought out marketing concept. Once that is fixed, in your mind and on paper, you can start with any element of the package. In most cases, I begin with the reply device, which encapsulates the marketing concept.

The outer envelope, which gives donors or prospects their first look at your package, bears special consideration and may take a lot of work — perhaps a third or more of the time allotted to copywriting and design, especially in the case of acquisition packages. An especially clever or provocative "teaser" calculated to entice prospects to open the envelope may be the hardest thing of all to write. But the very biggest challenge is to write outer envelope copy that is fully consistent with everything *inside* the envelope and leads recipients directly into the marketing concept.

All the pieces in a direct mail package must fit together neatly or they'll confuse rather than motivate. They'll prompt a response only if you've carefully thought through your marketing concept before you start to write.

Settling in for the Long Haul

4

I've described the ideal direct mail prospecting program as one that attracts new donors at an *acceptable* acquisition cost.

What's "acceptable" to you?

Take my word for it: the breakeven prospecting that may seem "acceptable" in the abstract could be impossible for you to attain. You could be making a big mistake to hold yourself to that standard simply because it seems "right." Building your donor base will mean a great deal to your organization. It may be worth paying a lot of money to keep your list growing.

Your challenge is to figure out how *much* it's worth.

In the next chapter, we'll examine several different methods for evaluating the worth of the donors you recruit through prospecting. You may then be able to apply specific numbers to your donor acquisition program, establishing criteria that relate uniquely to your organization's strategy and the role you've assigned to the direct mail program. In this chapter, we'll look at the possibilities and the pitfalls of sustaining a direct mail fundraising program over the long term. First, let's figure out whether it's worth trying.

Telling the Difference Between Success and Failure

You've finally gotten enough results from your initial test mailing to tell the story, and what they say is absolutely clear and unequivocal: *maybe* it's going to work:

❑　You've tested two slightly different versions of one package using samples from ten lists, splitting each of them down the middle. The total cost of this 50,000-piece test was $25,000. We project you'll receive a total of $12,500, and despite cautionary warnings, your Board of Directors had been expecting at least $20,000. From this initial test, you'll gain about 500 donors at an acquisition cost of $25 per donor — a level that is too high for your organization to sustain.

❑　Judging from the latest "flashcounts" — periodic list-by-list reports — one of the two package versions appears to be performing slightly better than the other; a statistical analyst who isn't too much of a purist would agree that it's a better bet for the future. It might even produce results as much as twenty percent higher than the other one's — and we're all convinced in hindsight that we

Package A

25,000 letters
mailed to Lists 1-10
at $12,500 cost

273 Contributions
averaging $25 each,
$6,825 total revenue,
Lists 1-3 break even,
acquisition cost $21
per donor.

Package B

25,000 letters
mailed to Lists 1-10
at $12,500 cost

227 Contributions
averaging $25 each,
$5,675 total revenue,
List 1 breaks even,
acquisition cost $30
per donor.

ILLUSTRATION 21: Mailing results often vary by package

could substantially boost the returns even more with several simple changes in the copy.

❏ Even with the better of the two existing packages, your mailing broke even on only three of the ten lists. Notably, however, two of those three are very large lists, with substantial potential for further mailing.

❏ We project that you'll be able to recover three-quarters of the costs and fees you might invest in a second, "continuation" or "roll-out" mailing of 75,000 pieces. Our more favorable projections are based on using the more successful of the two packages, mailing to substantial numbers of new, yet unmailed names from the three most responsive lists, and making what we believe are improvements in the copy. Also, the increased quantity and diminished start-up costs will lower the mailing's unit cost. As a result, we expect you'll recover about $22,500 out of $30,000, gaining 900 new donors at a cost of $8.33 each. Because your capital is limited and your rudimentary fundraising program is unlikely to derive more than $20 in net revenue per donor per year, this acquisition cost is much closer to the level your organization can sustain.

❏ However, in a second mailing, we hope to learn enough from further list and package testing to lower that acquisition cost on subsequent mailings to the range of $3 to $5 — although there's no guarantee we can do so.

To proceed with a second mailing means either a fight with your board right now, or, possibly, a bigger conflict further down the line. What do you do?

The only way I know to deal with a problem of this sort — which is maddeningly common — is to decide *in advance* how to define a "successful" outcome for your direct mail test. There's no such thing as a workable universal definition, but here's a principle to start from:

The criteria that distinguish success from failure must be directly based on your organization's resources and strategic goals.

For some organizations, the scenario I've sketched above is very attractive. A well-capitalized group with an appealing action program and a handful of wealthy major donors might be nuts not to go ahead under these circumstances. So would one that's seeking to change prevailing attitudes on a matter of broad public policy and requires significant grassroots participation to do so.

Simple Flashcount for Hypothetical 50,000-piece Donor Acquisition Mailing

LIST	UNIVERSE	QUANTITY MAILED	GIFTS	REVENUE	PERCENT RESPONSE	AVERAGE GIFT	ACQUISITION COST/DONOR
LIST 1	100,000	5,000	120	$3,000	2.40%	$25	($4.17)
LIST 2	3,000	5,000	100	$2,650	2.00%	$27	($1.50)
LIST 3	250,000	5,000	88	$2,500	1.76%	$28	.00
LIST 4	4,000	5,000	55	$1,300	1.10%	$24	$21.82
LIST 5	450,000	5,000	50	$1,100	1.00%	$22	$28.00
LIST 6	10,000	5,000	40	$750	.80%	$19	$43.75
LIST 7	25,000	5,000	21	$603	.42%	$29	$90.33
LIST 8	50,000	5,000	12	$342	.24%	$29	$179.83
LIST 9	750,000	5,000	8	$155	.16%	$19	$293.13
LIST 10	1,500,000	5,000	6	$100	.12%	$17	$400.00
TOTAL		50,000	500	$12,500	1.00%	$25	$25.00
TEST PACKAGE A		25,000	273	$6,825	1.09%	$25	$20.79
TEST PACKAGE B		25,000	227	$5,675	0.91%	$25	$30.07

ILLUSTRATION 22: Periodic flashcounts show returns for each list mailed

Similarly, an organization committed to a long-range membership growth *strategy* — with sufficient capital on tap to make it work — might well decide it's worth paying even $25 per donor. A $25 new member acquisition cost — corresponding, in the hypothetical case sketched out above, to returns of fifty cents on the dollar in prospecting — might be well worthwhile for such an organization. They'll recover their investment within less than a year, given the generous returns they receive from membership dues, special donor appeals and collateral fundraising efforts that feed off the membership list.

By contrast, a narrowly based and underfunded effort to launch a new organization through the mails might wisely decide to leave the field with results like the above. The same goes for a well-established charity with a fully staffed development department. For a large organization, the case *against* direct mail in this scenario is even stronger if this, its first foray into direct mail donor acquisition, was a wistful effort to diversify its funding base. (More than once, I've seen half-hearted, compromised efforts at direct mail undertaken by cautious organizations and quickly ended because they never were convinced their work lent itself particularly well to the emotional rough-and-tumble of direct mail. Some groups might be better off not trying.)

Every organization is unique. Your challenge is to make direct mail work uniquely for *you*.

Choosing Lists for the Next Mailing

As you set out to select prospect lists for the second mailing in your donor acquisition campaign, you'll be forced once again to address those strategic considerations that determine the levels of investment and risk acceptable to your organization.

Let's assume we've identified fifteen possible lists to be used in your continuation mailing: Lists "A" through "O." They range in size ("universe") from 3,000 names to 250,000, with a total universe of one million names. Four months ago, you mailed to ten of them — "A" through "J" — so we can project the response rate and average contribution we anticipate from each of them. If we use all ten in your roll-out, we'll be "re-mailing" four small lists, re-mailing portions of two others, and mailing to additional, yet untouched names on six lists. The other five lists — "K" through "O" — are to be newly tested, and it's anybody's guess what will happen when we mail to them; to be conservative, I've assumed poor results.

In **Illustration 23** *(see pages 92-93)*, I've ranked the fifteen lists from best-performing to worst in terms of response rate. I've calculated the probable results of mailing to what appears from the test results to be the optimum quantity on each list. To simplify the picture, I've arbitrarily assumed that we won't run a merge-purge.

For each list, the chart presents the mailing cost and anticipated gross and net returns, the projected number of new donors, and the acquisition cost for that list. (Costs vary from one list to another because some are available to you only as rentals and others only on exchange.) On its farthest right column, the chart shows on each row the *cumulative* profit or loss of mailing to all the lists down to and including the one on that row.

For the top five lists — "A" through "E" — we anticipate mailing to every available name. For most of the others, we'll select only a percentage of the names available. (To "roll out" to all the available names on a large list without repeated testing is a risky proposition.) This points to a total mailing quantity of up to 150,000 packages — only fifteen percent of the total number of names available on the fifteen lists. With lists that perform only moderately well at best, it's often unwise to "roll out" to the full universe.

In the long run, mailing to Lists "K" through "O" — the five "test" lists — may be the most significant aspect of this second mailing. Together, they constitute half of the universe for the mailing as a whole. Each consists of at least 25,000 names. List "N" alone contains 250,000. To succeed with any of the five will make a meaningful contribution to the success of your direct mail program. Every prospect mailing should include list tests of this sort to explore new markets. You can and should mail more than once to those lists that constitute the core of your donor acquisition program because they work so very well, but there's a limit to remailing. List testing is never-ending.

On the final row of the chart you can see the total and cumulative impact of mailing all fifteen lists in the quantities indicated: a response rate of 1.6% and an average gift of $18. With a budget of $65,000 and projected gross revenue of $44,020, the mailing is projected to lose $20,980, acquiring 2,465 new donors at an acquisition cost of $9 per donor.

Now here's where your strategy takes specific tactical shape:

☐   If your strategy requires you to *build your donor list as quickly as possible* — and you've got the money to do so — your best tactical move is to mail all 150,000 names, and perhaps more besides. At an acquisition cost of $9, you may feel you're getting a bargain on

List Selection Model for Hypothetical Donor Acquisition
Mailing Described in Accompanying Text

LIST	UNIVERSE	QUANTITY	PCT RESPONSE	AVERAGE GIFT	GROSS INCOME
A	5,000	5,000	4.0%	$20	$4,000
B	10,000	10,000	3.5%	$18	6,300
C	3,000	3,000	3.0%	$18	1,620
D	15,000	15,000	2.5%	$16	6,000
E	5,000	5,000	2.0%	$18	1,800
F	75,000	25,000	1.8%	$20	8,750
G	150,000	25,000	1.5%	$18	6,750
H	25,000	12,000	1.3%	$16	2,400
I	5,000	5,000	1.0%	$14	700
J	200,000	20,000	.8%	$18	2,700
K	150,000	5,000	.8%	$16	600
L	25,000	5,000	.8%	$16	600
M	52,000	5,000	.8%	$16	600
N	250,000	5,000	.8%	$16	600
O	30,000	5,000	.8%	$16	600
	1,000,000	150,000	1.6%	$18	$44,020

ILLUSTRATION 23: *Projected overall mailing results determine individual list selection*

COST	NUMBER NEW DONORS	NET INCOME	CUMULATIVE INCOME	ACQUISITION COST
$2,000	200	$2,000	$2,000	($10)
4,500	350	1,800	3,800	(5)
1,200	90	420	4,220	(5)
6,750	375	(750)	3,470	2
2,000	100	(200)	3,270	2
11,250	438	(2,500)	770	6
11,250	375	(4,500)	(3,730)	12
4,800	150	(2,400)	(6,130)	16
2,000	50	(1,300)	(7,430)	26
9,000	150	(6,300)	(13,730)	42
2,000	38	(1,400)	(15,130)	37
2,000	38	(1,400)	(16,530)	37
2,000	38	(1,400)	(17,930)	37
2,250	38	(1,650)	(19,580)	44
2,000	38	(1,400)	(20,980)	37
$65,000	**2,465**	**($20,980)**	**($20,980)**	**$9**

nearly 2,500 new donors. Capital permitting, you might opt to mail 50,000 names or more on List "G," and all 25,000 names on List "H." If you're feeling really lucky, you might also test larger quantities on some of the new test lists.

❐   If, however, your strategy requires that you *conserve capital* — or if your cash flow is simply inadequate to the task — you might mail only the top six or seven lists. Using Lists "A" through "F" will yield an estimated 1,553 new donors, and a net profit of $770. Mailing to 10,000 or 20,000 names on List "G" will eat up that profit, and more. But you'll still cut the projected loss in half, and the resulting acquisition cost for the mailing as a whole will be only about $5 — a level you might well find acceptable.

Nearly one-third, or $6,300, of the projected loss for the mailing as a whole will come from List "J," and more than one-half from Lists "J" and "G" combined. Those two lists, however, represent 350,000 prospective donors — more than one-third of the total universe for this mailing. If you're following a growth strategy — and particularly if workable large lists are few and far between for your program — you have to mail to these and other large lists despite painful losses.

Note that we're projecting a profit on only *three* of the fifteen lists individually. If you limit your prospect mailing to those three alone, you'll have a total of only 18,000 names available — a quantity too small to mail cost-effectively. The profits we project on Lists "A," "B" and "C" are significant only in that we expect them to cancel out the losses on Lists "D," "E" and "F." Even if your strategy is particularly cautious, you'll be well-advised to mail the largest possible quantity that will produce break-even results for the mailing <u>as a whole</u>.

You'll play out this process of prospect list selection again and again over the years, and at every stage your strategic goals will guide you in this selection. From time to time, cash flow considerations — or headline-grabbing events — may arbitrarily limit your freedom of action, but if they do so consistently, you'll need to reexamine your strategy and look for a way to capitalize your direct mail program.

The First Three Years

Let's assume you've chosen to take the plunge and proceed with a donor acquisition program, despite the equivocal results of your initial test. I'll assume further that your organization is new and under-funded and that this is your first foray into the mails: you don't have either a large pool of capital or a significant existing donor list to underwrite an aggressive growth strategy.

If the response to your second mailing improves, here's a schedule of the mailings you might conduct in the first three years. For the sake of simplicity, I'll assume we received test results in the fall, and that your first-year program will get underway in January. The following chart depicts your first year's mailing schedule and the increasing size of your donor list as the year unfolds:

Year One	Prospecting Volume	Resolicitation Volume	List Size
January	75,000		500
February			1,500
March		1,350	1,500
April	125,000		1,500
May			3,250
June		3,000	3,250
July	150,000		3,250
August			5,350
September		4,750	5,350
October	150,000		5,350
November			7,350
December		6,500	7,350
YEAR ONE TOTAL	**500,000**	**14,600**	**7,350**

In the first year, we've mailed a little over half a million letters. The lion's share of the effort consisted of progressively larger donor acquisition mailings, conducted about once every three months.

Through quarterly donor resolicitation mailings we've netted enough to underwrite your investment in prospecting. (Note that in none of the resolicitation efforts have we remailed *all* of the donors we've acquired; some gave gifts so small that they're unlikely to be cost-effective to mail again. There are other, profitable uses for such names.)

If yours is a typical experience, you'll end the year at breakeven after all of this activity, despite its unexciting beginning. Here, now, is what the second year's program might look like:

Year Two	Prospecting Volume	Resolicitation Volume	List Size
January	200,000		7,000
February		6,500	10,000
March			10,000
April	150,000	9,000	10,000
May			12,000
June		10,500	12,000
July	150,000		12,000
August		10,500	14,000
September			14,000
October	200,000	12,000	14,000
November			17,000
December		15,000	17,000
YEAR TWO TOTAL	**700,000**	**60,500**	**17,000**

By stepping up your donor acquisition program from 500,000 to 700,000 letters, we've added nearly 10,000 donors to your file. Meanwhile, we've increased the frequency of donor resolicitation efforts from four in the first year to six in the second. Chances are, you've posted a *significant net profit* from direct mail this year because your donor list has now reached a size at which resolicitation mailings are typically very cost-effective. (In mailings of 10,000 names or more, economies of scale are comparatively significant, and a list of that size will permit you to exercise greater selectivity when you decide *which* donors to mail to.)

In the third year, your direct mail fundraising program may unfold as follows:

Year Three	Prospecting Volume	Resolicitation Volume	List Size
January	200,000		16,000
February		14,000	18,500
March		3,500	18,000
April	150,000	15,500	18,000
May			19,500
June		16,000	19,500
July	150,000		19,000
August		17,000	21,000
September			20,500
October	200,000	16,000	20,500
November		5,000	22,500
December		20,000	22,500
YEAR THREE TOTAL	**700,000**	**107,000**	**22,500**

By sustaining the same 700,000-piece-per-year rate of donor acquisition efforts, we've added another 10,000 names to your file in this third year.

However, the size of your donor base has grown only half that much, because we've been weeding out dead wood all along the way. We've dropped most of those first-year contributors who haven't sent checks since then, and we've taken extra pains to improve the accuracy of the file through address correction procedures.

Even so, we haven't mailed all the available active donor names in *any* of the eight resolicitation mailings. In six resolicitations, we've increased your net profits through careful segmentation based on individual donor histories. Also, both early and late in the year we've added small mailings that *target only* your most generous and responsive donors. (In the next chapter, we'll discuss the targeting issues that arise in resolicitation programs.)

In this third year, you've seen your investment — and your patience — really start paying off in a big way. The continuing cost of acquiring new donors represents only a fraction of the net proceeds of your increasingly frequent and selective donor resolicitation efforts.

And the donor base you've already built will continue paying off in a big way for many years to come.

Investment Strategies: A Banker's View of Direct Mail

Direct mail fundraising runs on two tracks: donor acquisition and donor resolicitation. If you're starting from scratch, *acquiring* donors will dominate your attention for the first year (or two years, or even three, depending upon how much capital you have and how many risks you can take). As your list grows, however, *resoliciting* your donors will come to mean more and more to you. The profits from a single donor resolicitation mailing — just one of seven or ten you may conduct in your program's third year — could easily dwarf the net revenue from even a wildly successful initial test mailing, no matter how substantial it seemed at the time.

By the same token, those profits from resolicitation may make your initial losses from prospecting look downright puny.

To get a sense of how these factors play themselves out over time, let's take a look at two hypothetical examples: CITIZENS FOR and PEOPLE AGAINST.

❒   CITIZENS FOR is not well funded. The group started on a shoe-string two years ago and only recently managed to beg, borrow and steal $25,000 for an initial direct mail test. Fortunately, CITIZENS FOR's 50,000-piece test was a big success. It yielded 800 members whose average contribution was $22.50. The group grossed only $18,000 from this initial effort but was encouraged to proceed because six of the ten lists tested were at breakeven or better and one of two package variations substantially outper-formed the other. The successful package variation and six of the ten lists accounted for the lion's share of the $18,000 in revenue, strongly suggesting that in a second, "continuation" or "rollout" mailing that eliminated poorly performing lists, response to the winning package will be much higher overall.

❒   Following a contrasting strategy, PEOPLE AGAINST is also on the road to a successful long-term direct mail fundraising program. With an identical 1.6 percent response and $22.50 average gift, the well-funded group shrugged off its $7,000 loss and is ready to pull out the stops to launch a major nationwide campaign.

Because of their sharply different financial circumstances, CITI-ZENS FOR and PEOPLE AGAINST follow different strategies even though the results of their initial test mailings were statistically identical. CITIZENS FOR sets out to tap the profit potential of its direct mail fundraising program at the earliest possible opportunity, while well-heeled PEOPLE AGAINST has its sights set on a more distant future.

Neither strategy is "better" than the other: each serves the group's strategic requirements.

Here's what these two groups' contrasting experiences look like, year by year, in the five-year period following their initial tests:

Year One

CITIZENS FOR conducts four 75,000-piece donor acquisition mailings, for a total of 300,000 prospect letters, building its list from 800 at the outset to 5,300 by year's end. The proceeds from quarterly donor renewal mailings, combined with modest profits from prospecting, yield a net profit of over $45,000.

PEOPLE AGAINST aggressively pursues a growth strategy, mailing one million donor acquisition packages in the first year. While the list grows to more than 12,000 by the end of this period, profits from an intensive donor renewal program aren't enough to erase the loss. PEOPLE AGAINST ends the first year another $7,000 in the red.

Year Two

CITIZENS FOR continues to pursue its cautious, cash-flow-conscious approach, mailing just 300,000 acquisition appeals (as it will each year throughout the five-year period). The donor list passes the 9,000-mark by year-end; aggregate net profits for the full year top $81,000.

Having built an active donor list of over 12,000 names at a net cost of a little more than $1 per name, PEOPLE AGAINST calculates it's not being sufficiently aggressive. It steps up its prospecting effort to 1.5 million letters in the second year. Despite this increased investment, the program nets $217,000 because donor renewal efforts yield large profits.

Year Three

The CITIZENS FOR list passes the 12,500 mark and the organization tops $139,000 in net direct mail revenue after paying all program costs and fees.

PEOPLE AGAINST's file nears 50,000 names by year's end after another 2 million acquisition letters. Net profits for the year are $492,000.

CITIZENS FOR			
	PROSPECT	**LIST**	**RENEWAL**	**NET**
	50,000	800		($7,000)
YEAR 1	300,000	5,300	$12,200	45,600
YEAR 2	300,000	9,164	36,160	81,320
YEAR 3	300,000	12,564	86,913	139,370
YEAR 4	300,000	15,557	112,484	177,726
YEAR 5	300,000	18,190	134,986	211,478
TOTAL	**1,550,000**	**18,190**	**$382,743**	**$648,494**

ILLUSTRATION 24: Investment in direct mail can pay big dividends

Year Four

CITIZENS FOR's 300,000-piece prospecting program pushes the donor list to over 15,500. With stepped-up resolicitation efforts, net cash yield from the program is $177,000.

Dropping 2.5 million prospect letters, PEOPLE AGAINST's file tops 73,500. Net program revenue is $825,000 for the year.

Year Five

CITIZENS FOR has over 18,000 donors by the end of the year. Net profits for the year are $211,000.

PEOPLE AGAINST drops 3 million acquisition letters, and its file passes the 100,000 mark. Its net for the year is $1,200,000.

The Five-Year Period

CITIZENS FOR has mailed 1,550,000 donor acquisition letters and netted $648,000 from direct mail after paying all costs and fees. Its file includes 18,000 active donors.

PEOPLE AGAINST has dropped more than 10 million prospect letters and built an active donor list of 100,000 names. Its five-year net profit was $2,728,000.

PEOPLE AGAINST			
PROSPECT	**LIST**	**RENEWAL**	**NET**
50,000	800		($7,000)
1,000,000	12,300	$39,300	(7,400)
1,500,000	28,800	164,400	217,800
2,000,000	49,800	314,400	492,800
2,500,000	73,550	493,400	825,800
3,000,000	100,550	696,400	1,206,800
10,050,000	**100,550**	**$1,707,900**	**$2,728,800**

In other words, PEOPLE AGAINST — with the resources and the grit to push the limits of the market in its donor acquisition program — has built a file that is *five times* as large and netted more than *four times* as much as CITIZENS FOR.

This doesn't mean that the more aggressive strategy is "better" than the other. I confess that the entrepreneur in me finds PEOPLE AGAINST a more interesting organization. Its "high risk-high gain" philosophy is the way to make the most of what direct mail has to offer. But such a hard-hitting approach may be inappropriate and even impossible for CITIZENS FOR, no matter what its inclinations might be.

However, the capital — and the level of risk — actually involved in even the larger of these two programs was quite small compared to the ultimate returns from the program:

❏ CITIZENS FOR and PEOPLE AGAINST advanced $25,000 each for their test mailings. CITIZENS FOR needed no more than another $15,000 to launch its first 75,000-piece "continuation" or "rollout" mailing, and nothing more thereafter. Its total investment was $40,000; measured against five-year net of nearly $650,000, that seems puny. It's a return on investment of *1,625 percent!* I don't

know about *your* banker, but mine thinks that's not a bad deal for
CITIZENS FOR.

❏   By contrast, though, PEOPLE AGAINST made out like a bandit.
    For its first 250,000-piece rollout, the group had to add about
    $40,000 to the $18,000 contributed in response to the initial test
    mailing. Its banker was a *little* worried, but from that point on, the
    program was self-sustaining. Profits from resolicitations funded
    the larger and more costly acquisition mailings in Years Three,
    Four and Five — and left a *lot* to spare. A total cash investment of
    $65,000 yielded more than $2,700,000 in net revenue available to
    finance PEOPLE AGAINST's programs — a return on investment
    of *4,154 percent.*

Admittedly, that's one of the more advantageous ways to view the
return on an investment in a direct mail fundraising program. A more
conservative method is to examine the amount of capital tied up in the
program at any one time — that is, the funds needed to pay the bills
for those large, repeated donor acquisition mailings — and compare it
with the net returns for that year only.

❏   For CITIZENS FOR, this amount never exceeded $40,000 — the
    approximate total cost of one of its 75,000-piece prospecting efforts
    plus one of its larger donor resolicitation mailings that might have
    been conducted at about the same time. In its first year, then, CITI-
    ZENS FOR's return on investment calculated in this manner was
    113%. In Year Five, it was 528%.

❏   For PEOPLE AGAINST, the capital required to finance continuing
    direct mail operations rose perceptibly as the scale of prospecting
    grew. In Years One and Two, PEOPLE AGAINST needed up to
    $130,000, and even in the second year net profits of $217,000
    represented a return of only 167%. By Year Five, the group needed
    to devote nearly twice as much cash to cover ongoing program
    costs; current capital investment of about $250,000 yielded net
    profits of over $1,200,000 — a return of 480%.

Of course, there's another thing about bankers (as well as the
trustees and executives of most charities): they don't like risk.

Without question, CITIZENS FOR's strategy entailed lower risks
than that of PEOPLE AGAINST. While we tell our clients — and
ourselves — that the risks are very limited in a carefully managed
direct mail fundraising program, they're nonetheless real.

I've never yet lost a mailing because a mail truck caught fire — but
such things have happened to others (on *rare* occasions). And from

time to time we've seen mailing results dip, sometimes very sharply, because of headline-grabbing catastrophes such as a stock market crash or a massive earthquake. It makes no sense to deny these problems — and even less to let them stop you.

The only way I know to address the problem of risk is to *manage* it, expecting occasional setbacks and maintaining the program's momentum in spite of them. As the leader of almost any successful new enterprise — whether a business, a nonprofit organization or a political campaign — will tell you, the only reliable way to achieve success is to keep plugging away, day after day, week after week. The rewards don't often come quickly. But, ultimately, the profits from a well-conceived and well-managed direct mail fundraising program may justify not just a little risk but a whole lot of hard work as well.

The approaches followed by CITIZENS FOR and PEOPLE AGAINST represent just two of many possible alternative strategies. Among others:

☐ seeking huge numbers of donors at gift levels under $10 on the average and resoliciting them as frequently as every week; programs of this type may entail tens of millions of prospect letters annually, and donor files consisting of hundreds of thousands of names

☐ investing large sums in costly prospect packages in order to acquire new donors at a high entry level ($50 and up for single gifts, and $10 to $25 per month in "pledge" or "sustainer" programs), and investing more in "upgrading" them to even more generous levels of support

☐ establishing an arbitrarily low initial membership fee of $5 or $10 to build the largest possible membership with attractive (and expensive) benefits that cost you a lot more than the entry-level dues — and then identifying and upgrading those members willing and able to provide significant gifts

☐ acquiring "qualified" (proven) prospective donors at little or no cost through some form of sweepstakes offer, thus allowing more cost-efficient donor acquisition and building large lists that will generate substantial rental revenue

While the possibilities aren't genuinely endless, they might as well be. After all, there are more than 90 million households in the United States, and there's probably somebody in the industry who thinks that just about every one of them is a good candidate for someone's direct mail fundraising program.

Are We Having Fun Yet?

I'm sure it's becoming clear by now: if you've turned to direct mail as a way to grow, to diversify your sources of funding, and to broaden your financial base, direct mail is likely to be a waiting game for you.

In the hypothetical cases of CITIZENS FOR and PEOPLE AGAINST as sketched out above, you can detect some of the tradeoffs you're likely to confront — often a matter of time versus money. To cast a little more light on these issues, here are two concrete, real-life examples:

The Campaign

Two years and seven months have gone by — and *finally* The Campaign's direct mail fundraising program has gone into the black. We've mailed 800,000 prospect letters, yielding 12,400 new donors at a net cost of $49,000, or $3.95 per name. Donor resolicitation profits of $130,000 have barely covered this loss plus other costs and fees totaling $81,000. After raising a grand total of $557,000, The Campaign has netted the munificent sum of $1,500 through its direct mail fundraising program.

What could possibly make this program a good deal for The Campaign? Here are three of the reasons:

(1) *Major donor revenue*: From the outset, The Campaign has been systematically approaching the most generous donors acquired in our direct mail program — treating them as *prospects* for larger gifts. In this aggressive effort, The Campaign's development department has netted more than $300,000 in just the first two years and seven months. They'll derive hundreds of thousands, perhaps eventually millions more, from these same donors in the years ahead.

(2) *Public relations value*: The Campaign's message has already reached over a million people through direct mail, including a great many national opinion leaders. The Campaign's public profile has risen perceptibly in these first few years, in part due to the added exposure afforded by direct mail. As a public advocacy organization with a continuing need for publicity, this has great value for The Campaign — estimated to be worth $250,000 at the very least.

(3) *Future direct mail revenue*: Starting virtually from scratch, we've already built an active donor list of 13,000 names. While profits from The Campaign's donor resolicitations were limited in the first two years, averaging about $6,000 per mailing, they've been

running two or three times that much in the third year (in part because of the greater economies of mailing to a larger list). In the next twelve months that list will *net* The Campaign more than $200,000 in direct mail revenue alone — *after* deducting all consulting and program management fees and the continuing costs of acquiring new donors at the rate of $4 to $6 per name.

(4) *List rental revenue*: The Campaign may now choose to increase its current revenue by offering its list of 13,000 donors for rental to approved nonprofit and political mailers. If it pursues this option aggressively, it can net upwards of $25,000 per year for the next year or two.

In other words, even this seemingly lackluster program hasn't just broken even. The Campaign has directly received costly services, or cash from collateral fundraising, to the tune of more than $550,000 (adding $300,000 in net revenue from major donor fundraising to $250,000 in public relations value and *not* counting potential list rental revenue). This has *doubled* the immediate returns from the program. Because of the contribution made by direct mail to The Campaign's major donor fundraising program — which is properly seen as a long-term development effort — the real net value of the thirty-one month campaign was probably nearer $1 million.

In this case, a $38,000 investment in an initial direct mail fundraising test accomplished exactly what it was supposed to do. Direct mail has planted a tree that will go on bearing fruit for The Campaign for many years to come.

The Institute

With another organization, The Institute, our experience has been much closer to a case study custom-made for a textbook on fundraising:

❑ In six years, The Institute's direct mail fundraising program has netted $3.4 million from gross receipts of $6.5 million.

❑ Beginning with just 200 donors, The Institute has acquired a total of more than 50,000 contributors. The average contribution of their resolicitation gifts was an unusually high $64.

❑ A grand total of 4.6 million letters has yielded 114,000 contributions averaging $50 — gross revenue of $5.7 million. (Telephone fundraising and other collateral efforts produced another $800,000.)

❑ The Institute posted a net profit from direct mail operations of $119,000 in its very first year. In Year Two, net revenue topped

$290,000. By Year Five — the high point of the program — the net approached $900,000.

❑   The dramatic growth of The Institute's direct mail fundraising program paralleled the growth of its operating budget — from $300,000 in Year One to $2.5 million in Year Five. Many of the new funds raised in large gifts came from donors originally acquired through direct mail.

In this apparently idyllic picture, however, there are hidden massive problems. They're best highlighted by the fact that The Institute's net from direct mail dropped precipitously, from almost $900,000 in the fifth year to barely more than $500,000 in the sixth — and the seventh year promises to be far worse.

How could such a thing happen, with a donor list of 50,000 names? It occurred for one simple reason:

The Institute decided to stop prospecting.

After a massive prospecting binge, The Institute virtually ended its donor acquisition efforts. Because response rates were dropping — and The Institute's management was preoccupied with internal management issues — the organization cut its prospecting volume from 1.7 million letters in the fifth year to fewer than 300,000 in the sixth.

Not only did this short-sighted decision curtail The Institute's future growth, it also cut off the rich supply of fresh, responsive new donors that made it possible for the group to have netted almost a million dollars in a single year.

Some people speak of direct mail fundraising as a treadmill: if you're among the minority of nonprofit organizations able to get up to speed, you can climb on the belt — but getting off is a lot more difficult. The Institute's experience illustrates one aspect of this problem. The principal lesson its program illustrates is this:

You can't expect to build a list of loyal and responsive donors through direct mail and then simply leave the game, expecting them to sustain your continuing operations at the same level indefinitely.

Direct mail fundraising requires *continuous* prospecting because of "attrition." People die or move without leaving forwarding addresses, their financial circumstances change, and so do their interests and loyalties.

Direct mail is a *process*, not a passing event.

There's no point at which the process ends or achieves perfection. It's a continual search for new marketing concepts that serve *your* strategic needs because they work a little better than the old ones.

The way we develop those new concepts is through "testing."

Testing, Testing, Testing – Until You're Blue in the Face

Every once in a rare while, we'll hit the nail on the head with a powerful marketing concept — a seemingly perfect marriage of package and lists — at the very beginning of a new program. Our "control" package — the standard-bearing donor acquisition appeal we keep mailing, over and over again — may emerge more or less wholly formed from a successful initial test. I've seen it happen more than once. But, much more often, it takes two or three tries, and months or years of step-by-step refinements, to produce a workhorse prospecting package that will build a large, responsive donor file. And then, sometimes quite suddenly, that package will "die" and you'll have to come up with another one very quickly.

A donor acquisition program might not hit its stride until the third or fourth year, or even later. This may be due to the organization's gradual accumulation of credibility and public recognition, to some shift in public sentiment about the issues it's addressing, or to changed attitudes in the organization's top management. But chances are it has a lot more to do with the cumulative value of thoughtful, systematic testing.

Now here's what I mean by a *"test"*:

You might, for example, want to know whether the response to your prospect package will rise significantly if you suggest a lower minimum gift in the letter and on the response device. Currently, the package urges a contribution of $25 or more; you decide to test whether suggesting a $15 minimum will lift the response rate sufficiently — without forcing the average gift to drop in proportion — so as to lower the overall donor acquisition cost. To determine this, you'd take two equal and statistically equivalent groups of names from the same pool of lists, mailing one group a package with the $25 "ask" and the other with the $15 suggested minimum.

The theory behind direct mail testing such as this is that scientific principles will enable you to discover the perfect combination of offer, package and postage — and ride off into the sunset, forever financially secure.

The reality's a little different.

For one thing, there are literally *innumerable* possible tests in a direct mail fundraising program. It's sometimes damnably difficult to figure out what's important to test and what isn't — particularly when your budget is strictly limited. Too much testing can eat up all the profits from your direct mail program.

In a program of modest scope, it's especially important to test only those elements that are "significant." A wholly new acquisition package built around a new marketing concept is likely to be a significant test. Most of the time, so are meaningful variations in the offer (or "ask"), in the copy that appears on the outer envelope (the "teaser") or in the type of postage used. But any or all of these might be *in*significant under some circumstances.

Another problem with the proposition that rigorous testing will show the way to optimal results is that it's often difficult to design tests that are statistically meaningful. In most situations, it requires many tens of thousands of names to establish confidence in the results of such things as price or postage testing. And even when you're able to test in these relatively large quantities, you'd be well advised to view the results with caution — no matter what the statisticians tell you.

MINIMUM GIFT SUGGESTED	ACTUAL AVERAGE GIFT	RESPONSE RATE	COST PER DONOR ACQUIRED	NUMBER OF DONORS ACQUIRED IN 1 YEAR WITH $50,000 INVESTMENT
$15	$17	1.3%	$7	7,142
$25	$23	0.9%	$11	4,545

ILLUSTRATION 25: The amount you ask for can have extensive implications

Time and again, I've seen results vary twenty percent or more on even very large samples on which the variation was supposed to be no greater than five or ten percent. According to experts in statistics, variations this great shouldn't have occurred more often than one to five percent of the time. I suspect it *often* occurs, and so do some other direct mail fundraisers.

To test the validity of this proposition, on two occasions my colleagues and I arranged what we were assured were rigorous conditions: we split large groups of letters into two statistically identical groups to see what effect random variation might have. There was *no* difference between the two groups in package, postage, list or any other controllable factor. All we were testing was the extent to which two or more equal samples would produce equal results when simultaneously mailed identical packages. On both occasions, random variation had a greater effect than statistical theory said it should. Other consultants have had similar experiences.

No doubt there's some obscure theory of statistics that can explain away even these anomalous experiences. Rather than chase it down, however, I'd prefer to hold my clients' losses to a minimum and trust as little as possible in statistics — *except* when mailing quantities and testing budgets are big enough to add an extra margin of safety.

Why, then, when the results may not be statistically reliable, do we bother to test such things as offers, teasers or postage? The answer is simple: by and large, testing works. Testing works because we test with expectations, and we incorporate the results of our tests into future packages when our expectations are confirmed. Over time — sometimes even *re*testing vital elements two or three times — we're likely to learn valuable lessons that will enable us to upgrade a tolerably workable control package into one that is truly responsive.

Through testing — lifting response by ten percent with this little change and five percent with that one — we may eventually cut the donor acquisition cost by fifty or seventy-five percent. Testing may, and often does, literally bring new life into a prospecting program by permitting us to expand the volume and more quickly build large donor files. In larger donor resolicitation programs, too, it can sometimes dramatically increase net revenue by helping establish the most cost-effective use of postage, packaging techniques, suggested contributions and the like.

Testing is *not* limited to large direct mail programs. Almost any mailing of 10,000 names or more affords opportunities to test. Smaller quantities limit the options and make testing a long, drawn-out process. They demand extra care and greater patience, but the payoff can be just as dramatic in the end.

And remember, a "test" is just as real a mailing as one that's called something else. One person's small test is another's huge prospect mailing. They both have to be evaluated in terms of costs and benefits.

Be sure you don't fall prey to the common but costly mistake of evaluating test results only in terms of their actual costs. Testing is often expensive, because it may involve added creative, production and even management costs — all of which need to be factored out when analyzing the outcome of a test. Otherwise, you'll be comparing expensive apples to cheap oranges. Testing costs should be considered part of the overhead of the direct mail fundraising program as a whole.

Now, it's not enough to design the tests — you've got to read and *use* the results, and that may be more easily said than done. They may conflict with the findings of earlier tests or with each other. With different goals in mind, interpretations may vary. Furthermore, errors in the "lettershop" (where your mailing is addressed and assembled) may call the validity of the results into question.

But the biggest danger in testing is that equivocal results — or anxiety about poor results — might tempt you to delay future mailings.

Important as your test results might be, the chances are that in a successful, ongoing direct mail fundraising program you'll be better off mailing blind than waiting for a definitive reading — because your biggest mistake may be not to mail at all.

Getting the Most From Your Donors

5

The Four Stages of a Donor's Life

Most donors acquired by direct mail will support your organization in an active way for only a short time. A smaller number will remain with you for many years, completing the full cycle of donor life. That cycle has the following four stages:

(1) *Interest*: Among those relatively few recipients of your donor acquisition package who spend more than the four seconds it takes to decide to throw it away, you'll create some level of awareness about your organization and its work. A minority of those people will, in turn, demonstrate their interest by mailing you a first-time gift. You can't count on these people as committed donors; they're simply declaring that they've gotten a good first impression of you. Now you've got to convince them that you're really worthy of their support.

(2) *Support*: Through the conversion process which your donor resolicitation program is designed to promote, you'll convince a majority of your one-time donors that you're worth more active support. The second, often more generous, gift you elicit from a new donor is a more meaningful statement of conviction. She may well be a candidate now for an ever more substantial role in your organization.

(3) *Commitment*: In response to your efforts to upgrade your donors, many will enter onto a level of financial commitment meaningful to you as well as to them. But to take this big step toward a major gift may require substantial personal contact as well as months or years of donor education through such means as newsletters and in-depth reports on your activities. It's important, too, that you do everything possible to make the donor's experience rewarding for her as well as for you — by publicly recognizing her contribution, if she wishes, and by thanking her not just with an impersonal note but warmly and often.

(4) *Legacy*: A continuing process of cultivation, education and appreciation will induce some of your major donors to regard their participation in the work of your organization as one of their major contributions in life. These are the people who will serve as volunteers — perhaps even on your board of trustees, talk about your work among friends and family, make sizable annual gifts or establish planned giving programs, and remember you in their wills. Ultimately, the bequests and other major gifts you receive from these exceptionally strong supporters may dwarf the contributions from all your other donors combined. They're a living reminder that fundraising is a long, long process.

You'll derive the *full* value from your direct mail fundraising program only if your development efforts are capable of working with your donors at every one of these four stages. Direct mail can start — even, in some cases, jump-start — the development process. But fundraising is a flesh-and-blood relationship that ultimately requires personal contact to realize its true potential.

What's a Donor Worth?

Sentimental or political considerations aside, it's entirely possible for an organization with at least a four-year track record in direct mail

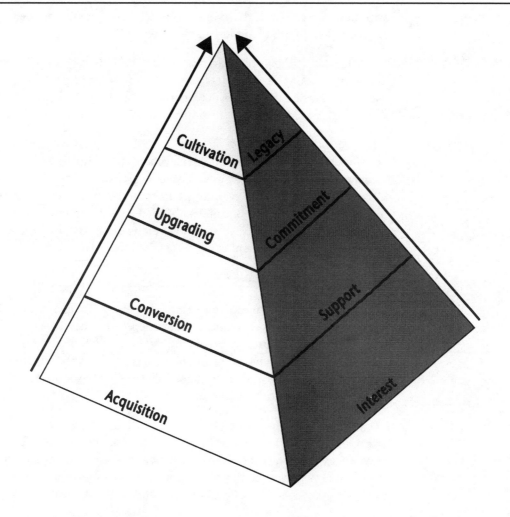

ILLUSTRATION 26: The four stages of donor life

to calculate with meaningful precision the value it derives from the average new donor. It's rarely *easy* to do so. But there are at least three methods that may help you get a handle on this fundamental question.

Method One

By studying your donor renewal rates, you may be able to determine the average "life" of your donors. In direct mail fundraising, that averages out to about 2.6 years, or 31 months. During that time, the typical donor's two or three renewal gifts will average about twenty to twenty-five percent higher than her first gift. If she joined you with a contribution of $25, that means you'll likely receive another $90 (three times $30).

If the *average* gift in your acquisition program is as high as $25, this arithmetic is realistic. If the average is much lower, it may not be true: donors of less than $15 are less likely to renew.

After deducting applicable renewal costs and fees, your net from this source should be about $60. Add to that figure another $10 in net list rental revenue (five years at $2 per year), and the total value of that donor is $70, or about $27 per year during the donor's "lifetime" of giving to your organization.

If you have a sophisticated development department, with an aggressive major donor program and other opportunities to elicit more frequent and larger-than-average gifts, that number may be twice as high, or even higher. Some well-established national public interest groups, for example, expect to net an average of more than $70 *per year* from newly acquired members.

Method Two

By listing all the fundraising efforts you expect to undertake in the coming three years to elicit additional support from newly acquired donors or members, and by projecting the returns you might reasonably expect to receive, you can calculate the total expected revenue per donor. (It's easier if you do so for 1,000 or 10,000 donors and then divide accordingly, as in **Illustration 27**.)

Judging from the first method, it seems that each new donor is worth a total of $70 to you. Using the second method, it's $71. Either way, an acquisition cost of $5 to $10 per name seems eminently reasonable — and two or three times that much, or even more, would make perfectly good sense if fast growth is essential to your strategy.

Setting that level, however, is a matter of tactics. The strategic problem is to determine how quickly you want your donor base to grow — and how much you can afford to invest in growth.

	QUANTITY MAILED	COST PER 1000	RESPONSE RATE	CONTRI- BUTIONS	AVERAGE GIFT AMOUNT	GROSS REVENUE	*NET REVENUE
Year One							
Acquisition Mailing	100,000	$300	1.00%	1,000	$25	$25,000	($5,000)
Special Appeal 1	1,000	500	9.00%	90	43	3,870	3,370
Special Appeal 2	1,000	600	6.00%	60	36	2,160	1,560
Special Appeal 3	1,000	700	8.00%	80	38	3,040	2,340
Special Appeal 4	1,000	450	5.00%	50	34	1,700	1,250
Special Appeal 5	1,000	500	8.00%	80	38	3,040	2,540
Renewal 1**	950	500	19.00%	181	25	4,513	4,038
Renewal 2	770	500	16.00%	123	23	2,832	2,447
Renewal 3	646	500	11.00%	71	22	1,564	1,241
Renewal 4	575	500	9.00%	52	22	1,139	851
Renewal 5	524	500	6.00%	31	21	660	398
Renewal 6 (phone)	492	2,000	14.00%	69	35	2,411	1,427
Pledge Commitments	1,000	1,000	3.00%	30	240	7,200	6,200
TOTALS/YEAR ONE	**109,957**					**$59,128**	**$22,662**
Renewal Rate			**52.68%**				
Net Revenue Per New Member							**$22.66**
Year Two							
Special Appeal 1*	750	500	10.40%	78	49	3,857	3,482
Special Appeal 2	750	600	6.90%	52	41	2,142	1,692
Special Appeal 3	750	700	9.20%	69	44	3,015	2,490
Special Appeal 4	750	450	5.80%	44	39	1,701	1,363
Special Appeal 5	750	500	9.20%	69	44	3,015	2,640
Renewal 1*	750	500	21.90%	164	29	4,722	4,347
Renewal 2	586	500	18.40%	108	26	2,851	2,558
Renewal 3	478	500	12.70%	61	25	1,536	1,297
Renewal 4	417	500	10.40%	43	25	1,098	889
Renewal 5	374	500	6.90%	26	24	623	436
Renewal 6 (phone)	348	2,000	16.10%	56	40	2,256	1,559
Additional Pledges	750	1,000	2.00%	15	180	2,700	1,950
TOTALS/YEAR TWO						**$29,516**	**$24,705**
Renewal Rate			**61.06%**				
Net Revenue Per New Member							**$24.71**
Year Three							
Special Appeal 1*	563	500	12.00%	68	57	3,839	3,557
Special Appeal 2	563	600	7.90%	44	48	2,116	1,778
Special Appeal 3	563	700	10.60%	60	50	2,996	2,603
Special Appeal 4	563	450	6.70%	38	45	1,695	1,441
Special Appeal 5	563	500	10.60%	60	50	2,996	2,715
Renewal 1*	563	500	25.20%	142	33	4,687	4,405
Renewal 2	421	500	21.20%	89	30	2,713	2,503
Renewal 3	332	500	14.60%	48	29	1,408	1,243
Renewal 4	283	500	12.00%	34	29	989	847
Renewal 5	249	500	7.90%	20	28	547	422
Renewal 6 (phone)	229	2,000	18.50%	42	46	1,965	1,506
Additional Pledges	563	1,200	1.50%	8	170	1,434	759
TOTALS/YEAR THREE						**$27,385**	**$23,780**
Renewal Rate			**66.75%**				
Net Revenue Per New Member							**$23.78**
TOTAL/THREE YEARS						**$116,029**	**$71,147**
Net Revenue Per New Member Over 3 Years							**71.15**

*Assumes a 25% shrinkage of list over previous year—and 15% increase in response rate and in average gift amount.
**Assumes 95% of members will receive renewal notices.

ILLUSTRATION 27: *There is a simple way to calculate the long-term value of a new member*

YEAR	ONE	TWO	THREE	FOUR
Number of members retained	1,000	600	420	328
Average gift including dues	$25.00	$27.50	$30.25	$33.28
Average number of gifts per member	1.3	1.3	1.3	1.3
Other income from same members	$1,000	$660	$462	$360
Number of monthly sustainers	20	44	57	63
Average annual income per sustainer	$163	$171	$180	$189
GROSS INCOME	$36,764	$29,650	$27,162	$26,462
Acquisition cost per member	$5.00			
Membership renewal cost per member	$.00	$1.95	$1.76	$1.58
Special appeal cost per member	$4.80	$5.28	$5.81	$6.39
Fundraising cost per sustainer	$8.40	$8.40	$8.40	$8.40
Other fundraising cost per member	$2.00	$2.20	$2.42	$2.66
TOTAL FUNDRAISING COST	$36,968	$6,028	$4,668	$4,013
NET INCOME	($204)	$23,622	$22,494	$22,450
COST PER DOLLAR RAISED	$1.01	$.20	$.17	$.15

ILLUSTRATION 28: There is a complicated way to calculate the "Lifetime Value" of a direct mail donor

Method Three

This task becomes easier if you bring a truly long-term perspective to bear in your strategic planning. View direct mail fundraising over a *ten-year* period, and the picture will look genuinely rosy. Just take a look at **Illustration 28** (which deals with a hypothetical organization different from the one depicted in **Illustration 27**). In this third method of calculating the "Lifetime Value" of a donor or member, we take into account not only dues income but profits from special appeals, a lucrative monthly sustainer program, and other fundraising efforts, such as through merchandising, events, travel or other products and services offered to members. The upshot is that one thousand donors, acquired in Year One at an acquisition cost of $5 per donor, yield a total of $203,904 over ten years, or $204 per donor. That's net revenue averaging more than $20 per year for a decade. Doesn't $5 seem downright paltry by comparison?

FIVE	SIX	SEVEN	EIGHT	NINE	TEN	TOTAL
278	242	218	198	181	164	
$36.60	$40.26	$44.29	$48.72	$53.59	$58.95	
1.3	1.3	1.3	1.3	1.3	1.3	13
$306	$266	$240	$218	$199	$181	$3,893
66	63	60	57	54	51	
$198	$208	$219	$230	$241	$253	
$26,636	$26,056	$25,902	$25,859	$25,782	$25,668	$275,942
$1.42	$1.28	$1.15	$1.04	$.93	$.84	
$7.03	$7.73	$8.50	$9.35	$10.29	$11.32	
$8.40	$8.40	$8.40	$8.40	$8.40	$8.40	
$2.93	$3.22	$3.54	$3.90	$4.29	$4.72	
$3,722	$3,492	$3,381	$3,313	$3,253	$3,200	$72,038
$22,914	$22,564	$22,521	$22,546	$22,529	$22,468	$203,904
$.14	$.13	$.13	$.13	$.13	$.12	$.26

However, the donor's "Lifetime Value" and the "donor acquisition cost" are statistical concepts. The truth is, all your donors are not worth the same amount. Lifetime Value varies by the year in which a donor joins an organization, the list source and giving characteristics.

Gift level may be the most significant of these variables. Of every 1,000 new donors you acquire through direct mail prospecting, 50 may give initial gifts of $50 or more, while 100 each contribute less than $15. Those at the bottom of the scale may, in effect, be worth nothing at all to your organization, because testing repeatedly shows that donors of less than $15 are difficult to upgrade. By contrast, your new $50 donors may be worth a great deal indeed. They're by far the most likely of your new donors to remit additional gifts and are more likely to increase the level of their support. *There is a very high correlation between the level of the donor's original gift and the likelihood that that donor will still actively support you more than a year later.* A rigorous Lifetime Value analysis of a fundraising program should break out the value of an organization's donors in categories determined by the size of their initial gifts. Among other things, an analysis of this sort might point the way toward a new approach to prospecting, emphasizing lists that yield above-average gifts.

Donor Renewal Concepts

If you're paying good money to recruit new donors, you'd better get your money's worth. That's what donor "renewal," or "resolicitation," efforts are all about.

The fundamental principle of all professionally managed donor resolicitation programs is to *mail early and often*. Many people — especially, it seems, those who serve on nonprofit boards — find this maddeningly counter-intuitive. Chances are you eat, sleep and breathe your work. It may be difficult for you to accept the fact that for someone who sent you a $25 check two or three months ago, your organization might not be the most important thing in her life this week. She *may* recall sending you a check, but the odds that she'll remember what you told her in your acquisition letter are very slim.

Something important is lurking in the background here:

Direct mail fundraising is a form of advertising, which is based on repetition.

Unless you get back in touch with that new donor very quickly, and repeat the same themes and symbols in your resolicitation, she may no longer be a good prospect for additional support. Also, the chances are you'll have to ask her *several times* before you get a second gift.

You needn't take my word for this. Just try calling at random a few dozen of your new donors acquired by direct mail two or three months after you receive their first gifts (and before you mail them anything else). I predict that you'll emerge the humbler from the experience.

It's conventional in the direct mail fundraising business to define everyone who's given you a single gift as a "donor." But in a real sense, a first-time contributor is really just a *qualified prospect*: she may be aware of your work, but she probably knows little about it, and she's clearly not a committed supporter. To tap the financial potential she represents, you'll have to educate and motivate her.

Psychologically, it's a big step for most people to send a *second* contribution: that implies a level of commitment many people are never willing to demonstrate. In fact, it's likely that anywhere from one-third to one-half of your first-time contributors will *never* give you a second gift. But once people have given *two* gifts, they're much more likely to contribute yet again, and perhaps much more generously.

In general, it's prudent to expect that no more than half your new donors will renew their support within the twelve-month period following their first gift. Of those who do so, a much larger proportion are likely to give again within the subsequent year. The progression is likely to look something like this:

Of your new donors, 50-60% renew in Year 1

Of donors renewed in Year 1, 60-70% renew in Year 2

Of donors renewed in Year 2, 68-78% renew in Year 3

Of donors renewed in Year 3, 75-85% renew in Year 4

Of donors renewed in Year 4, 80-87% renew in Year 5

Of donors renewed in Year 5, 83-90% renew in Year 6

Of donors renewed in Year 6, 85-91% renew in Year 7

Of donors renewed in Year 7, 87-91% renew in Year 8

Of donors renewed in Year 8, 88-91% renew in Year 9

Of donors renewed in Year 9, 89-91% renew in Year 10

The upper limit is imposed by death, illness, changing fortunes, shifting interests and addresses lost when donors move.

In an organization that's been in operation for many years, it's common for more than sixty-five percent of *all* donors to renew their support in any given year.

The most urgent task of a donor renewal program is to convert the largest possible percentage of your recent first-time contributors into *donors*. Increasing their renewal rate from forty percent to fifty percent, or from fifty to sixty, can have profound financial implications for your fundraising program in later years. Just as you've invested in acquiring new donors, it's worth spending money to persuade them to become active supporters. This process, sometimes called "donor conversion," typically entails a quick thank-you in response to the first gift and then a series of donor resolicitation letters about once every two or three months for the next year or year and a half.

A nearly equal priority in your donor renewal program is to *upgrade* your donors — to convince them to give bigger gifts.

Donor upgrading techniques favored by many public interest organizations include "gift clubs" and "monthly sustainer" programs. Both are devices to involve donors more intimately in the organization's work and to provide them with special rewards or recognition.

☐ "Gift clubs" provide a sense of belonging and special purpose to those donors who contribute large amounts of money. For example, you might offer "Life Membership" or special status within "The President's Circle" for $1,000 (paid in one sum or installments), conferring attractive privileges, benefits and recognition not available to your other donors. Or you might choose to confer special status on those donors whose cumulative lifetime giving has exceeded that amount. A fully developed gift club can raise substantial sums from a large donor base, but it requires careful attention by staff. Many gift clubs are assigned full-time staff to deliver the promised benefits, privileges and recognition and to attend to donors' correspondence and special requests.

☐ "Monthly sustainer" or "pledge" programs offer new giving opportunities to small donors, whose gifts can add up very fast. At $10 per month, a donor's annual contribution is $120 — far more than she's likely to give through dues notices and special appeals if her initial gift was a typical $15 or $20. Thoughtfully designed and managed with skill and persistence, a sustainer program can attract as much as ten percent of your donors and become the financial backbone of your direct mail fundraising program. In one organization with which I'm familiar, 4,500 of 45,000 donors contribute monthly gifts; in the aggregate, those monthly sustainers account for nearly one-third of the organization's $4.5 million operating budget. Like any successful gift club, however, a monthly pledge program requires patience, considerable staff time and special attention.

Ultimately, however, your success in *cultivating* donors may have the greatest impact on your organization's long-term financial health. A handful of your direct mail donors may eventually become *major donors* whose individual gifts or bequests could possibly equal all the support you receive from the rest of your contributors combined.

Because your donors will become more and more valuable over time, your donor renewal program should seek to retain them as long as possible once you've converted them from one-time contributors into committed donors. "Donor retention" is a function of the impact and attractiveness of your programmatic work at least as much as it is of your fundraising efforts — but an effective donor renewal program can easily lift donor retention by ten percent or more each year. Over.

After 10 years of haphazard resolicitation, 10 out of 100 donors remain.
With 10% improvement in results each year, more than 30 remain.

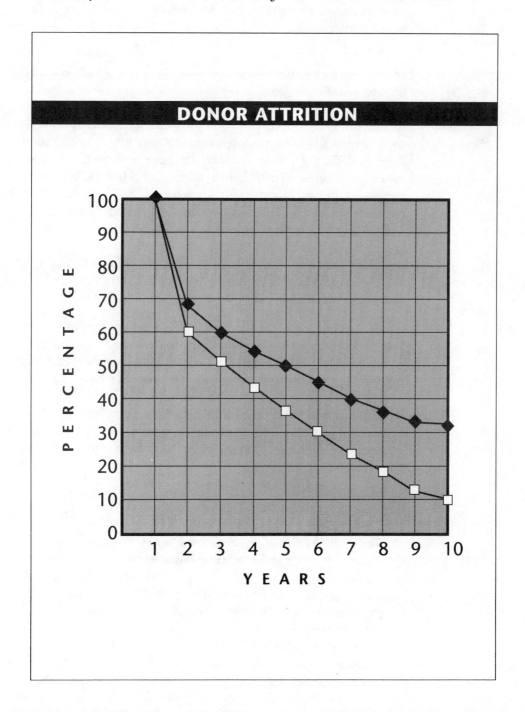

DONOR ATTRITION

ILLUSTRATION 29: *Through care and cultivation, you can retain many more donors*

the long haul, that ten percent lift will have a profound impact on your budget: a ten percent annual improvement over typical donor renewal rates will *more than triple* the number of donors remaining active on your file after ten years!

For many public interest organizations, a *membership* system makes good sense. Individuals recruited as members will expect you to ask for next year's dues. Because they've *chosen* to identify with your organization, they'll be actively interested in receiving news about your current activities, and they're good prospects for special appeals. One-third or more of your active members will send gifts over and above their dues. They'll feel more involved in your work and may more readily respond to invitations to become more active, perhaps as volunteers. But they'll expect you to deliver on your promises. If your membership acquisition letter says members receive a quarterly newsletter, you'd better be sure you send one every three months. If you've promised a "premium" for gifts above a certain level, you're in trouble if you don't have a system in place to send it out quickly. Membership systems have many advantages, but they demand discipline and efficiency that carry pricetags of their own.

Grassroots organizations often use "emergency" appeals to boost their fundraising revenue. Threatening to close the doors if there's poor response to an emergency letter may be an effective short-term fundraising technique, but it's unlikely to work as well the second time around. More important, it's short-sighted to "cry wolf." Few donors will invest sizable sums in an organization that's on the brink of bankruptcy. A public interest group's long-term self-interest lies in enhancing, not undermining, the public's confidence in its integrity and stability.

Your approach to donor renewal must relate to your organization's strategy:

☐ For example, if your organization has a strong development department with a well-established fundraising program that includes major donor "gift clubs," planned giving, bequests, and other special donor opportunities, your direct mail donor renewal program should probably emphasize donor education and *cultivation*. By using such tactics as highly personalized thank-you packages and phone calls, donor newsletters and other free publications, and "High-Dollar" direct mail packages designed to elicit much larger gifts, your direct mail donor renewal program may prove to be a rich source of prospects for your major donor fundraising efforts. The large contributions that ultimately result will represent a handsome return on a relatively modest investment in donor cultivation.

❐   By contrast, if your organization has had neither the time nor the opportunity to build a strong overall development effort, your direct mail program may constitute a large share of your "major donor" fundraising efforts. If this is the case, your direct mail program needs to be as profitable as possible while also providing sufficient opportunities for donor *upgrading*, so you can get the most from your donors. This may mean mailing very selectively to your donors and treating the most generous of them to particularly strong, personalized packages and friendly phone calls. In effect, this approach mimics the personal attention major donors would get from a professionally run development department.

Sticking to the Schedule

While you need to plan the frequency of your renewal mailings in the context of your organizational strategy, the rule of thumb we follow is to mail *more* often rather than less. In all likelihood, your net profits from direct mail will rise as you increase the frequency of appeals to your donors. For example, a friend once conducted a systematic, year-long test of this proposition. He divided a large, statistically homogeneous segment of his file into two equal groups, mailing one group only four special appeals that year and the other group eight. As might be expected, those donors who received eight letters didn't respond in such great numbers to each *individual* appeal as those who received only four. But the *net* returns from the group that received eight appeals were more than thirty percent higher. *(See* **Illustration 30** *on next page.)*

Sticking to the schedule is the key to making a donor renewal system work consistently well. If your mailing schedule calls for eight donor resolicitations this year — roughly six weeks apart from one another — a slippage of ten days to two weeks for each of the first three mailings will mean that you're likely to mail seven times, not eight. Another month's delay could cut your program down to six renewals. In that case, you won't be getting full value from your donors. The financial impact can be sizable. *(See* **Illustration 31** *on page 125.)*

An intelligent donor renewal system can easily be undermined by undue attention to our old nemesis, the fundraising ratio (the cost of a dollar raised). Let's say your board's fundraising chair tells you it's unacceptable to continue paying $0.38 to raise every dollar in your direct mail donor resolicitation program; she says you have to drive the ratio below $0.30.

Three-Year Monthly Schedule for Representative Fundraising Program

MONTH	DONOR ACQUISITION QUANTITY	DONOR RESOLICITATION QUANTITY	NEWSLETTER QUANTITY	TELEPHONE FUNDRAISING QUANTITY	TOTAL
Year 1					
Jan	50,000				50,000
Feb			500		500
Mar		500			500
Apr			500		500
May	100,000				100,000
Jun		1,000			1,000
Jul			1,500		1,500
Aug					
Sep	150,000	1,500			151,500
Oct			2,000		2,000
Nov					
Dec		3,000			3,000
Year 2					
Jan	150,000		2,500		152,500
Feb		4,000			4,000
Mar					
Apr		4,500	3,500		8,000
May	100,000				100,000
Jun		5,000			5,000
Jul			4,000	3,000	7,000
Aug		5,500			5,500
Sep	150,000				150,000
Oct		6,000	5,000		11,000
Nov					
Dec		7,000		2,000	9,000
Year 3					
Jan	250,000		5,000		255,000
Feb		8,000			8,000
Mar				4,000	4,000
Apr		9,000	7,000		16,000
May	100,000			3,000	103,000
Jun		9,000			9,000
Jul			7,500		7,500
Aug		9,000			9,000
Sep	200,000				200,000
Oct		10,000	8,000		18,000
Nov				6,000	6,000
Dec		11,000			11,000
TOTAL	**1,250,000**	**94,000**	**47,000**	**18,000**	**1,409,000**

ILLUSTRATION 30: Managing a long-term direct mail fundraising campaign is complex and demanding

In this hypothetical resolicitation program, net profit from eight mailings is more than double the net profit from one mailing — and far more donors will remain active next year because they renew their support this year.

NUMBER OF RESOLICITATION MAILINGS PER YEAR	AVERAGE RESULTS FOR EACH MAILING INDIVIDUALLY		TOTAL NET ANNUAL PROFIT
8	Quantity mailed Percent response Average gift Cost per 1,000 Net revenue	30,000 7.5% $30 $750 $45,000	$360,000
7	Quantity mailed Percent response Average gift Cost per 1,000 Net revenue	30,000 8.0% $30 $750 $49,500	$346,500
6	Quantity mailed Percent response Average gift Cost per 1,000 Net revenue	30,000 8.5% $30 $750 $54,000	$324,000
5	Quantity mailed Percent response Average gift Cost per 1,000 Net revenue	30,000 9.0% $30 $750 $58,500	$292,500
4	Quantity mailed Percent response Average gift Cost per 1,000 Net revenue	30,000 10.0% $30 $750 $67,500	$270,000
3	Quantity mailed Percent response Average gift Cost per 1,000 Net revenue	30,000 12.0% $30 $750 $85,000	$256,500
2	Quantity mailed Percent response Average gift Cost per 1,000 Net revenue	30,000 15.0% $30 $750 $112,500	$225,000
1	Quantity mailed Percent response Average gift Cost per 1,000 Net revenue	30,000 20.0% $30 $750 $157,500	$157,500

ILLUSTRATION 31: One added resolicitation mailing can make a big difference

That may be easy to accomplish, as you can see in the accompanying chart. Simply reduce the frequency of your resolicitations (which will improve the response rate on each mailing), stop mailing to less recent and less generous donors (which will raise both the average gift and the response rate), and mail cheaper packages (which might lower the average gift and the response rate but is also likely to raise proportionally more money for every dollar expended). In the example illustrated here, this combination of choices will succeed in raising the response rate from six percent to eight percent and the average gift from $35 to $40. The cost of the direct mail donor resolicitation program accordingly will drop from $128,000 to just $50,000. The fundraising ratio thus will plunge from thirty-eight percent to twenty-six percent, an improvement that will please your fundraising chair — until you explain the disadvantages.

	CURRENT RESOLICITATION SCHEDULE	REVISED RESOLICITION SCHEDULE	DIFFERENCE
Number of resolicitations	8	4	4
Average number of donors resolicited per mailing	20,000	15,000	5,000
Year's total resolicitation quantity	160,000	60,000	100,000
Number of gifts received	9,600	4,800	4,800
Average percent response per resolicitation mailing	6%	8%	33%
Year's total gross resolicitation revenue	$336,000	$192,000	$144,000
Year's total cost of resolicitation mailings	$128,000	$ 50,000	$ 78,000
Net resolicitation revenue	$208,000	$142,000	$ 66,000
Cost per dollar raised	$0.38	$0.26	32%

ILLUSTRATION 32: Cutting costs can be a losing proposition

In this case, overemphasis on efficiency in your donor renewal system would be counterproductive because (1) your net revenue will drop by $66,000, or nearly thirty-two percent, and (2) your donor list will shrink by several thousand individuals. By mailing 100,000 fewer resolicitation letters, you won't just be cutting costs; you'll also be missing opportunities to convert new donors into active supporters and to persuade lapsed donors to come back into the fold. Your organization would continue paying the price of this short-sightedness for many years to come.

Remember: your donors are your friends, and they *want* to hear from you.

Taking Good Care of Your Donors

At first, nearly all the donors you acquire from direct mail acquisition will be, for all intents and purposes, of equal importance. Initially, you'll have just a few thousand on file. Your biggest challenge then will be to find cost-effective ways to stay in touch with them and build their understanding of your work. If you're lucky, you'll net at least modest amounts, which will help subsidize your prospecting program.

Once you're beyond the four- to six-thousand donor level, you can begin "segmenting" your file. "Segmentation" is the key to a profitable donor renewal program over the long term.

Segmentation is based on one simple truth: some people give more money than others.

In direct mail fundraising, segmentation — the division of your donor list into subgroups or "segments" — is usually based on the three fundamental distinguishing characteristics of each donor:

❏ *Recency*: the date on which you received a donor's most recent contribution

❏ *Frequency*: how many gifts you've received from that donor — either cumulatively or within the current calendar year — or how many years the donor has actively supported you

❏ *Gift amount*: generally stated as the highest previous contribution, but often inconveniently — and less usefully — presented as cumulative total giving or year-to-date total

The fundamental principle of segmentation is this:

*Those who've contributed most generously, most fre-
quently and most recently are your best prospects for
additional gifts.*

These are the people to whom you should be paying the most
attention and in whom you should be investing the most in your donor
renewal efforts. We call them "Maxi-Donors." Depending upon the
precise definition, they may include anywhere from fifteen to thirty
percent of your file — but the chances are they contribute three-
quarters or more of the *net* income from your fundraising program.
(*See* **Illustration 34** *on next page.*)

You may be tempted to refrain from resoliciting anyone who's just
given you a gift, or even to methodically eliminate from later appeals

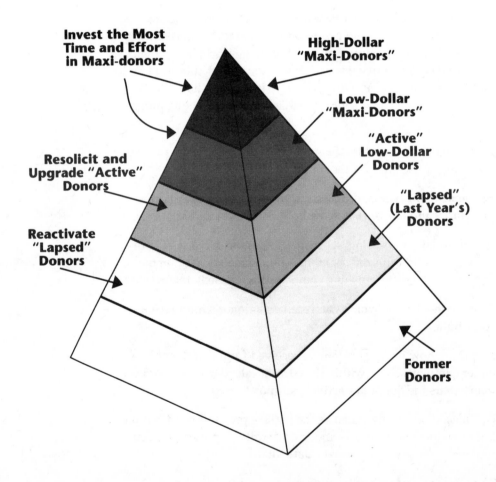

ILLUSTRATION 33: Some donors are more equal than others

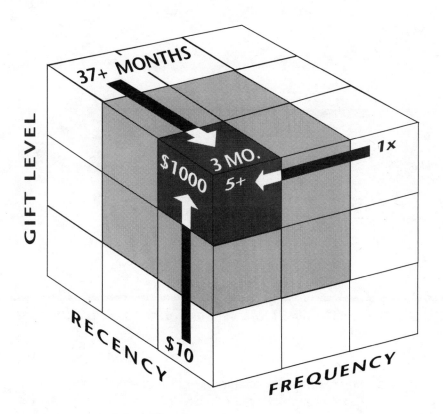

ILLUSTRATION 34: Recency, frequency and gift level define donor segments

those who respond to the first or second letter you've sent this year. In most cases, this is a very big mistake, for three reasons:

❒ The special appeals you write are — or should be — one of your donors' primary sources of information about your work. Not to inform the donors who have shown the *most* interest in your organization reflects misguided priorities. Resolicitation is part of the process of "bonding" and cultivating your donors, some of them potential major contributors.

❒ Remember, your donors contribute to you from their *current* income. Most write checks that are small by their own standards, and many are willing to do so several times a year. By failing to solicit them regularly, you'll lose a great deal of money.

❒ Recent contributors are *most* likely to give again. They're the most interested, the most responsive, and the best prospects for special opportunities such as monthly sustainer programs or gift clubs.

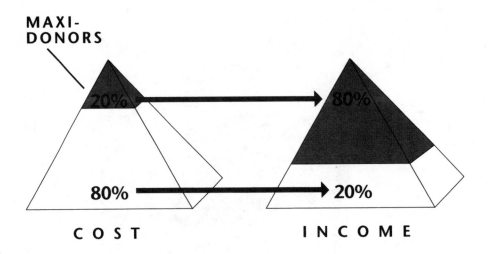

MAXI-DONORS

COST

INCOME

ILLUSTRATION 35: The 80-20 Rule means dollars invested in resolicitation bring unequal dividends

An intelligent approach to segmentation requires that you establish the most cost-effective frequency of contact with each segment of your donor file. You might choose to group the individuals on your list into four broad categories:

(a) "Maxi-Donors," including your most generous, most frequent and most recent contributors;

(b) "Active Donors," who aren't quite so generous, frequent or recent as Maxi-Donors;

(c) "Lapsed Donors," whose last gift arrived at least a year or eighteen months ago but not longer than two or three years ago; and

(d) "Former Donors," who haven't contributed for two or three years or more.

It's simply not worth treating all four of these groups in the same way.

❐ The only segment that's really worth your full attention at all times are your *Maxi-Donors*: you should be in touch with them no less frequently than once every two months (six times per year) and perhaps more often than once per month.

❐ Your *Active Donors* may not respond well to such frequent contact. Four to six times per year should suffice.

❐   You may recapture a significant proportion of your *Lapsed Donors* with two, three or four mailings this year.

❐   The more recent of your *Former Donors* may be worth one or two last direct mail efforts this year — but probably not more.

The biggest cliche in fundraising is the "80-20 Rule": twenty percent of your donors will contribute eighty percent of your fundraising revenue, even though they may require only twenty percent of your fundraising budget. The other eighty percent — soaking up four-fifths of the budget — will yield only twenty percent of your revenue. Identifying and cultivating your Maxi-Donors — and treating other significant segments of your donor file in different but appropriate ways — is an effort to turn the "80-20 Rule" on its head. *(See* **Illustration 35**.*)*

Through segmentation, you can invest greater resources to maximize the returns from your most productive segments and minimize the cost of working with those that are less productive. This will help ensure that you get the highest possible net profit from your direct mail fundraising program.

In the long run, however, your direct mail program may pay off even more handsomely with *major* gifts from a few individuals. As your donor list grows, you should put into place a system of "donor research" to determine whether new donors are good prospects for large gifts. These are the individuals you'll want to cultivate carefully. You'll write and call them personally and arrange face-to-face visits, if possible. Their contributions — amounting to many thousands of dollars — may represent the *real* payoff for all the hard work that's gone into your direct mail fundraising program.

You may wish to conduct donor research in-house, checking the local library's *Who's Who*, the *Foundation Directory*, Standard & Poor's *Register of Corporations, Directors and Executives* and other likely sources of information about wealthy individuals. Chances are, though, you'll find that donor research is as taxing and distracting as other labor-intensive aspects of your fundraising program.

Some large nonprofit institutions, especially colleges and universities, support substantial donor research departments. If you have little or no development staff, you may conclude it's worth paying someone else to do the job of donor research. A variety of professional services are available in this important field. For example, the Information Prospector (Falls Church, Virginia) compiles detailed reports on major gift prospects on the basis of publicly available information. Marts & Lundy, Inc. (Lyndhurst, New Jersey) and the Donor Research Institute

(Garrison, New York) use computers (in sharply different ways) to identify the best major gift prospects on an organization's donor file. The directories of vendors published by fundraising trade periodicals contain the names of other firms that provide similar services.

"Back-end" Services

As your donor base grows, you'll probably begin paying more and more attention to two of the most nettlesome questions about direct mail fundraising: Who's going to count the money? And how are you going to keep track of all the people who give it to you?

It's a good idea to think through your answers to these questions *before* you mail your initial test. The decisions you make in this area of so-called "back-end" services are fateful — and they may not be obvious.

Here's the fundamental principle on which an intelligent back-end system for direct mail fundraising is based:

> *Donors are people, and they deserve to be treated as individuals. They also tend to give more money when they're treated well.*

In practice, this means you'll need:

❑ a quick-turnaround donor acknowledgment program;

❑ an extensive database maintenance system that includes almost every scrap of useful information your fundraising results can provide about each individual donor;

❑ a meticulous system of data entry with built-in quality control procedures to maintain a file of the highest possible accuracy; and

❑ a working system for your staff to respond to individual donor questions and complaints in a timely and polite manner.

A system to deliver all these services may cost you $2 to $3 per donor per year. Admittedly, such a costly back-end system may not work well for a direct mail fundraising program involving hundreds of thousands of $5 or $10 donors. Three dollars per year per donor will probably eat up too much of the profits. But a program in which the average gift is $15 or higher — thus allowing for upgrading — may not live up to its potential *without* the sort of labor-intensive back-end system necessary to ensure that your list will lend itself to credible, personalized appeals.

About every six months, almost like clockwork, one of our long-standing clients asks me, "How big a computer do I need to hold my list? How much will a computer like that cost?" The question may appear disingenuous — obviously, there's more involved than computer hardware — but it highlights one of the enduring sources of confusion in direct mail fundraising: whether to hire additional staff or train volunteers to provide back-end services instead of retaining a service bureau.

The best answer to that question — like most other things about direct mail — has its roots in your organizational strategy. With a multi-million-dollar direct mail fundraising program involving many tens or hundreds of thousands of donors in an intensive program of communications and resolicitation, an in-house service bureau might make sense. It might also be cost-effective at the other end of the scale, with a small, inactive direct mail program if your staff or an exceptionally well-trained, disciplined, *long-term* volunteer can handle the job in a timely and consistent manner.

But most of the time — for direct mail fundraising programs of the type and the scale described in this book — keeping the work in-house makes no sense at all. An in-house system for back-end processing will burden your organization with specialized staff and computer hardware and software, and it will subject you to all the headaches entailed by running what is, after all, a business. Very few nonprofits or political campaigns can run such a business in a consistently efficient and cost-effective manner.

Once again, it's worth taking a leaf from the annals of the business world and asking yourself the single most critical question you can pose about your organization: *What business are you in?* With an aggressive direct mail fundraising program and a growing donor file to match, you could easily discover that you're really in the data processing business if you try to build an in-house service bureau — no matter what your mission statement might say. Willy-nilly, the tail wags the dog. To avoid this problem, some organizations find it worthwhile to pay professionals to do the job *even if* they're convinced they can do it just as well and perhaps even more cheaply.

Back-end services require a respect for complex procedures and a compulsive attention to detail. The job looks deceptively easy — but it may require an investment of tens or hundreds of thousands of dollars in systems analysis, programming, training and maintenance for you to do it right. The cost of the computer hardware is a minor consideration by comparison.

One alternative favored by many organizations is to buy or lease a specialized fundraising software program. There are many on the market, some offered in conjunction with dedicated hardware systems, others sold "in the can," with or without continuing technical assistance. If it works — and I've never actually seen that happen — a system of this sort might lower your investment in an in-house service bureau. But it begs the question of where the job should be done. I believe that, in most circumstances, your wisest course is to retain a specialized service bureau to manage all your back-end operations — and be held accountable for doing the job right.

There are at least four separate (though not necessarily separable) tasks in a back-end system:

(1) *"Cashiering"* — processing and depositing contributions to your bank account;

(2) *"Caging"* — processing and recording the list-by-list and package-by-package information encoded on the response devices in your mailing and outputting it in the form of "flashcounts" (progress reports on your mailing that break down the results by list or segment);

(3) *"Donor acknowledgment"* — thanking your donors, and perhaps asking for another gift at the same time; and

(4) *"List maintenance"* — updating your donor file, recording both new information and corrections to the old, and providing periodic analytical reports that depict the cumulative impact of all your fundraising programs, segment by segment.

In the earliest stages of your direct mail fundraising program, it may be most efficient for your staff to tend to cashiering, caging and donor acknowledgments. If you have an effective list maintenance system in place, it may also be worthwhile to fold in the early test results. But once your direct mail program is underway, it makes sense to transfer your list maintenance to professionals. Ideally, you'll find a service bureau that caters to direct mail fundraisers and offers an integrated system of caging, list maintenance and donor acknowledgments.

It may make sense for you to continue cashiering your direct mail returns in-house, especially if they're just one of several active sources of income and you're already equipped to process large numbers of checks. In such circumstances, however, you'll need to transfer the raw data from your direct mail program to the service bureau on a timely basis.

As your direct mail fundraising program grows in scope and complexity, the demands on your back-end systems will increase geometrically. And just wait until you're ready to start using telephone fund-raising, too!

The Many Uses of the Telephone

Now, let me guess: you don't *like* the idea of telephone fundraising.

Chances are, you've got five or six objections to using what most people in the industry so clumsily refer to as "telemarketing." Calling your donors on the phone seems intrusive. It's a technique widely known to be used by fraudulent charities. It puts your organization's reputation at risk because you may not be able to exert direct control over the individuals who make the phone calls. And, besides, you just hate it when somebody calls *you* at dinnertime to ask for money — and so does everyone you know!

Then why do so many organizations use the telephone so extensively in their fundraising programs?

The answer I give to that question is precisely the same as my response to those who ask why so many nonprofit groups use direct mail:

It works!

Now, please don't confuse telephone fundraisers with bucket-shops peddling tickets by phone to charitable events. These high-pressure operations — most of them local, and some of them fly-by-night ventures that skip from one city to the next — are responsible for the lion's share of the public's complaints about telephone fundraising and for most of the fraud. Doubtless, some are honest, hardworking and sincere. But many such operators exploit their employees, their clients (if in fact they're legitimate) and the public. To me, telephone fundraising means using the telephone as a communications tool linking a public interest organization with its supporters, almost always its previous donors.

It's impossible to estimate with any accuracy how much money legitimate nonprofit groups and political campaigns raise by telephone in a year, but I'm certain that the figure runs to many billions of dollars. So explosive has been the growth of telephone fundraising in recent years that what was a mere handful of firms offering these services at the beginning of the 1980s has become a large industry involving many hundreds of companies. And countless charities and public interest groups have established in-house phone banks operated either by volunteers or by professional staff.

Whenever you contact thousands of people — whether by telephone or by mail — some of them are bound to become irritated. There's no more effective or efficient method of communicating with members and supporters than by telephone — and no more efficient way to annoy at least a few of them.

Without telephone fundraising, however, many groups would raise substantially less money to support their programs. Most nonprofit organizations conclude — with varying degrees of regret — that they simply can't avoid using the telephone. Measured on a revenue-to-cost basis, or in terms of sheer net profits, there's often no way to beat it.

Yes, there are complaints. And, yes, individual donors *matter*. We've found that it's cost-effective to exert the utmost effort to mollify those few individuals — fewer than one percent — who become angry when we call them.

But it's a mistake to dwell upon donors' complaints. Many people — especially those who don't reside on either coast — actually *enjoy* the telephone calls we make on behalf of our clients. Typically, the number of those who thank you for calling far exceeds the number who complain. Many people appreciate getting long-distance calls from groups they support. Each call is an opportunity to pass along a great deal of useful information to your members or donors, often correcting mistaken impressions or reminding them of past successes.

Whether conducted by a specialized telephone fundraising company, a commercial telemarketing service bureau, or an in-house phone bank, telephone fundraising has six principal applications in public interest fundraising:

(1) *Reactivating lapsed members* — After you've reached the end of your rope through direct mail, and one more renewal notice simply isn't cost-effective, your best shot at recapturing lapsed members or donors is by phone. Normally, this is a breakeven proposition, but only in a short-term perspective. After all, now you know how much your donors are worth! Some groups find they're worth enough — and telephone reactivation is effective enough — that it pays for them to call early in the renewal cycle, as the second or third effort in a series. (Keep in mind, though, that donors who are "recaptured" by telephone tend to be more responsive to future telephone appeals than to mail.)

(2) *Special appeals* — To vary the rhythm and the medium of your contact with your donors, you'll probably find it very profitable to conduct one or two special appeals each year by telephone. (Contact more frequently than every six months may be ineffective or even counter-productive.) But if your donors pledge to contribute, it's important to follow through with several reminders to hold them to their word — and not let them easily off the hook with direct mail appeals, which may request a lot less money than they've promised on the phone.

(3) *Upgrading donors* — Through such means as specially named "gift clubs," monthly pledge or sustainer programs, you can use telephone fundraising to increase the level of your donors' support for you. The phone allows a caller — a representative of your organization — to negotiate with the donor for a *specific* level of support. The caller can even negotiate convenient payment terms.

(4) *Donor acknowledgments* — It may well be worth your while to call at least the more generous of your donors to thank them for their support. A thoughtful gesture of this sort may increase in donor loyalty over the long term. For many groups, gifts of $100 or more are big enough to justify this type of red-carpet treatment.

(5) *Combined mail/phone appeals* — Especially for your most generous donors, the considerable expense of combining one or more direct mail contacts with at least one telephone call — all for a single appeal — may pay off in a very big way if it's wisely planned and well executed.

(6) *Prospecting for new donors* — Some nonprofit groups use the telephone to acquire new donors. In some circumstances, this may make a lot of sense. If your issue or project is hot enough, and available lists are strong enough, telephone acquisition may produce a high rate of response and even produce net revenue for your organization. Especially if you combine telephone acquisition with aggressive donor resolicitation efforts, your overall cost of fundraising may be entirely reasonable. Most of the time, however, I think telephone prospecting is a poor idea. It's often a more expensive mode of prospecting than direct mail. It's far more intrusive than calling your own donors, who are much more likely to want to hear from you. It may risk conflict with state charitable fundraising regulators. And, generally speaking, phone-acquired donors can only be resolicited cost-effectively by telephone.

In nearly every type of professionally executed telephone fundraising campaign, donors are asked to commit themselves to contribute a specific amount of money. That amount is then cited on a follow-up

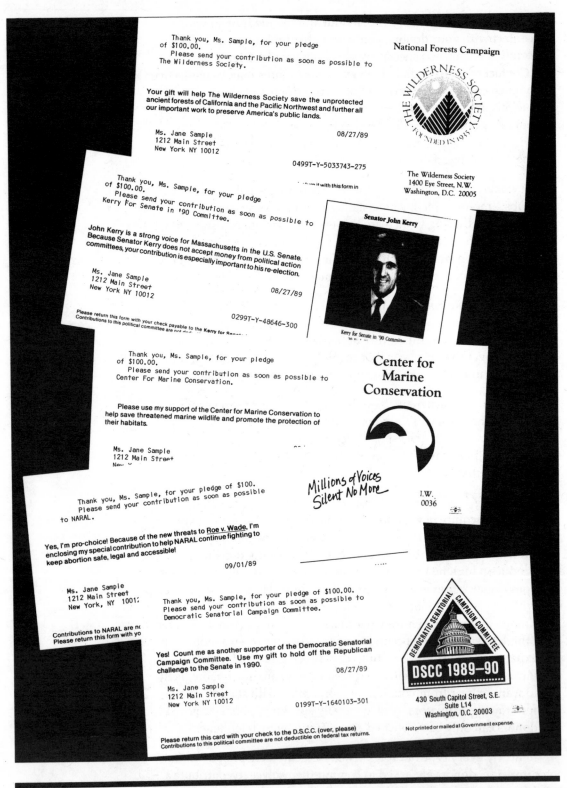

ILLUSTRATION 36: Pledge cards remind donors they promised to help

mailing, sometimes called a "pledge card" or "pledge reminder," mailed as quickly as possible after the phone call, ideally within 24 hours. Some firms mail slightly different versions of their pledge cards to donors who indicate support but won't commit themselves to specific amounts.

While your specific objectives will surely vary from one type of telephone fundraising program to another, all six types have several advantages in common:

❑ *Net revenue* — This may be deferred revenue in the case of reactivation or prospecting efforts, but it's almost always the principal reason to employ telephone fundraising techniques.

❑ *Donor education* — By conveying a brief and clearly focused message in a comprehensive telephone "script," your donors are much more likely to *remember* you than if you mail an appeal to them, because the telephone is a "warmer," more intimate form of communication.

❑ *Two-way communications* — Unlike all but the rarest direct mail appeal, a telephone program gives your donors a chance to talk back and to feel more involved in your work.

❑ *Donor loyalty* — This may ultimately be the greatest advantage of telephone fundraising. Studies show that donors who are contacted by phone tend to remain donors longer and give more generously and more frequently than those who are contacted by mail alone.

Some organizations run telephone fundraising programs independently of their other development work. This is usually unwise. Telephone fundraising efforts are typically — and appropriately — conducted in conjunction with the overall direct mail program. The telephone is best seen as one more implement in the fundraiser's toolbox.

Think strategically. *Integrate* your direct mail and telephone fundraising efforts — even if you find, as some groups do, that their telemarketing efforts contribute as much as half of the net profits from the combined "direct response fundraising" program. The mails and the telephone are different ways to communicate a common vision and sense of purpose to your donors.

For most members of a large national organization, the only *personal* contact available is by telephone. Intelligently managed telephone fundraising can add a warm, personal dimension to the relationship between you and your members, reinforcing your donor communications and fundraising programs (including direct mail) and building individual interest and loyalty. Nothing else but face-to-face contact can match telephone fundraising as a way to *intensify* your organization's relationship with its members. The telephone is one of very few tools widely available to public interest groups that makes *person-to-person fundraising* possible.

However, telephone fundraising is fundamentally a financial proposition. The strongest case for it is that it makes money, and it usually does so in a way that's readily predictable. The numbers tell the most important part of the story.

What to Expect from a Telephone Appeal

Assume that your organization has 30,000 "current" donors on file — contributors who, in this case, have sent you at least one gift within the past twelve months. You've contracted with a professional telephone fundraising firm to conduct a special appeal designed to maximize net revenue and upgrade as many of your donors as possible. Here's what the numbers might look like:

❑ Of your 30,000 donors, the telephone fundraising firm you've hired feels that only 20,000 qualify as good prospects for telephone contact. The rest haven't given large enough gifts at any one time.

❑ A service bureau retained by the telephone fundraising firm will run a computer-match against your remaining 20,000 donors to find their telephone numbers. With a little luck, they'll find sixty percent, or 12,000.

❑ Working on the basis of a script that you and the firm should devise together, paid callers will use WATS lines to contact those 12,000 donors, generally between the hours of 5:30 and 9:30 pm. Depending on how persistently they're told to keep trying if they get a busy signal, no answer or an answering machine, the callers will reach about seventy percent, or 8,400.

❑ It's reasonable to expect that between thirty and fifty percent of the 8,400 donors you reach will pledge a contribution of a specific amount. (The qualifier is important, because many will also make vague promises or drop hints but not agree to specific pledges. Nonspecific pledges are much less likely to be fulfilled.) In an active donor resolicitation program, a forty percent pledge rate is typical. That means you'll have 3,360 pledges.

❒ The "fulfillment rate" — the percentage of donors who actually send in checks — may range from less than half to more than one hundred percent (in which case the number of non-payers is equalled or exceeded by the number of nonspecific pledges that are fulfilled.) For a well-run telephone fundraising program, a seventy percent fulfillment rate is acceptable. For you, this means 2,352 gifts.

❒ If the average contribution to all your direct mail resolicitations is $30, removing the 10,000 least responsive donors should raise that average by at least ten percent — and the "warmth" and innate persuasiveness of telephone contact should add another ten percent to the average gift. This means an average of about $36 for each of the 2,352 gifts you receive from this telephone fundraising project, or a gross of $84,672. (Naturally enough, the average gift almost *always* depends on whom you call.)

❒ But don't expect all $85,000 to come in at once. Telephone contact may take time — several weeks, perhaps, to contact all 8,400 donors. Your telephone fundraising firm then has to mail out pledge cards, and you have to wait for the donors to respond. Many don't; most programs follow up once or twice by mail and sometimes by phone as well. Generally, seventy to eighty percent of the proceeds from a telephone fundraising program will be received within 120 days of the date of the first contact with donors. The *last* contributions should be received within 120 days of the date of the last contact. As you can see, telephone fundraising is rarely a quick way to raise a buck.

❒ While the length and character of the script will determine how much time each phone contact requires, it's likely that callers will average anywhere from four to twelve contacts per hour. The median is almost squarely in the middle of that range, or about eight contacts per hour. At that rate, it will take 1,050 hours of calling to complete the job. If the firm is charging you $50 per caller-hour (including direct mail follow-up costs), the cost of the effort will be $52,500. Eventually, you'll net $32,172.

❒ The ratio of revenue to costs in this hypothetical project is 1.6 to 1. In other words, you won't even double your money. But the chances are you'll be getting gifts from many more than the number of donors who would respond to a direct mail appeal, you'll get larger gifts from many of them than they've ever given before by mail, and you'll have established personal contact with more than one-third of your best donors, which will educate them and build their loyalty.

Telephone Pledge Package

A telephone pledge card package may contain several items. The package illustrated on this and the following three pages is typical. It includes a standard, business-size window envelope, a two-page letter (printed on one sheet), a pledge card and a Business Reply Envelope. Some telephone pledge packages contain additional items, such as lift letters, buckslips, stickers or other front-end premiums.

NATIONAL WOMEN'S POLITICAL CAUCUS

1275 "K" Street, N.W., Suite 750, Washington, D.C. 20005   (202) 898-1100

Dear Friend,

I'm glad we were able to speak with you on the phone the other night. We called to thank you for your past support and to bring you up to date on the recent Supreme Court ruling.

As we had feared, the <u>abortion battleground</u> <u>has</u> <u>now</u> <u>shifted</u> <u>to</u> <u>the</u> <u>states</u>. Women can no longer look to the Supreme Court to protect their reproductive freedom. The right to reproductive choice will have to be fought for STATE BY STATE. And this is a battle we cannot afford to lose.

By upholding the state of Missouri's right to restrict access to abortion, the Supreme Court has sent a loud signal to every state that such restrictions are now possible. In short, <u>the</u> <u>Court</u> <u>has</u> <u>taken</u> <u>the</u> <u>right</u> <u>to</u> <u>choose</u> <u>FROM</u> <u>women</u> <u>and</u> <u>given</u> <u>it</u> <u>to</u> <u>state</u> <u>legislatures</u>.

The National Women's Political Caucus is moving forward to propel the silent pro-choice majority into political action. NO American who supports a woman's right to choose can afford to sit on the sidelines any more. And no candidate -- incumbent or challenger will be able to skirt this issue for another day.

Abortion will be <u>the</u> cutting edge issue for the 1990 gubernatorial and statehouse elections.

And that's why I'm writing you today -- to urge your immediate and generous support for our <u>**1990**</u> <u>**STATE**</u> <u>**LEGISLATIVE**</u> <u>**PLAN**</u>. This plan is designed to promote an effective electoral strategy that focuses on <u>candidates</u> and <u>voters</u>.

Our <u>**1990**</u> <u>**STATE**</u> <u>**LEGISLATIVE**</u> <u>**PLAN**</u> is designed to prepare as many women as possible for grassroots political leadership and to use our proven techniques to win the battles that lie ahead. Our strategy includes three major components.

(over, please)

-2-

<u>First</u>, we will conduct our national campaign training program designed for women running for seats at the state level. Women who are current or former elected officials will help prepare women candidates to run <u>successfully</u> for state legislative seats. We've already tested the program in three pilot states -- Minnesota, Texas and New Jersey -- and now we are ready to expand it into as many states as possible in order to prepare for the 1990 elections.

<u>Second</u>, we will target pro-choice candidates for state legislative seats. Through a successful program now in use, we will develop an information bank of voters who <u>will</u> vote across party lines on this issue.

And <u>third</u>, we will provide "issue briefs" for qualified candidates to address sensitive personal issues, like freedom of choice, child care and parental leave, in a positive manner. It is crucial that our women candidates are equipped with the best information available when they campaign for public office. These briefs will provide our candidates with position statements that will promote support for their candidacy, rather than controversy.

For 18 years, the National Women's Political Caucus has established a solid organization with a proven track record of success. But we need your support to implement our <u>**1990 STATE LEGISLATIVE PLAN**</u>. Your gift of $1,000, $500, $250, $100, $50, or $25 will make a difference in providing women with a strong political voice across the country. With our own broad-based, grassroots political leaders, we will gain new power to protect our rights and improve the quality of our lives by achieving greater equality.

<u>Please</u> <u>give</u> <u>as</u> <u>generously</u> <u>as</u> <u>you</u> <u>can</u>. I look forward to hearing from you soon.

Sincerely,

Irene Natividad

Irene Natividad
National Chair

P.S. We must move forward immediately with our plan in order to harness the electoral clout of ALL PRO-CHOICE advocates in this country. If we are going <u>to</u> <u>protect</u> <u>our</u> <u>right</u> <u>to</u> <u>choose,</u> <u>we</u> <u>have</u> <u>to</u> <u>prepare</u> <u>as</u> <u>many</u> <u>PRO-CHOICE</u> <u>women</u> <u>as</u> <u>possible</u> <u>for</u> <u>political</u> <u>leadership</u> at the grassroots level. And we have to mobilize AGAINST those politicians who are anti-choice. Thank you for your ongoing commitment to women's rights.

1275 K Street, N.W. #750
Washington, D.C. 20005

NWH-B-04

Your stamp will save us postage.

BUSINESS REPLY MAIL
FIRST CLASS   PERMIT NO 10775   WASHINGTON, D C

POSTAGE WILL BE PAID BY ADDRESSEE

 National Women's Political Caucus
P.O. Box 66500
Washington, D.C. 20035-6500

NO POSTAGE
NECESSARY IF
MAILED IN THE
UNITED STATES

Thank you, Ms. Sample, for your pledge
of $100.00.
Please send your contribution as soon as possible to
National Women's Political Caucus.

Your special contribution to the **National Women's Political Caucus**
will help more women take their places as leaders and decision-
makers at all levels of government.

08/27/89

Ms. Jane Sample
1212 Main Street
New York NY 10012

1699T-Y-23142-253

Please return this card with your check payable to NWPC. Contributions to
the NWPC are not tax-deductible as charitable contributions. (Over, please)

NATIONAL WOMEN'S
POLITICAL CAUCUS

NWPC

1275 K STREET, N.W., SUITE 750
WASHINGTON, D.C. 20005

If you prefer to fulfill your pledge by credit card, please indicate below:
Amount to be charged $ _____.
Card # _____   ☐ MasterCard   ☐ Visa
Name on Card _____   Expiration date _____
Thank you very much!   Signature _____

In fact, the numbers I've used in this hypothetical example are conservative. A pledge rate of forty-five percent with eighty percent fulfillment and a $40 average gift is by no means out of the question: in this example, that would mean gross revenue of $120,960. You'd turn a profit of $68,460, with a revenue-to-cost ratio of 2.3 to 1. Integrated mail and phone programs commonly achieve even higher ratios.

An especially effective telephone fundraising program — one carefully segmented to deliver the most powerful message to each segment or type of donor — can upgrade the average contribution by more than ten percent. Some programs successfully generate major gifts: single contributions of $10,000 or more are not unknown. Careful direct mail follow-up can substantially raise fulfillment rates.

Illustration 38 (*on the following page*) depicts the bottom-line impact of modest increases or decreases in the average contribution, the response rate and the fulfillment rate — the difference between competent and mediocre telephone fundraising efforts. Professionals in this demanding and highly competitive industry have developed techniques, often proprietary, to improve results as measured by any or all of these important criteria. Performance varies widely.

But, in any case, don't be mesmerized by dollars and cents. Telephone fundraising can play a strategic role for your organization by converting many of your one-time "donors" into genuine supporters, by generating real enthusiasm among many of your reliable donors and coaxing them to give much larger gifts, and by conveying the message to your supporters in the most intimate way available to you that their support really *matters*.

Fees charged by telephone fundraising firms vary greatly, and each firm seems to have its own peculiar list of inclusions and exclusions from the base rate. They tend to run from about $30 per caller-hour to $70 or more, or — to look at it a different way — from around $3.50 per contact to $12.00 or more. Experience and levels of talent also vary. Chances are, you'll get what you pay for. You're not likely to find any bargains.

Cost is only one of a great many issues to consider about telephone fundraising. Normally, you can lower the cost by limiting the duration of the contact (the "script"), by cheapening the quality of the printed materials sent to those who pledge to contribute, by avoiding "lead letters" or postcards to the donors you're going to call, and by simplifying the methods and terms of collecting payments. It may or may not be smart for you to do any of these things.

When you look around the telephone fundraising field, you should also find out whether a firm you're considering is properly registered

By raising or lowering your pledge rate, fulfillment rate or average gift, a high-quality telephone fundraising program can greatly improve results.

ASSUMPTIONS	
All Donors	30,000
Qualified donors	20,000
Qualified w/phone #	12,000
Completed calls	8,400
Cost	$52,500

PLEDGE RATE		FUFILLMENT RATE	AVERAGE GIFT	NET REVENUE	ABOVE/ BELOW AVERAGE
Effect of change in pledge rate					
Above Average	45%	70%	$36	$42,756	$10,584
Average	40%	70%	$36	$32,172	$0
Below Average	35%	70%	$36	$21,588	($10,584)
Effect of change in fullfillment rate					
Above Average	40%	75%	$36	$38,220	$6,048
Average	40%	70%	$36	$32,172	$0
Below Average	40%	65%	$36	$26,124	($6,048)
Effect of change in average gift					
Above Average	40%	70%	$40	$41,580	$9,408
Average	40%	70%	$36	$32,172	$0
Below Average	40%	70%	$30	$18,060	($14,112)

ILLUSTRATION 38: Skill and experience can pay big dividends in telephone fundraising

to do business in the states where your donors live. Regulation of telephone fundraising has become a controversial issue of considerable staying power, and I'm sure you'll agree it's essential to conduct your affairs with scrupulous regard for both legal and ethical standards.

An Inside Look at One Campaign

6

Eight Packages for 295,000 Individuals

To launch its initial campaign for San Francisco-based TURN — Toward Utility Rate Normalization — Mal Warwick & Associates, Inc. designed and produced what was in effect a mailing in eight parts, or segments. All eight were based on a detailed "copy platform" — in effect, a "case statement" summarizing the arguments for supporting TURN — that was conceived, edited and approved by TURN's executive director. In other words, TURN dictated every substantive aspect and factual detail of the message delivered to donors and prospects, and later edited and approved every word appearing in the eight finished letters.

Three similar packages were mailed to different segments of TURN's active and lapsed donors — a total of 32,786. At about the same time, we mailed five versions of a donor acquisition package to selected portions of a much larger collection of prospective donor lists (plus 8,158 inactive and low-dollar TURN donors). In the following pages, you can see exactly what we mailed.

PACKAGE	QUANTITY	COST PER PIECE	RESPONSE RATE	NUMBER OF GIFTS
"Maxi-Donor" Year-End Renewal	5,870	$1.99	46.7%	2,737
"Active Donor" Year-End Renewal	12,728	$0.54	20.6%	2,624
Lapsed Donor Reactivation	14,188	$0.44	10.6%	1,497
Acquisition Control Package	130,841	$0.29	2.4%	3,137
Survey Test Package	29,917	$0.29	2.6%	767
Free Sticker Test Package	29,921	$0.33	1.6%	480
Teaser Test Package	29,925	$0.29	1.8%	528
Price Test Package	29,921	$0.29	2.2%	650

ILLUSTRATION 39: *The TURN kickoff campaign consisted of four mailings using eight packages*

TURN
Toward Utility Rate Normalization
693 Mission Street
San Francisco, CA 94105

Mr. John Doe
123 Main Street
Anytown, AS 00000

Maxi-Donor Year-End Renewal

TURN's Maxi-Donors — its most loyal, most frequent and most generous contributors — received a high-quality personalized package. This included the items reproduced here and on the following pages: a "closed-face" outer envelope (one, that is, without a window), a personalized letter and response device, and a reply envelope bearing a "live" first-class stamp. Only about eighteen percent of TURN's prime donor list were in this Maxi-Donor group. We mailed 5,870 of these packages at a cost of about $1.99 apiece. Nearly forty-seven percent of the recipients responded generously. The mailing produced a *very* significant profit.

TURN

Toward Utility Rate Normalization
693 Mission Street
San Francisco, CA 94105

Sylvia M. Siegel
Executive Director

December 22, 1988

Mr. John Doe
123 Main Street
Anytown, AS 00000

Dear Mr. Doe,

What's in store for your natural gas, electricity, and phone
bills next year? I'll give you my best forecast in a moment.
But first, I want to say a big THANK YOU for your past support
of TURN.

Without it, we could never have accomplished all we did in
1988. And <u>what</u> a year 1988 has been!

Your gas, electric, and telephone companies outdid themselves.
They dreamed up the most complicated and outlandish schemes yet
to get their hands on <u>more</u> of <u>your</u> money while giving you <u>less</u> in
return.

TURN beat back those schemes, thanks to your support.
TURN's hardworking staff put in overtime to keep OUTRAGEOUS
overcharges off your bills:

o TURN went all the way to Washington, D.C. -- to argue for
   lower rates on your phone bill before the U.S. House of
   Representatives Telecommunications and Finance Committee.
   And TURN joined an appeal of a FCC decision that initiated
   the access charge scam.

o TURN went to the state legislature in Sacramento to keep
   your natural gas bills from going through the roof.

o And TURN spent weeks on end with the Public Utilities
   Commission in San Francisco to keep ALL your utility bills
   down.

Just look at how TURN's hard work (and your support) has
paid off. In 1988, we chalked up these important victories:

** TURN got <u>Pacific Bell toll call charges lowered by</u>
<u>between 5% and 32%</u>. And we convinced the PUC to <u>slash AT&T's</u>
<u>long-distance rates by 28%</u>. Sprint and MCI slashed their rates
similarly.

Page 2

** TURN successfully opposed a $2 charge for blocking "976" programs from your telephone. Why should you pay to remove an unsolicited service from your telephone?

** TURN stopped a DISGRACEFUL plan to raise your natural gas and electricity rates. It all started when last year's cold winter sent southern California heating bills sky high.

SoCal Gas was giving its big industrial users whopping discounts. Then, it tacked exorbitant charges onto the bills of ordinary households that went over the "baseline rate" in order to finance its giveaways to big users.

Now, the obvious solution to this problem is for SoCal Gas and other California natural gas companies to <u>stop</u> <u>undercharging</u> <u>big</u> <u>customers</u> <u>and</u> <u>stop</u> <u>overcharging</u> <u>small</u> <u>customers</u>. But did they agree to do that? No way.

Instead, they had the gall to go to the state legislature and try to get the <u>baseline rate outlawed</u>. That would have raised <u>your</u> gas and electricity bill.

It would have raised gas and electricity bills for <u>all</u> but the <u>wealthiest</u> Californians.

In the worst case, it could have meant illness or even death for senior citizens, single mothers, and other people who just barely get by. For those who barely manage to pay their winter heat bills, even a few dollars in higher rates can mean catastrophe!

TURN stopped that one in Sacramento. And we'll be there <u>every</u> <u>time</u> the gas and electric companies try these tricks. We'll fight <u>any</u> plan to shift costs from big industrial users onto households like yours.

** Another decisive victory that helped you in 1988 was <u>halting</u> <u>PacBell's</u> <u>abusive</u> <u>marketing</u> <u>practices</u>.

Pacific Bell had been tricking people into ordering services like Call Forwarding and Call Waiting -- even when they didn't want them. Then, the unsuspecting customers paid for these services <u>every</u> <u>month</u>, even if they NEVER used them. But the charge was hidden on the bill!

Because TURN and other consumer advocates blew the whistle on this swindle, the PUC made PacBell stop. Even more, we won <u>refunds</u> for the people who were cheated ($27 million so far). And we won a ruling that forced PacBell to set up a $16.5 million trust fund to educate the public about their <u>rights</u> <u>as</u> <u>telephone</u> <u>consumers</u>.

Page 3

There's no mystery about how TURN wins all these victories.
It's just plain old hard work. We always have justice on our
side. But we have to sort through mountains of boring documents
and check endless columns of figures to prove it.

The phone, gas, and electric companies try to make it all so
complicated, ordinary folks can't understand what they're up to.

That's why ordinary Californians need TURN. We argue on
your behalf every day of the year. To make sure you don't pay
one penny more than you should.

Now back to my forecast for your bills in 1989. Just take a
look at what's in store:

(1) California's phone, natural gas, and electricity
companies are making a big push for deregulation.

This would mean they could raise your bills as high as they
want -- and you would have nowhere to turn. The Public Utilities
Commission would no longer provide a forum for stopping their
rate hikes. No one would stop them.

Even worse, nothing would stop the utilities investing the
proceeds from your electric bill (or your gas or phone bill) in
anything they wanted. Risky mergers. Foreign real estate.
Questionable loans. Anything.

And if their risky investments hurt their credit rating,
they could get back the higher finance costs they'd have to pay,
simply by upping the charges on your phone, gas, or electric
bill.

This is clearly outrageous. TURN is pledged to stop it, but
it will be a hard fight. I ask for your support once again.
I assure you that if we have it, we will win.

(2) The second big fight in 1989 will be over the Diablo
Canyon Nuclear Power Plant. PG&E is trying to sock its customers
with the $5.8 billion the plant cost. PG&E ran up big bills on
engineering mistakes and design flaws building this costly
boondoggle.

TURN insists that PG&E's stockholders should bear the cost.
We've been fighting this one for a long time. The Public
Utilities Commission is exhausted from wading through PG&E's
piles of paper. (One set of arguments was so big, PG&E had to
use a Bekins moving van to deliver it!)

The PUC is trying to cut a deal. But TURN says NO DEAL!

This deal will mean higher electric bills for the next 30
years! If the PUC makes this deal, TURN is ready to fight it all
the way to the U.S. Supreme Court!

Page 4

(3) We're also out to win <u>metropolitan</u> <u>phone</u> <u>rates</u> for you. This will mean no more of those "zone" charges when you call nearby communities.

<u>Your</u> <u>basic</u> <u>phone</u> <u>rate</u> <u>should</u> <u>cover</u> <u>your</u> <u>entire</u> <u>metropolitan</u> <u>area</u>. And you should get that service for the same basic rate you pay now -- or even lower.

So, what's going to happen to your utility bills next year? Just as we won in 1988, TURN can win in 1989. And if we do, <u>we'll</u> <u>save</u> <u>you</u> <u>money</u> <u>on</u> <u>your</u> <u>phone</u>, <u>gas</u>, <u>and</u> <u>electric</u> <u>bills</u>. But we rely on your support to keep up the fight.

The utilities never contribute a dime to keep TURN alive. And big businesses don't support us, either. We've stopped <u>them</u> too many times from getting lavish discounts at <u>your</u> expense.

<u>We're</u> <u>counting</u> <u>on</u> <u>support</u> <u>from</u> <u>you</u>. Please make a special, year-end contribution to help TURN gear up to save you money in 1989. Send back your contribution with your personal reply form in the postage-paid reply envelope enclosed.

Your tax-deductible donation will go a long way. Because at TURN, we make every penny count.

We don't have fancy offices. Our staff of experts could get more than double the salaries they earn at TURN if they went over to the other side. But they'll never do that.

We're dedicated to making sure that you -- and other California consumers -- get a fair shake. In 1989, just like in 1988, just like every year since 1973 -- TURN will be there.

TURN has saved the average Californian hundreds of dollars over the years. But the natural gas, electricity, and phone companies are poised with a whole bag of new tricks, waiting to snatch it all back and then some. They'll do it, too, if they get the chance.

Please lend your support to make sure they don't. Because if you keep TURN there, you can bet your bottom dollar that your gas, electric, and phone companies won't get the chance to rip you off.

Sincerely,

Sylvia M. Siegel

Sylvia M. Siegel
Executive Director

P.S. The phone, gas, and electric companies are pushing hard for deregulation as soon as possible. If they win, they'll be able to raise your bills <u>as</u> <u>high</u> <u>as</u> <u>they</u> <u>like</u>, <u>with</u> <u>NO</u> <u>limit</u>. TURN needs your contribution right now to make sure we have the resources to stop them. So I ask you, please, to send your contribution <u>within</u> <u>the</u> <u>next</u> <u>10</u> <u>days</u>.

TURN
Financial Processing Service
2550 Ninth Street, #1038
Berkeley, CA 94710

Mr. John Doe
123 Main Street
Anytown, AS 00000

Dear Sylvia,

Yes, I want to help TURN stop the new tricks
the utilities are using to raise my gas, electric
and phone bills. Here's my special, tax-deductible,
year-end contribution to help you fight for fair
utility rates for all Californians in 1989:

[ ] $200

[ ] $1,000

[ ] $_____

I have made my tax-deductible contribution
payable to TURN and I am returning it in the
postage-paid envelope provided.

0200

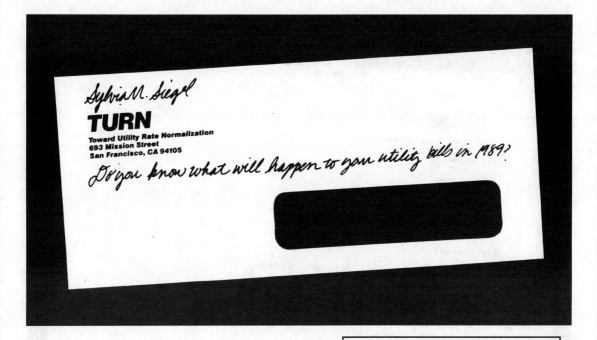

Active Donor Year-End Renewal

Thirty-nine percent of TURN's donors received a "generic" (non-personalized) version of the Maxi-Donor appeal. The text of the letter was virtually identical to that of the Maxi-Donor appeal, but the message was packaged far less expensively. We affixed a "Cheshire" mailing label to a pre-printed reply device and mailed it in a window carrier along with a Business Reply Envelope, all of which you can see above and on the following pages. We mailed 12,728 of these packages costing about fifty-four cents each. A heartening twenty percent responded with gifts, adding substantially to TURN's net profit from the project as a whole.

Sylvia M. Siegel
Executive Director

TURN
Toward Utility Rate Normalization
693 Mission Street
San Francisco, CA 94105

Dear Friend,

What's in store for your natural gas, electricity, and phone bills next year? I'll give you my best forecast in a moment. But first, I want to say a big THANK YOU for your past support of TURN.

Without it, we could never have accomplished all we did in 1988. And <u>what</u> a year 1988 has been!

Your gas, electric, and telephone companies outdid themselves. They dreamed up the most complicated and outlandish schemes yet to get their hands on <u>more</u> of <u>your</u> money while giving you <u>less</u> in return.

TURN beat back those schemes, thanks to your support. TURN's hardworking staff put in overtime to keep OUTRAGEOUS overcharges off your bills:

o TURN went all the way to Washington, D.C. -- to argue for lower rates on your phone bill before the U.S. House of Representatives Telecommunications and Finance Committee. And TURN joined an appeal of a FCC decision that initiated the access charge scam.

o TURN went to the state legislature in Sacramento to keep your natural gas bills from going through the roof.

o And TURN spent weeks on end with the Public Utilities Commission in San Francisco to keep ALL your utility bills down.

Just look at how TURN's hard work (and your support) has paid off. In 1988, we chalked up these important victories:

** TURN got <u>Pacific Bell toll call charges lowered by between 5% and 32%</u>. And we convinced the PUC to <u>slash AT&T's long-distance rates by 28%</u>. Sprint and MCI slashed their rates similarly.

38029

Page 4

(3) We're also out to win <u>metropolitan</u> <u>phone</u> <u>rates</u> for you. This will mean no more of those "zone" charges when you call nearby communities.

<u>Your</u> <u>basic</u> <u>phone</u> <u>rate</u> <u>should</u> <u>cover</u> <u>your</u> <u>entire</u> <u>metropolitan</u> <u>area</u>. And you should get that service for the same basic rate you pay now -- or even lower.

So, what's going to happen to your utility bills next year? Just as we won in 1988, TURN can win in 1989. And if we do, <u>we'll</u> <u>save</u> <u>you</u> <u>money</u> <u>on</u> <u>your</u> <u>phone</u>, <u>gas</u>, <u>and</u> <u>electric</u> <u>bills</u>. But we rely on your support to keep up the fight.

The utilities never contribute a dime to keep TURN alive. And big businesses don't support us, either. We've stopped <u>them</u> too many times from getting lavish discounts at <u>your</u> expense.

<u>We're</u> <u>counting</u> <u>on</u> <u>support</u> <u>from</u> <u>you</u>. Please make a special, year-end contribution to help TURN gear up to save you money in 1989. Your tax-deductible donation of $20, $35, $50, $75, or $100 will go a long way. Because at TURN, we make every penny count.

We don't have fancy offices. Our staff of experts could get more than double the salaries they earn at TURN if they went over to the other side. But they'll never do that.

We're dedicated to making sure that you -- and other California consumers -- get a fair shake. In 1989, just like in 1988, just like every year since 1973 -- TURN will be there.

TURN has saved the average Californian hundreds of dollars over the years. But the natural gas, electricity, and phone companies are poised with a whole bag of new tricks, waiting to snatch it all back and then some. They'll do it, too, if they get the chance.

Please lend your support to make sure they don't. Because if you keep TURN there, you can bet your bottom dollar that your gas, electric, and phone companies won't get the chance to rip you off.

Sincerely,

Sylvia M. Siegel

Sylvia M. Siegel
Executive Director

P.S. The phone, gas, and electric companies are pushing hard for deregulation starting as soon as possible. If they win, they'll be able to raise your bills <u>as</u> <u>high</u> <u>as</u> <u>they</u> <u>like</u>, <u>with</u> <u>NO</u> <u>limit</u>. TURN needs your contribution right now to make sure we have the resources to stop them. So I ask you, please, to send your contribution <u>within</u> <u>the</u> <u>next</u> <u>10</u> <u>days</u>.

NO POSTAGE
NECESSARY IF
MAILED IN THE
UNITED STATES

38024

BUSINESS REPLY MAIL
FIRST CLASS PERMIT NO. 3506   BERKELEY, CA

POSTAGE WILL BE PAID BY ADDRESSEE

TURN
Toward Utility Rate Normalization
Financial Processing Service
2550 Ninth Street, Suite 1038
Berkeley, CA 94710

TURN
Toward Utility Rate Normalization
693 Mission Street
San Francisco, CA 94105

Dear Sylvia,

Yes, I want to help TURN stop the new tricks the utilities are using to raise my gas, electric and phone bills. Here's my special, tax-deductible, year-end contribution to help you fight for fair utility rates for all Californians in 1989:

☐ **$25**   ☐ **$35**   ☐ **$50**   ☐ **$75**   ☐ **$100**   ☐ **$250**   ☐ **$____**

SAMPLE
Mr. John Doe
123 Any Street
Any Town, AS 00000

"I'm not going to let those utilities rip you off in 1989."

Please make your check payable to **TURN.**
Your gift to TURN is tax-deductible.

38022

Thank you.

Lapsed Donor Reactivation

To "reactivate" lapsed donors — those forty-three percent of TURN supporters who hadn't sent contributions in more than eighteen months — we affixed a handwritten note to the letter we'd written for active supporters and added a special note from the executive director along with a "Strategy Survey" to induce greater participation. Then we packaged these items in the same window carrier we'd printed for active donors. The whole package cost about forty-four cents per piece. On the following pages, you can see the handwritten note as it appeared on page one of the letter, along with the executive director's note and and the combined survey and contribution form. Typically, response is poor to lapsed donor appeals of this type. But nearly eleven percent of the 14,188 who received these packages returned gifts to TURN. *(See next pages).*

TURN

Toward Utility Rate Normalization
693 Mission Street
San Francisco, CA 94105

Sylvia M. Siegel
Executive Director

*Here's your copy of a
letter I sent to all our
current supporters.
—Sylvia*

Dear Friend,

What's in store for your natural gas, electricity, and phone bills next year? I'll give you my best forecast in a moment. But first, I want to say a big THANK YOU for your past support of TURN.

Without it, we could never have accomplished all we did in 1988. And <u>what</u> a year 1988 has been!

Your gas, electric, and telephone companies outdid themselves. They dreamed up the most complicated and outlandish schemes yet to get their hands on <u>more</u> of <u>your</u> money while giving you <u>less</u> in return.

TURN beat back those schemes, thanks to your support. TURN's hardworking staff put in overtime to keep OUTRAGEOUS overcharges off your bills:

o   TURN went all the way to Washington, D.C. -- to argue for lower rates on your phone bill before the U.S. House of Representatives Telecommunications and Finance Committee. And TURN joined an appeal of a FCC decision that initiated the access charge scam.

o   TURN went to the state legislature in Sacramento to keep your natural gas bills from going through the roof.

o   And TURN spent weeks on end with the Public Utilities Commission in San Francisco to keep ALL your utility bills down.

Just look at how TURN's hard work (and your support) has paid off. In 1988, we chalked up these important victories:

** TURN got <u>Pacific Bell toll call charges lowered by between 5% and 32%</u>. And we convinced the PUC to <u>slash AT&T's long-distance rates by 28%</u>. Sprint and MCI slashed their rates similarly.

38041

From the desk of
Sylvia M. Siegel

Dear Friend,

In the past, you supported TURN when we really needed it. Without you, TURN wouldn't have been able to save Californians over $7 billion on phone, electricity and natural gas bills.

But we haven't heard from you in a long time now.

I'm enclosing a copy of a letter I sent all TURN's current supporters. I want to let you in, too, on what we've accomplished in 1988. The utility companies came close to outright gouging on your bills. And TURN stopped them in the nick of time.

But the utilities are already at work on new scams for 1989. And it doesn't take a crystal ball to see that if TURN isn't there to fight them, your rates will go up.

Please, read the whole story in the enclosed letter. When you do, you'll see TURN really needs old friends like you more than ever now. Please give careful consideration to supporting TURN once again.

Sincerely,

Sylvia M. Siegel

Sylvia M. Siegel

P.S. One thing we've really missed are your ideas. Now, I need your help to determine TURN's strategy for next year. Won't you please take a few moments to fill out the special "1989 TURN Strategy Survey" I've prepared for you?

38046

1989 TURN Strategy Survey

NUMBER C1039Z   PREPARED FOR:

Please return this 1989 TURN Strategy Survey along with your check in the enclosed envelope. Make checks payable to TURN. Contributions to TURN are tax-deductible.

SAMPLE
Mr. John Doe
123 Any Street
Any Town, AS 00000

38042

1

What do you think should be TURN's number one priority in 1989?

☐ Fair telephone rates
☐ Fair natural gas rates
☐ Fair electricity rates
☐ All three

2

Should TURN work hardest:

☐ To keep phone, natural gas and electricity service affordable for senior citizens and the poor
☐ To keep phone, gas and electric rates as low as possible for the majority of California households
☐ Both are equally important

3

Are your present phone rates:

☐ Too high
☐ Too low
☐ Just about fair

4

Because of TURN, local and long-distance phone rates went down in 1988. Metropolitan phone rates would mean no extra "Zone" charges for calling nearby communities. Should TURN fight for metropolitan rates in 1989?

☐ Yes
☐ No

5

Are your present gas and electric rates:

☐ Too high
☐ Too low
☐ Just about fair

6

California's telephone companies want less regulation. This would let them set their rates as high as they like. Should TURN fight this step toward deregulation in 1989?

☐ Yes
☐ No

7

(Optional) Please give suggestions that will help TURN better serve California consumers like yourself in 1989 (use back of page).

8

Are you willing to invest $2 per month toward TURN saving California utility customers millions of dollars in 1989?

☐ Yes, Sylvia, and here's my tax-deductible contribution to help you save me and other Californians those millions of dollars:

☐ $15 ☐ $24 ☐ $35 ☐ $50
☐ $75 ☐ $100 ☐ $_____

☐ No.

TURN
Toward Utility Rate Normalization
693 Mission Street
San Francisco, CA 94105

Toward Utility Rate Normalization
693 Mission Street
San Francisco, CA 94105

IMPORTANT NOTICE
about your
telephone bill

Please read
before paying

Acquisition Control Package

Prospective TURN donors received one of five Cheshire label packages in an effort to determine the most cost-effective donor acquisition strategy. The only common elements in all five packages were a news clipping and a Business Reply Envelope. Other elements varied from one package to another. Above is reproduced the outer envelope in which the "control," or standard, package was mailed. On the next six pages you can view the control letter, the news clipping, the Business Reply Envelope and the reply device included in the control package.

Toward Utility Rate Normalization
693 Mission Street
San Francisco, CA 94105

Dear Friend,

Your phone rates should be going <u>down</u>. But instead -- just when the phone companies should be passing on their lower costs to you -- they're dreaming up a whole raft of schemes to hang on to <u>your</u> money!

And if they get their way, <u>your phone bills will go through the roof</u>!

Suppose the legislature passed a tax that took hundreds of dollars from your pocket. And then they turned around and gave it to the phone companies to spend any way they please.

If the phone companies get their way, <u>the effect</u> on <u>you will be exactly the same as if the legislature passed that tax</u>.

Dollars out of your pocket. Millions into the hands of the phone company.

It makes me fighting mad to see the phone companies hire high-priced experts whose only job is to think up new ways to overcharge you. And then they turn around and tack the cost of those same experts onto <u>your</u> phone bill.

I'm determined to stop this outrageous phone robbery. But I'm going to need your help to do it.

And I assure you that if you join me in this fight, <u>we can win</u>.

I know we can, because since 1973, <u>every time</u> Pacific Bell or General Telephone or PG&E or SoCal Edison or SoCal Gas has arrived at the Public Utilities Commission demanding more of your hard-earned dollars, TURN has been there to fight on your behalf.

For example, two years ago, Pacific Bell tried to make your home phone <u>into a pay phone</u>. They wanted to charge for every local call you made, just like for long distance calls.

Your telephone would have racked up charges for every minute you spoke, even if the call was to your next-door neighbor!

TURN beat back that one. And believe me, if we hadn't been there, your phone bill might well be double or triple

Page 2

what it is now.

Soon, you should see your share of a $230 million refund on your phone bill. TURN helped win that for you earlier this year. PacBell has been stalling on paying it, but TURN will make sure you get it.

This refund is not the first money we've won for you. Since 1973, we've saved the average California utility customer hundreds of dollars -- a total of over $7 billion for all ratepayers.

And we never let up. TURN constantly keeps an eagle eye on your utility rates. We know if we relax for even one season, Pacific Bell will sneak back with its outrageous plan to make your home phone just like a pay phone. And the gas and electric companies will slide through exorbitant rate hikes.

Our name, TURN, means Toward Utility Rate Normalization. It simply says that those who use the most electricity, the most gas or telephone service -- like big corporations and big factories -- should pay their fair share instead of getting huge discounts.

And right now, we're fighting hard to keep your phone rates down. With your help, we'll succeed.

PacBell's latest scam is to make you -- the residential user -- subsidize their investment in fancy $50 million digital switches.

This equipment isn't necessary to transmit voices over the phone lines. It isn't even needed to send information between home computers.

The only customers who need this equipment are the biggest businesses that transmit huge amounts of data. And other information service companies can help them do that -- companies that don't get to tack their investment costs onto your phone bill.

The Public Utility Commission's own staff says PacBell overcharged you and other phone customers $700 million to buy this high-tech gear. That's a $70 refund for the average phone customer.

TURN aims to win back as much of that as we can -- every penny that's coming to you. And we aim to see that PacBell doesn't get the $640 million more they want to sock you with.

You see, TURN has uncovered solid evidence that phone company costs are down. They have fewer employees, and so their

Page 3

labor costs are lower. They have more efficient equipment (that you paid a bundle for). Their other expenses -- their income tax for example, which is also charged to you -- are down, too.

TURN is fighting to make sure those lower costs get passed on to you -- as lower phone bills.

What's more, we believe your local phone charge should cover all your calls to your entire metropolitan area. No more of those "zone" charges to call a nearby community.

We recently won the first step toward victory on this. TURN got the local calling area that's included in your basic rate boosted from 8 miles away to 12 miles away. While that's good, it's not good enough.

We won't stop there. You deserve Metropolitan Area Rates -- for the same local rate you pay now, or even lower.

The most dangerous scheme on the horizon is that the phone companies want to set their own rates and charge you whatever they want.

Local phone service is still a monopoly. It would be outright robbery to let the phone companies charge whatever they please!

What's more, there are many low-income elderly people who are able to stay independent, living in their own homes, simply because there's a telephone at their elbow. Even a $5.00 per month increase in their phone rates threatens their independent life!

Throughout the year, TURN is at the California Public Utilities Commission, fighting to keep your bills as low and as fair as possible. When necessary, we even go to Washington, D.C., to represent your interests before the Federal Communications Commission, the U.S. Congress, and even the Supreme Court.

Fighting to keep rates down has become so complex, it would be very hard for you to do it on your own. One set of arguments was so big, PG&E had to use a Bekins moving van to deliver it! We spend hundreds of hours on research and hearings for every case.

We go over every word, every figure. And it pays off. We once found an arithmetic error that would have cost you and me and other consumers $50 million! We ferret out every trick they use to try to rob you -- and we stop them every chance we get.

Page 4

Because TURN's work benefits millions of Californians, many of whom cannot help themselves, I ask you to contribute what you can to make sure we're there when you need us most.

If TURN defeats the phone companies' latest schemes, we'll be saving you up to $100 a year or more on your phone bill alone. And that's not even counting what we'll save you on gas and electricity.

Your tax-deductible contribution of $20, $25, $50, $100, or more is a smart investment in keeping your phone and utility rates down.

As a TURN contributor, you'll receive our informative newsletter four times a year. It keeps you up to date on all the fights we wage on your behalf. And it gives you chances to make your own voice heard -- by telling you when to send a letter or make a strategic phone call to turn on the pressure.

One thing is certain: your phone bills will go up substantially unless TURN succeeds -- as we have for 15 years -- in beating back these rate hikes.

Remember, the money we save will be your own. And with your help, we will win.

                              Sincerely,

                              Sylvia M. Siegel

                              Sylvia M. Siegel
                              Executive Director

P.S. We have to be ready for crucial hearings in just a few weeks
     -- hearings that decide if money will come out of your pocket.
     We're a lean, shoestring organization and we're counting on
     your support to be ready. So please, send your contribution
     as soon as you can.

38031A

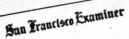

San Francisco Examiner

Dwight Chapin

Professional underdog

THE PILES OF paper would have gladdened any pack rat's heart, but Sylvia Siegel said things weren't quite as chaotic as usual.

"I've tried to clean up a little," she said, "because '60 Minutes' has been following me around."

Siegel is a short, plump, white-haired woman who says she's old enough to retire but won't go further than that ("My age is nobody's damned business").

Once in awhile, you can find her in her Mill Valley home, making chopped liver. Most of the time you can find her in one of three other places: her none-too-fancy office on Mission Street, working the phones or those stacks of stuff; a courtroom or a hearing room, taking on PG&E or Pacific Bell; or out among the people, ringing doorbells, raising money, spreading the word.

Siegel is a consumer activist, the executive director of Toward Utility Rate Normalization (TURN), which for the last 10 years plus has fought hard and with surprising effectiveness for the little guy and the middle-sized guy.

It's estimated that Siegel and her staff, which now includes three lawyers, an educational outreach worker, a secretary and five to 10 canvassers who go door to door passing out information and raising funds, have saved Californians more than $7 billion in gas, electrical and phone rates.

SIEGEL IS not a lawyer, but she's mastered the highly complex ways of utility regulation to the point where she's won many significant victories in the courts and before the state Public Utilities Commission.

Several years ago, Siegel helped force the utilities to establish "life-line" rates — low-cost, basic service for the elderly and the poor.

Recently, TURN won the right (through the PUC) to insert promotional and fund-raising mailing into PG&E bills and is seeking the same access to telephone bills.

At the same time, Siegel and her group are battling hard to cut back Pacific Bell's $446 million rate increase.

"We're carrying a new briefcase every day," she says. "We usually have four or five major cases going on at a time. I don't look at my calendar much anymore. It just makes me tired."

Siegel has been involved in unusual pursuits most of her life.

"I knew I wasn't destined for any ordinary pursuit," she says. "I'm a Taurus. I'm persistent. I have no patience with anything dull."

38038

BUSINESS REPLY MAIL

FIRST CLASS PERMIT NO. 3506 BERKELEY, CA

POSTAGE WILL BE PAID BY ADDRESSEE

NO POSTAGE
NECESSARY IF
MAILED IN THE
UNITED STATES

TURN

Toward Utility Rate Normalization
Financial Processing Service
2550 Ninth Street, Suite 1038
Berkeley, CA 94710

Dear Sylvia,

YES, I want to keep home phone rates from going sky high. Here's my tax-deductible contribution to help TURN keep on saving millions of dollars for me and other California utility customers:

☐ $20 ☐ $50 ☐ $100 ☐ $500 ☐ $____

I can fight even harder for you with a contribution of this size.

Sylvia M. Siegel

TURN
Toward Utility Rate Normalization
693 Mission Street
San Francisco, CA 94105

SAMPLE
Mr. John Doe
123 Any Street
Any Town, AS 00000

"The phone company is trying to rob you — and I'm fighting mad!"

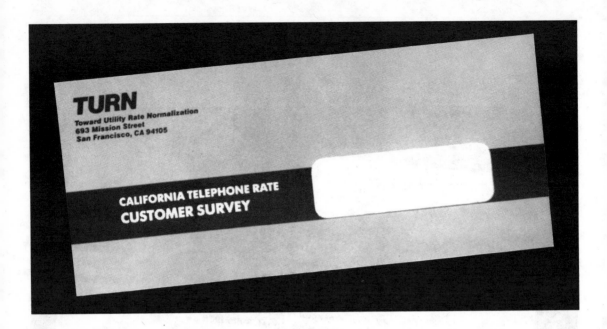

Acquisition Survey Package

One test version of the TURN acquisition package contained a "California Telephone Rate Customer Survey" integrated into the reply device along with a version of the control letter slightly altered to note the inclusion of the survey. The front of the outer envelope is reproduced above, followed by the letter and the survey. (As with the other three acquisition test packages, the news clipping and the Business Reply Envelope used in the control package were also present.)

TURN
Toward Utility Rate Normalization
693 Mission Street
San Francisco, CA 94105

Dear Friend,

Your phone rates should be going <u>down</u>. But instead -- just when the phone companies should be passing on their lower costs to you -- they're dreaming up a whole raft of schemes to hang on to <u>your</u> money.

And if they get their way, <u>your phone bills will go through the roof</u>!

The fight to stop this outrageous phone robbery begins in just a few weeks. If I have hard evidence that informed Californians are against this scam, it will help me win.

That's why I'm asking you, after you read this letter, to <u>complete the California Telephone Rate Customer Survey</u> I've <u>enclosed</u>.

Suppose the legislature passed a tax that took hundreds of dollars from your pocket. And then they turned around and gave it to the phone companies to spend any way they please.

If the phone companies get their way, <u>the effect on you will be exactly the same as if the legislature passed that tax</u>.

Dollars out of your pocket. Millions into the hands of the phone company.

It makes me fighting mad to see the phone companies hire high-priced experts whose only job is to think up new ways to overcharge you. And then they turn around and tack the cost of those same experts onto <u>your</u> phone bill.

I'm determined to stop this outrageous phone robbery. But I'm going to need your help to do it. And I assure you that if you join me in this fight, <u>we can win</u>.

I know we can, because since 1973, <u>every time</u> Pacific Bell or General Telephone or PG&E or SoCal Edison or SoCal Gas has arrived at the Public Utilities Commission demanding more of your hard-earned dollars, TURN has been there to fight on your behalf.

For example, two years ago, Pacific Bell tried to make your home phone <u>into a pay phone</u>. They wanted to charge for every local call you made, just like for long distance calls.

Page 2

Your telephone would have racked up charges for every minute you spoke, even if the call was to your next-door neighbor!

TURN beat back that one. And believe me, if we hadn't been there, your phone bill might well be double or triple what it is now.

Soon, you should see your share of a $230 million refund on your phone bill. TURN helped win that for you earlier this year. PacBell has been stalling on paying it, but TURN will make sure you get it.

This refund is not the first money we've won for you. Since 1973, we've saved the average California utility customer hundreds of dollars -- a total of over $7 billion for all ratepayers.

And we never let up. TURN constantly keeps an eagle eye on your utility rates. We know if we relax for even one season, Pacific Bell will sneak back with its outrageous plan to make your home phone just like a pay phone. And the gas and electric companies will slide through exorbitant rate hikes.

Our name, TURN, means Toward Utility Rate Normalization. It simply says that those who use the most electricity, the most gas or telephone service -- like big corporations and big factories -- should pay their fair share instead of getting huge discounts.

And right now, we're fighting hard to keep your phone rates down. With your help, we'll succeed.

PacBell's latest scam is to make you -- the residential user -- subsidize their investment in fancy $50 million digital switches.

This equipment isn't necessary to transmit voices over the phone lines. It isn't even needed to send information between home computers.

The only customers who need this equipment are the biggest businesses that transmit huge amounts of data. And other information service companies can help them do that -- companies that don't get to tack their investment costs onto your phone bill.

The Public Utility Commission's own staff says PacBell overcharged you and other phone customers $700 million to buy this high tech gear. That's a $70 refund for the average phone customer.

Page 3

TURN aims to win back as much of that as we can -- every penny that's coming to you. And we aim to see that PacBell doesn't get the $640 million more they want to sock you with.

You see, TURN has uncovered solid evidence that phone company costs are down. They have fewer employees, and so their labor costs are lower. They have more efficient equipment (that you paid a bundle for). Their other expenses -- their income tax for example, which is also charged to you -- are down, too.

TURN is fighting to make sure those lower costs get passed on to you -- as lower phone bills.

What's more, we believe your local phone charge should cover all your calls to your entire metropolitan area. No more of those "zone" charges to call a nearby community.

We recently won the first step toward victory on this. TURN got the local calling area that's included in your basic rate boosted from 8 miles away to 12 miles away. While that's good, it's not good enough.

We won't stop there. You deserve Metropolitan Area Rates -- for the same local rate you pay now, or even lower.

The most dangerous scheme on the horizon is that the phone companies want to set their own rates and charge you whatever they want.

Local phone service is still a monopoly. It would be outright robbery to let the phone companies charge whatever they please!

What's more, there are many low-income elderly people who are able to stay independent, living in their own homes, simply because there's a telephone at their elbow. Even a $5.00 per month increase in their phone rates threatens their independent life!

Throughout the year, TURN is at the California Public Utilities Commission, fighting to keep your bills as low and as fair as possible. When necessary, we even go to Washington, D.C., to represent your interests before the Federal Communications Commission, the U.S. Congress, and even the Supreme Court.

Fighting to keep rates down has become so complex, it would be very hard for you to do it on your own. One set of arguments was so big, PG&E has to use a Bekins moving van to deliver it! We spend hundreds of hours on research and hearings for every case.

Page 4

We go over every word, every figure. And it pays off. <u>We</u> <u>once</u> <u>found</u> <u>an</u> <u>arithmetic</u> <u>error</u> <u>that</u> <u>would</u> <u>have</u> <u>cost</u> <u>you</u> <u>and</u> <u>me</u> <u>and</u> <u>other</u> <u>consumers</u> <u>$50 million</u>! We ferret out every trick they use to try to rob you -- and we stop them every chance we get.

Because TURN's work benefits millions of Californians, many of whom cannot help themselves, I ask you to contribute what you can to <u>make</u> <u>sure</u> <u>we</u> <u>are</u> <u>there</u> <u>when</u> <u>you</u> <u>need</u> <u>us</u> <u>most</u>.

If TURN defeats the phone companies' latest schemes, we'll be saving you up to $100 a year or more on your phone bill alone. And that's not even counting what we'll save you on gas and electricity.

Your tax-deductible contribution of $20, $25, $50, $100, or more is a smart investment in keeping your phone and utility rates down.

As a TURN contributor, you'll receive our informative newsletter four times a year. It keeps you up to date on all the fights we wage on your behalf. And it gives you chances to make your own voice heard -- by telling you when to send a letter or make a strategic phone call to turn on the pressure.

One thing is certain: your phone bills will go up substantially unless TURN succeeds -- as we have for 15 years -- <u>in</u> <u>beating</u> <u>back</u> <u>these</u> <u>rate</u> <u>hikes</u>.

We have to be ready for crucial hearings in just a few weeks -- hearings that decide if money will come out of your pocket. We're a lean, shoestring organization and we are counting on your support to be ready. So please, send your contribution <u>as</u> <u>soon</u> <u>as</u> <u>you</u> <u>can</u>.

Remember, the money we save will be your own. And with your help, <u>we</u> <u>will</u> <u>win</u>.

Sincerely,

Sylvia M. Siegel
Executive Director

P.S. I really need your opinions on the enclosed survey to back up my arguments when I go before the Public Utilities Commission. Please give a few minutes of your time to fill it out and return it today -- so we have it before the hearings start. You'll be helping save yourself and other Californians millions of dollars.

380319

TURN

*Toward
Utility Rate
Normalization*

693 Mission Street   San Francisco, CA 94105

QUESTIONNAIRE

PREPARED FOR   NO. A-432681

INSTRUCTIONS

Please fill in your answers to the questions on the California Telephone Rate Customer Survey.

Then, please take a moment to complete the Reply Memorandum below. Make your check payable to TURN.

Return this entire form in the enclosed postage-paid envelope.

REPLY MEMORANDUM

Dear Sylvia,

☐ I've completed the "California Telephone Rate Customer Survey."

☐ I want to keep home phone rates from going sky high. Here's my tax-deductible contribution to help TURN keep on saving millions of dollars for me and other California utility customers:

☐ $20   ☐ $25   ☐ $50   ☐ $100   ☐ $800   ☐ $_____

CALIFORNIA TELEPHONE RATE CUSTOMER SURVEY ▶

38032E

CALIFORNIA TELEPHONE RATE CUSTOMER SURVEY

Pacific Bell should be required to refund the $700 million (an average of $70 for each of us) that they overcharged residential customers last year.

☐ Agree
☐ Disagree

When phone company costs drop, as they have in recent years, raising rates for residential customers is outrageous. Lower costs to the phone company should be passed on to us.

☐ Agree
☐ Disagree

Residential and small business phone users should not have to pay more so Pacific Bell and General Telephone can invest billions in fancy high-tech services for big business.

☐ Agree
☐ Disagree

Local phone rates should cover the whole metropolitan area for the price we pay now—or lower. Zone charges should be discontinued.

☐ Agree
☐ Disagree

It's dangerous for the government to stop regulating phone companies. If they're allowed to set their own rates, our phone bills could go sky high.

☐ Agree
☐ Disagree

If you agree with me on at least three out of these five questions, please join me in fighting the phone companies' exorbitant price hikes. Remember, the money we save will be your own. Sylvia M Siegel

12-5-88

Acquisition Free Sticker Package

To one test version, we added a sheet of eight "peel-off" stickers. The stickers, the distinctive envelope in which we mailed them, and the response device are all pictured. The letter, the news clipping and the Business Reply Envelope were all identical to those included in the control package.

Acquisition Teaser Test Package

Yet another TURN acquisition test package used an outer envelope with a photo and distinctive "teaser" copy. The envelope is pictured here, along with the response device it contained. All other elements of this package — the letter, news clipping and Business Reply Envelope — were identical to those of the control package.

Dear Sylvia,

YES, I want to keep home phone rates from going sky high. Here's my tax-deductible contribution to help TURN keep on saving millions of dollars for me and other California utility customers:

☐ $15   ⊘ $25   ☐ $50   ☐ $100   ☐ $500   ☐ $_____

I can fight even harder for you with a contribution of this size.

Sylvia M. Siegel

TURN
Toward Utility Rate Normalization
693 Mission Street
San Francisco, CA 94105

SAMPLE
Mr. John Doe
123 Any Street
Any Town, AS A0000

"The phone company is trying to rob you — and I'm fighting mad!"

38032D

Acquisition Price Test Package

In the fifth version of our initial donor prospecting test for TURN, we suggested a $15 minimum gift instead of a $20 minimum, as on the other four versions. The response device is reproduced above, and the very slightly different fourth page of the control letter appears next. In all other respects, this version was identical to the control package.

Page 4

Because TURN's work benefits millions of Californians, many of whom cannot help themselves, I ask you to contribute what you can to <u>make</u> <u>sure</u> <u>we're</u> <u>there</u> <u>when</u> <u>you</u> <u>need</u> <u>us</u> <u>most</u>.

If TURN defeats the phone companies' latest schemes, we'll be saving you up to $100 a year or more on your phone bill alone. And that's not even counting what we'll save you on gas and electricity.

Your tax-deductible contribution of $15, $25, $50, $100, or more is a smart investment in keeping your phone and utility rates down.

As a TURN contributor, you'll receive our informative newsletter four times a year. It keeps you up to date on all the fights we wage on your behalf. And it gives you chances to make your own voice heard -- by telling you when to send a letter or make a strategic phone call to turn on the pressure.

One thing is certain: your phone bills will go up substantially unless TURN succeeds -- as we have for 15 years -- <u>in</u> <u>beating</u> <u>back</u> <u>these</u> <u>rate</u> <u>hikes</u>.

Remember, the money we save will be your own. And with your help, <u>we</u> <u>will</u> <u>win</u>.

Sincerely,

Sylvia M Siegel

Sylvia M. Siegel
Executive Director

P.S. We have to be ready for crucial hearings in just a few weeks -- hearings that decide if money will come out of your pocket. We're a lean, shoestring organization and we're counting on <u>your</u> support to be ready. So please, send your contribution <u>as</u> <u>soon</u> <u>as</u> <u>you</u> <u>can</u>.

38031D

■ ■ ■ ■ ■

All together, we mailed a quarter-million prospect packages. Of the "Important Notice," the control package, we produced about 130,000. It was the standard against which we tested results for the other four versions. We printed and mailed approximately 30,000 of each of the four at a unit cost of between twenty-nine and thirty-three cents.

While from our point of view, this mailing was an "initial test," it was simply a continuation of a long-running direct mail fundraising program, as far as TURN was concerned. We began our work with extensive knowledge of the market, based on TURN's previous mailings. This enabled us to mail a much larger number of letters than is ordinarily the case in an initial test.

Overall, the response rate was 2.2 percent, but it varied from one package to another. The survey version yielded 2.6 percent, the control 2.4 percent, and the other three varied from 1.6 to 2.2 percent. However, the average contribution also varied considerably.

Because of TURN's proprietary interests, it's inappropriate to report here the average gifts received (and thus the total revenue realized). Take my word for it, though: in this case, it's not valid to conclude that the version with the highest response rate was the most successful.

The results TURN obtained from both prospect and resolicitation packages were extraordinary, running between fifteen and forty percent over projections. The effectiveness of these packages clearly had something to do with the excellent results. So, too, did the long time that had elapsed since the last previous resolicitation. But more than any other factor, this direct mail success story is best explained by TURN's remarkable effectiveness in battling for the rights of California utility consumers. And it didn't hurt a bit that TURN's founder and then-executive director, Sylvia Siegel, is one of the state's best-known and most beloved consumer advocates, and a wonderfully quotable and colorful person to boot. Direct mail fundraising doesn't operate in a vacuum.

One Month's Work for Jesse Jackson

7

What's Different About Political Direct Mail?

Electoral politics is a strategy favored by many would-be world-changers — but they rarely know what they're getting into. With its intense time-pressures, high visibility and its own peculiar logic and vocabulary, the billion-dollar business of politics has made work for legions of consultants, lawyers and accountants. Since the post-Watergate political reforms of 1974, the world of political campaigns has become progressively more complicated and inaccessible to the general public.

Despite the specialized knowledge required to run a large-scale political campaign, the applications of direct mail fundraising are surprisingly similar in politics and in the larger world of public interest organizations. That's why a consultant who specializes in political direct mail is also likely to do business with nonprofits, perhaps under a different corporate name.

While candidates, campaign managers and political party officials usually feel their problems are unique, they're only partly right. In strategic terms, there are really only two meaningful differences between nonprofit and political direct mail fundraising: deadlines and legal requirements.

1. Deadlines

Everything in politics revolves around the unavoidable deadline of Election Day. Legislative candidates must think in terms of "election cycles," which are two-, four- or six-year periods separated by elections. For each election, there is also a "filing deadline" by which candidates must declare their intention to run, and usually there are "disclosure" deadlines too, when information must be made public about how candidates' funds are raised and spent. Initiative or referendum campaigns face the same deadlines, and often more besides. Ballot measures need to be drafted, published, circulated and certified by government officials within prescribed periods of time. PACs and political party organizations face similar deadlines. For all of them, the underlying reality is that *time is limited*. After Election Day, there may literally be no tomorrow. Direct mail fundraising programs that don't take election deadlines into account are doomed.

Unfortunately, the gubernatorial candidate who faced the daunting task of building a huge donor base in too short a time (in Case Study Four in Chapter 1) is not an exception. Politicians almost always wait until it's too late to embark upon direct mail fundraising. This helps account for the diminishing use of direct mail fundraising in electoral politics. At least nine out of every ten candidates and campaign managers I've ever talked to about this subject have made this mistake, whether running campaigns for legislative office or for the Presidency of the United States. The same goes for most of those who undertake campaigns for statewide ballot measures. On the other hand, political parties and Political Action Committees tend to plan from a somewhat longer-term perspective, so they're a little less likely to commit the error of waiting too long — but not much. It's ironic that so many people in politics should have such a poorly developed sense of the strategic uses of *time*; while their election campaigns are often laid out on paper, week by week and day by day, months or even years before Election Day, their fundraising plans are often made far too late.

2. *Legal requirements*

Under the impetus of election "reform," fundraising for political campaigns has become circumscribed by layer upon layer of federal and state law, judicial and quasi-judicial rulings, and administrative regulations. Candidates and campaign managers for federal office and in many state campaigns need a sophisticated understanding of these restrictions just to know *from whom* they may raise funds, *how much* they may accept, *when* and in *what form* they may accept funds, where they may *bank* contributions, how they may *spend* them, what *information* they must request of contributors, and where and how they must *report* it.

The laws that apply to presidential and Congressional campaigns are different. Many states and some localities have their own limitations and reporting requirements, virtually none of which match one another, much less the federal laws. The penalties for failure to comply with this bizarre hodge-podge of laws and regulations are sometimes severe, at least on paper. At best, violations are embarrassing and a potential political liability.

One exceptionally important special feature of the statutes relating to presidential campaigns offers an opportunity of strategic importance to candidates for the White House. An election reform law passed in the mid-seventies in the wake of the Watergate scandal makes taxpayer funds available to many candidates in presidential primary campaigns. Before the parties choose their nominees, contending candidates may (and almost always do) choose to abide by spending limits so that they may receive "matching funds." Within limits, every dollar they raise up to a maximum of $250 per donor is matched on a dollar-for-dollar basis by the federal government. (The money comes from taxpayers who voluntarily "check off" $1 contributions on their income tax returns.)

For presidential direct mail fundraising programs, these matching funds are a godsend. To break even in acquiring donors, a presidential campaign must theoretically collect only fifty cents on the dollar in direct contributions. (In practice, sixty-five cents may be closer to the mark, because the reporting requirements are very exacting and not all contributions will qualify to be matched.) This allows any presidential candidate with sufficient capital — and broad enough appeal — to build a donor list with astonishing speed.

There are other, less meaningful differences between nonprofit and political direct mail fundraising:

☐ The *idiom* of political direct mail is distinctive. Buzzwords and symbols abound. Any self-respecting nonprofit organization might be ashamed to send out letters like those of some of the most respected politicians in the land.

☐ Most candidates have broad latitude in choosing their *issues*. With a pliable candidate and public opinion polling data in hand, a direct mail copywriter can have a field day. This places an especially high premium on integrity, a quality that is not in notably great supply in the business of politics.

☐ Bequests, planned giving and many other forms of *major donor fundraising* are absent from most political campaigns. Political party organizations sometimes make remarkably effective use of these techniques. But in most political fundraising, the payoff from direct mail must be more immediate.

Otherwise, political campaigns and political parties must live with the same direct mail fundraising realities as any nonprofit organization. Their *constituents* may be willing to vote for them — but turning constituents into *donors* is quite a different matter.

The direct mail fundraising techniques described in this book apply as well to political campaigns as to nonprofit public interest groups. Using those methods, my colleagues and I have created successful fundraising packages and managed fundraising programs for two major presidential campaigns, more than thirty political committees and unnumbered candidates for Congress and other offices. By the same token, what we've learned from raising money for political campaigns has been of immense value in our work for nonprofit organizations, most of it transferable without alteration. In this chapter, you'll see some of the fruits of that experience.

Thirty-One Days in March

Shortly before Labor Day 1987, Changing America, Inc., the political fundraising affiliate of Mal Warwick & Associates, Inc., launched a direct mail fundraising program for the Rev. Jesse L. Jackson's 1988 Presidential campaign. The effort ended eleven months later, having raised a total of more than $7 million from 73,000 contributors.

From mid-February until early May 1988, when the Jackson campaign was featured almost nightly on network news, contributions poured in from the direct mail fundraising program at the rate of more than $1 million per month (not including federal matching funds). For a grassroots campaign starting so late and virtually from scratch, this was a heady experience. For the direct mail consultants, it was a headache.

PACKAGE	QUANTITY	COST PER PIECE	RESPONSE RATE	NUMBER OF GIFTS	AVERAGE GIFT
Presidential Issues Survey	400,794	$0.44	3.7%	14,666	$32
"Hope Stamp" Acquisition	90,525	$0.50	3.5%	3,149	$31
"Kitchen Cabinet" Acquisition	90,524	$0.47	3.6%	3,230	$30
Bill Cosby Acquisition	49,276	$0.45	2.1%	1,046	$30
"Hope Stamp" Resolicitation	94,085	$0.44	7.2%	6,804	$38
Action Alert	16,145	$0.82	12.3%	1,979	$55
High-Dollar "Kitchen Cabinet" Acquisition	8,932	$3.25	6.8%	610	$93
Telephone Fundraising	6,755	$3.70	14.0%	943	$66

ILLUSTRATION 48: One month's work for Jesse Jackson employed seven different direct mail packages

To give you a sense of the fast-changing character of political direct mail fundraising at its most frenzied, and to depict the intense concentration and wide variety of the work we crowded into a very short period, I reproduce in the following pages the *seven* direct mail packages Changing America mailed for the Jackson campaign between March 1st and March 31st. Two were donor resolicitations while five were donor acquisition packages. There were four separate acquisition mailings and two resolicitation mailings plus two telephone appeals — a total of six nationwide direct mail and telephone fundraising projects within thirty-one days.

The *acquisition* program in March consisted of 640,051 letters that ultimately yielded gifts totaling $767,109 (some of which was received in April or May). The effort generated 22,691 gifts averaging $34 — a response rate of 3.5%.

Resolicitation efforts consisted of 116,985 letters and telephone contacts. These produced $431,462 in contributions, a response of 8.3% with an average gift of $44.

Thus, the direct response fundraising program in March produced total revenue of $1,198,571, plus matching funds which later pushed the effective total near $2 million.

Jesse Jackson

1988 PRESIDENTIAL ISSUES SURVEY

Presidential Issues Survey Package

This donor acquisition package, with its heavy emphasis on donor involvement, had long since been established as the workhorse "control" package for the Jackson campaign's donor acquisition program. The over-whelming majority of the more than 640,000 prospects addressed by the Jackson campaign in March 1988 were mailed the "Presidential Issues Survey" package. It was sent via first class mail at a cost of approximately forty-two cents per package.

Jesse Jackson

Dear Fellow American Citizen,

I'm writing you because I believe you and I share the
same views on many of the most pressing issues of our time.

As one who has consistently demonstrated your commitment to the principles of dignity, humanity, and justice, I
greatly value your aid and counsel.

I invite you to play a very special role as a Charter
Member of my 1988 Presidential campaign. I want you by my
side in this historic effort to shape our nation's political
agenda as we approach the Twenty-First Century.

I want and need your support because -- like you -- I
know that America deserves better leadership.

When the President of the United States vetoes a bill
imposing sanctions on a government that jails and kills
South African children, what value does he place on children's lives?

America deserves better leadership.

When the government of the United States denies help to
students who want to go to college, and farmers who want to
save their farms ... yet gives money to kill students and
farmers in Central America ... what does that say about our
values as a nation and as a people?

America deserves better leadership.

We live in what is called the "Reagan Era" because
Ronald Reagan has offered the American people a coherent
vision, an ideology based on fighting communism and promoting the growth of American corporations around the world.

I hope you'll agree with me that it's time for us to
offer a vision that's just as coherent -- one based on fighting poverty, disease, and oppression, and promoting economic
development that meets the needs of people around the world.

I want you to join my campaign because I feel this
nation must reject the distorted values of the Reagan Administration ... which places private greed over public need

Page 2

and service ... and emphasizes military posturing over peaceful negotiations.

Everywhere I go in this beautiful country of ours, I hear a similar concern for the future. Not just the loss of jobs, but the loss of pride.

Not just the closing of a factory or the auction of a farm, but the end of community.

Not just the loss of hope, but the growth of fear.

At the same time, I hear renewed determination -- a determination that we can confront these troubled times and rise above them. We can provide equal opportunity to all, regardless of race, creed, color, or national origin. We will not give in to the destructive pattern of economic violence and spiritual despair.

We're often reminded that we live in a great nation -- and we do. But it can be greater still if we follow a new definition of greatness.

Our nation's greatness is not in the size of our GNP. It's not our military might. It's not our educational and technological achievements -- as great and as necessary as each of those may be.

More fundamental to national greatness, by my definition, is how we treat children, the poor, and the elderly.

o If we care for our young, ensuring their proper nutrition and educating them to work in tomorrow's world, we'll be a great nation.

o If we provide decent, safe, and sanitary housing and food for the poor, then we'll be a great nation.

o If we provide health care and food and show respect for our elderly, then we'll be a great nation.

Greatness is in how we value and care for our people.

That is what I hope the American people will learn from my second campaign for the Presidency.

I've included with this letter a brief survey on twelve of the major issues of the 1988 Presidential election campaign. I ask you to spend a moment to complete the survey. Find out whether we do agree on these vital matters affecting our health and welfare, the nation's economy, and our role in the world around us.

Page 3

As you can see on the survey, I don't pull any punches on the issues. I don't think you want leadership that ducks and dodges. There've been too many years of evasion of the real problems facing our society.

If you do share many of my views, I invite you to join me in my campaign for the Democratic nomination for President in 1988 -- to put our views at the top of the nation's political agenda.

I invite you to become a Charter Member of my campaign with a contribution of $25, $35, $50, $100, or $250 to "JESSE JACKSON '88."

Despite my strong showing in Iowa, I must still demonstrate to skeptical reporters and the general public that there is deep, continued support for my candidacy.

At this crucial time, your gift will give my campaign a big boost. But the impact of your contribution will be twice as great because of so-called Federal "matching funds."

The Federal Election Commission will match every dollar you contribute up to a maximum of $250. So your gift of $25, $35, $50, $100, or $250 will mean twice as much for the campaign.

In 1984, we won five states, finished second in four others, and ended a strong third in eight more. We raised $9.1 million. We got 3.5 million primary and caucus votes -- over one of every five votes cast for all the Democratic candidates in 1984! And we got 465-1/2 delegate votes at the Democratic National Convention.

To accomplish all this, my support came exclusively from principled and committed individual citizens like you.

Now, in this 1988 campaign, I need your support.

And I ask that you join me within the next 10 days.

Your $25, $35, $50, $100, or $250 contribution to "JESSE JACKSON '88" will help me reach millions of voters in Illinois, Michigan, New York, Pennsylvania, and the other crucial primary states.

As a Charter Member, you'll have a personal investment in my campaign -- and I promise we'll keep you fully informed of all the major developments in the exciting months of campaigning ahead of us.

Page 4

Recently we've witnessed terrible scenes of spiritual despair. The racial violence at Howard Beach and Forsythe County, Georgia; the suicides of farmers in the Midwest and young people in New Jersey and Illinois; the epidemic of drug taking in our schools, and of babies making babies in our neighborhoods.

<u>Too</u> <u>many</u> <u>of</u> <u>our</u> <u>young</u> <u>people</u> <u>are</u> <u>losing</u> <u>hope</u>. They do not see a future for themselves -- but if we do not, as a people, take the lives of our children seriously, how can they?

If we do not, as a nation, invest our resources in our children's future, what can they look forward to?

If we do not, as grown-ups, set them an example of working together and talking together among ourselves, what kind of example have we set for them?

With your support now, my campaign for the Presidency will strive to restore the <u>hope</u> of our young people.

Together, we <u>will</u> save the children ... strengthen the cities ... heal the land ... invest in America ... and achieve peace in our time ... and we will do it <u>now</u>.

From the bottom of my heart, my deepest thanks to you for your support and encouragement.

With high hopes,

Jesse L. Jackson

P.S.   Please take just a moment to complete and return the "1988 Presidential Issues Survey" I've enclosed with this letter -- so you can see whether you and I agree on many of the major issues of the campaign. And if you <u>do</u> share my views on at least 7 of the 12 issues, I invite you to join my campaign as a Charter Member.

P.P.S.   Your gift of $25, $35, $50, $100, or $250 will be matched, dollar for dollar, by the Federal Election Commission.

Authorized and paid for by Jesse Jackson '88, Howard Renzi, Treasurer

QUESTIONNAIRE

#AA-6788329

Jesse Jackson '88

PREPARED FOR

INSTRUCTIONS

A) Please take a moment to complete the Reply Memorandum below. Make your check payable to "Jesse Jackson '88."

B) Fill in your answers to the questions on the 1988 Presidential Issues Survey.

C) Return this entire form in the enclosed postage-paid envelope.

D) IMPORTANT: Please complete the Contributor Information on the reverse before you mail.

My sincere thanks to you!

REPLY MEMORANDUM

To Jesse Jackson:

☐ I've completed your "1988 Presidential Issues Survey."

☐ I want to help launch your 1988 Presidential campaign and put *our* ideas for a peaceful and prosperous America at the top of the nation's political agenda.

To help you obtain Federal "matching funds" and take your message of hope to millions of voters in Illinois, Michigan, New York, Pennsylvania, and the other crucial primary states, I've enclosed a personal check (payable to "Jesse Jackson '88") in the amount of:

☐ $25   ☐ $35   ☐ $50   ☐ $100   ☐ $250   ☐ $_____

1988 PRESIDENTIAL ISSUES SURVEY

(1) JOBS & HUMAN NEEDS
We need an "invest in America" strategy to increase America's competitiveness by investing in people—as workers, as students, as homebuyers, and as farmers. We must meet the unmet human needs of our people, providing food for the hungry, homes for the homeless and jobs for the jobless.

☐ AGREE   ☐ DISAGREE

(2) ECONOMIC INEQUALITY
We can see the homeless on the grates, but we cannot see the families doubling up in substandard apartments because that is all they can afford—even though they work full-time. It is a disgrace that the world's wealthiest nation lacks a national housing policy and denies adequate health care to so many of its citizens.

☐ AGREE   ☐ DISAGREE

(3) CENTRAL AMERICA
The Reagan Administration is paying mercenaries to carry out a senseless slaughter for the sake of "anti-communism." This doesn't make us more secure, it *weakens* us, because it diverts resources from attending to our true national interests. President Eisenhower went to Korea to end the war there. As President, *I will go to Central America* to put an end to our country's shameful role in that tragic region.

☐ AGREE   ☐ DISAGREE

(4) EQUAL OPPORTUNITY
We must measure our nation's success by the same yardstick with which we measure other nations'—the standards of human rights. Our country—or any country—cannot be judged successful unless it truly guarantees all its citizens equal access to housing, employment, education, health care and political participation. Injustice anywhere is a threat to justice everywhere.

☐ AGREE   ☐ DISAGREE

(5) SOCIAL SECURITY AND MEDICARE
Our security as a nation comes from our security and well-being as individuals. Under Ronald Reagan, our society's most vulnerable members have grown *less* secure. We must *guarantee* that Social Security benefits will *never* be cut back—because Social Security, without that reassurance, breeds insecurity. We need a comprehensive and universal national health program.

☐ AGREE   ☐ DISAGREE

(6) MERGER MANIA
It's time to wake up and fight to *stop* the merger maniacs and the corporate raiders. Last year Wall Street "invested" enough in unproductive corporate mergers to hire and train all the nation's unemployed workers and put them to work at productive tasks to meet their needs, and society's. It's time to reorder our country's economic priorities.

☐ AGREE   ☐ DISAGREE

CONTINUED ON BACK

1988 PRESIDENTIAL ISSUES SURVEY – PAGE TWO

(7) AIDS

It's time for leadership in the White House on this tragic epidemic which threatens the very fabric of our civilization. It's time for programs targeted at people most at risk, including Blacks and Hispanics . . . for intensive public education about AIDS . . . for testing that is voluntary and confidential . . . and for affordable treatments.

☐ AGREE   ☐ DISAGREE

(8) FOREIGN TRADE

The major cause of our trade deficit is President Reagan's record budget deficits, which have driven up the value of the dollar and made U.S. products uncompetitive. It's time to put our trade problems in true perspective and come to grips with our nation's *real* economic problems: economic inequality and inadequate investment in meeting human needs for jobs, health, housing and education.

☐ AGREE   ☐ DISAGREE

(9) DRUG ABUSE

Our country is consuming an estimated $150 *billion* of drugs every year. No foreign power could do to our children what dope pushers are doing and survive our anger. It's time for a massive, coordinated effort—by the courts, the Congress, the State Department, and law enforcement officials—to *stop* the flow of dangerous drugs into our country.

☐ AGREE   ☐ DISAGREE

(10) EDUCATION

The price to the state of four years of education for one person could be about $28,000, while imprisoning that person for four years would cost more than $100,000. Education is not a social program. It's a national defense act. America needs leadership that insists on a national commitment to educate *all* our children.

☐ AGREE   ☐ DISAGREE

(11) STAR WARS AND NUCLEAR DISARMAMENT

Star Wars runs up our budget deficit, reduces our credibility among our allies, and robs our society of the means to meet its real needs. For the sake of our survival and the survival of our children, we must test and produce *fewer* nuclear weapons, not more. We must convert our nation's war economy to a *peace* economy, creating productive jobs for all who lack them.

☐ AGREE   ☐ DISAGREE

(12) THE IRAN-CONTRAGATE SCANDAL

Whatever President Reagan did or did not know, the fact is Col. North and Adm. Poindexter were carrying out *his* policy toward Nicaragua. If the President didn't know what was going on with regard to the operation, that's bad. If he knew about it and conveniently forgot, that's worse. But if he knew about it and actually forgot, that's really something to be concerned about.

☐ AGREE   ☐ DISAGREE

If you agree with me on at least seven out of these twelve issues, I invite you to join the 1988 Jesse Jackson Presidential campaign— to put *our* ideas at the top of the nation's political agenda in 1988.

Jesse Jackson

NOTE: There are *many* crucial issues I haven't dealt with in this brief listing: the preservation of our precious natural heritage; the composition of the U.S. Supreme Court and the protection of our civil liberties; the need for plant-closings legislation; a sane national energy policy; and many, many more.

POLITICAL CONTRIBUTOR INFORMATION

(1) Any individual may contribute up to $1,000 to JESSE JACKSON FOR PRESIDENT '88. Members of a family, or partners in an unincorporated business, may each contribute up to $1,000.

(2) The JESSE JACKSON FOR PRESIDENT '88 Campaign cannot accept contributions from any corporation, labor union, or church.

(3) Individual contributions to JESSE JACKSON FOR PRESIDENT '88 can be matched, dollar for dollar, up to a maximum of $250 by the Federal Election Commission.

(4) Personal checks or money orders of up to $250 qualify for Federal matching **if** they are accompanied by the contributor's name, full address, occupation, and employer's name.

The Federal Election Commission requires that we ask for the following information and **we need it to qualify for matching funds:**

Your Occupation

Your Employer

JESSE JACKSON FOR PRESIDENT '88 900 BRENTWOOD ROAD, N.E. P.O. BOX 96400 WASHINGTON, D.C. 20090

NO POSTAGE
NECESSARY IF
MAILED IN THE
UNITED STATES

BUSINESS REPLY MAIL
FIRST CLASS PERMIT NO. 16724 WASHINGTON, DC

POSTAGE WILL BE PAID BY ADDRESSEE

JESSE JACKSON '88
900 Brentwood Road, N.E.
P.O. Box 96400
Washington, D.C. 20077-7327

Jesse Jackson

FIRST CLASS MAIL

Your free stamps enclosed.

99303

"HOPE Stamp" Acquisition Package

Here is one of three new donor acquisition packages we tested against the "Survey" control package in March 1988. Like the two similar test packages that follow, the "HOPE Stamp" package was addressed by a computer-driven laser printer, so that the form showing through the outer envelope window would match the blue color of the envelope rather than shout out "Mailing label!" in white. This gave all three packages a more "upscale" appearance — and raised the cost. Producing the stamps added slightly to the bill, too. The resulting packages cost about forty-four cents apiece.

Please read this <u>important notice</u> before you use your JESSE JACKSON STAMPS.

We're sending you these stamps because we need your help to broadcast Jesse Jackson's message of hope across the land. Please use these stamps on your letters or bills—or put them on the back to seal the envelopes. But please *don't use them as postage stamps.* They're produced by the Jesse Jackson campaign, not the U.S. Postal Service.

99307A

HO HO HO HO
PE PE PE PE

Jesse Jackson for President / Jesse Jackson for President / Jesse Jackson for President / Jesse Jackson for President

HO HO HO HO
PE PE PE PE

Jesse Jackson for President / Jesse Jackson for President / Jesse Jackson for President / Jesse Jackson for President

99304

BUSINESS REPLY MAIL
FIRST CLASS PERMIT NO. 16724 WASHINGTON, DC

POSTAGE WILL BE PAID BY ADDRESSEE

JESSE JACKSON '88
900 Brentwood Road, N.E.
P.O. Box 96400
Washington, D.C. 20077-7327

NO POSTAGE
NECESSARY IF
MAILED IN THE
UNITED STATES

Jesse Jackson

Dear Fellow American Citizen,

I'm sending you these stamps because you've shown your commitment to justice -- and because I know you're one of those Americans who haven't lost hope.

Like me, you don't believe 20 million Americans must go hungry.

Like me, you don't believe we have to sit by and watch more Americans become homeless.

Like me, you don't believe that a growing number of America's children should have to settle for a second-class education.

And like me, and the thousands of people who have already joined my campaign, _you_ haven't given in to the politics of despair.

And so, I'd like to ask you to play a very special role in my 1988 Presidential Campaign. I'll tell you how you can help by using the stamps I'm sending, and I'll describe the other things you can do today -- but first let me tell you why I need your help.

I want and need your support because _too_ _many_ _of_ _our_ _citizens_ _are_ _losing_ _hope_.

I hear it from young people who know they'll never do any better than a dead-end job. From senior citizens who see their meager incomes threatened. From locked-out workers, sold-out farmers, and bought-out middle managers.

But at the same time, from citizens such as your-self, I hear renewed determination. I hear that we can, we will, we must confront these troubled times and rise above them.

There is a way up -- and out. But we must be smart enough to forge it and strong enough to take it.

JESSE JACKSON '88   900 BRENTWOOD ROAD N.E.   P.O. BOX 90900   WASHINGTON. D.C. 20090-0900

- 2 -

We hear about the crisis of the American family. I'm not a person who just reads up on problems facing poor families, or a candidate who gets briefed on the statistics. I lived it. I am the child of a teenage mother who was the child of a teenage mother.

My family was helped by getting a good home in a public housing project. By my daddy (who only went to the third grade) getting the "veterans 10 points" to boost him into a job at the post office. Momma worked too, and together they created a stable home that allowed me to get a high school education and earn a college scholarship.

I am living proof that government policies can make a difference in the crisis facing today's families.

We must put America back to work, so America's parents can support their children.

Raise the minimum wage, to lift up America's nine million working poor.

Ensure quality child care and dependent care for all families.

Provide a uniform, national allowance to all needy families -- single-parent and two-parent alike.

But what will help our families most is giving our children a vision and hope for the future. So they don't turn to suicide, or dope, or to uncaring sex that leads to babies having babies.

Protecting America's families is not simply a problem of the poor. It is a challenge to our entire society. We will either raise up the poorest of us, or gradually lower the standard of living for all of us.

I'm sure you agree with me that this nation is too great to go backward.

But we can become an even greater nation, if we follow a new definition of greatness.

Our nation's greatness is not in the size of our GNP, our military might, our technological achievements -- necessary as these may be.

- 3 -

If we provide decent homes for the homeless ... and better homes for working families doubled up in substandard housing, then we will be a great nation.

If we make good the promise of quality public education for all our children ... renew our commitment to equal opportunity for all, then we will be a great nation.

If we guarantee the right to food ... provide quality health care for all, then we will be a great nation.

<u>Greatness lies in how we value and care for our people</u>.

For too long, America has let Ronald Reagan tell us there's no money to stop hunger, solve homelessness, help our families in crisis.

But America <u>can</u> solve these problems. It <u>will</u> take better leadership. And it <u>will</u> take citizens like you, people willing to roll up <u>their</u> sleeves and get involved.

To do it, we must <u>put the human race ahead of the arms race</u>. That is what <u>I</u> hope the American people are learning from my second campaign for the presidency.

Because of your long commitment to human justice and dignity, I want to ask you to do three things.

<u>First, please take a stand</u>. Show you believe America still has hope by signing the enclosed "Declaration of Independence from the Politics of Despair." I want to get these Declarations from thousands of thoughtful Americans like you -- so I can show the news media and the politicians that people really do <u>care</u>.

<u>Second, please use the stamps</u> I've enclosed. Put them on your letters and also on your bills. (There's always a person on the other end who opens the bills -- someone who may well be one of the working poor.)

I'm asking you to use these stamps because my campaign is not a campaign of fat cats. We're a campaign of the grass roots. With your help, these stamps can broadcast the message of new hope across this land.

<u>Third</u>, I ask you to make a contribution to "JESSE JACKSON '88" <u>in the next 10 days</u>.

- 4 -

Your $25, $35, $50, $100, $250, or $1,000 will help me reach voters in the crucial primaries coming up in New York, Pennsylvania, Ohio, and California.

And the impact of your contribution will be twice as great because of Federal Matching Funds.

The federal government will match your gift -- dollar for dollar -- up to a maximum of $250. So your gift of $25, $35, $50, $100, or $250 will mean <u>twice</u> as much for the campaign.

During the years I marched at the side of the Rev. Dr. Martin Luther King, many people tried to make us lose hope. They said Jim Crow would never fall.

Those same people broadcast their message of despair to you and me today. But we can take strength from the message of Martin's life:

There may be storm clouds of despair over our national life ... But don't surrender ... to darkness, fear, hatred. Don't let them break your spirit. Hold out till morning comes.

I know morning will come.

Together, we <u>will</u> save the children ... protect our families ... house the homeless ... feed the hungry ... achieve peace in our time ... and we will do it now.

From the bottom of my heart, my deepest thanks to you for your support and involvement.

With highest hope,

Jesse Jackson

Jesse L. Jackson

P.S.   The stamps I've enclosed take the place of high-priced campaign ads. When you send them, they carry <u>your</u> personal endorsement -- a priceless campaign asset that money can't buy.

P.P.S.   Your gift of $25, $35, $50, $100, or $250 will be matched, dollar for dollar, by the Federal Election Commission.

Authorized and paid for by Jesse Jackson for President '88, Howard Renzi, Treasurer

99301A

Declaration of Independence from the Politics of Despair

YES, JESSE, I'll stand up with you! I refuse to give in to the politics of despair. Real patriotism means putting our minds, hearts and bodies to work for the best interests of our country.

With renewed determination, I'll join you to confront these troubled times and rise above them. I'll help you give America new leadership to:

- *Put the human race above the arms race, with a comprehensive program to end poverty: full employment, a higher minimum wage, a welfare system with built-in respect and dignity.*

- *Keep the promise of equal opportunity in education for every child.*

- *Guarantee the right to food for America's 20 million hungry citizens.*

- *Protect America's families—put America back to work and guarantee national allowances to needy families, quality childcare and dependent care, and access to health care for all.*

- *Provide homes to the homeless—and a national housing policy to give a better future to working families doubled up in substandard apartments.*

- *Truly guarantee to all citizens equal access to housing, employment, education, health care and political participation.*

Signature _____

Deborah Sample Agre

☐ I'll help broadcast your message of new hope for America by using "Jesse Jackson for President" stamps.

☐ And here's my contribution to help you reach voters in crucial upcoming primaries. I understand the federal government will match my gift—dollar for dollar—up to $250.

☐ $25   ☐ $35   ☐ $50   ☐ $100
☐ $250   ☐ $1,000   ☐ $_____

Jesse Jackson '88
FOR PRESIDENT

900 BRENTWOOD ROAD, N.E.
P.O. BOX 90970
WASHINGTON, D.C. 20090-0970

Deborah Sample Agre
P.O. Box 1282
Berkeley, CA 94701

3001B

IMPORTANT: Please read and complete this information.

(1) Any individual may contribute up to $1,000 to JESSE JACKSON FOR PRESIDENT '88. Members of a family, or partners in an unincorporated business, may each contribute up to $1,000.

(2) The JESSE JACKSON FOR PRESIDENT '88 Campaign cannot accept contributions from any corporation, labor union, or church.

(3) Individual contributions to JESSE JACKSON FOR PRESIDENT '88 can be matched, dollar for dollar, up to a maximum of $250 by the Federal Election Commission.

(4) Personal checks or money orders of up to $250 qualify for federal matching if they are accompanied by the contributor's name, full address, occupation, and employer's name.

The Federal Election Commission requires that we ask for the following information and **we need it to qualify for matching funds:**

_____
YOUR OCCUPATION

_____
YOUR EMPLOYER

99302A

"Kitchen Cabinet" Acquisition Package

Like both the "Presidential Issues Survey" and the "HOPE Stamp" packages, this invitation to join Jesse Jackson's "Kitchen Cabinet" stressed donor involvement, a common element in political direct mail fundraising. The "Kitchen Cabinet" package cost about forty-three cents to mail with first class postage.

Jesse Jackson

Tuesday morning

Dear Fellow American Citizen,

Ronald Reagan has his "Kitchen Cabinet." It's a tiny group of rich men from Southern California who are about the same age as he.

When President Reagan wants advice, he doesn't turn to the Congress, or to those who've devoted their lives to studying the issues. He turns to his friends.

Well, I want <u>you</u> to join <u>my</u> "Kitchen Cabinet"!

Along with this letter, I'm sending you an informal "Kitchen Cabinet" poll on foreign policy issues. I want you to complete it and return it to me this week.

I need your commitment to humanity, justice and peace to help shape the foreign policy agenda of the 1988 Presidential campaign.

I'm writing you because I believe you share my grave concerns about America's role in the world.

Because your concern springs from the deep vein of caring and goodness that represents the best of America, I want and need your support.

My Presidential candidacy is a chance to turn America around in 1988. It's a chance to get beyond the bankruptcy of the Reagan Era and to form a new vision based on our common hopes and values.

For me, the starting point is this inescapable fact:

Never before has our fate as a nation depended so much on the state of the rest of the world.

The Reagan Administration has spent billions of dollars on Star Wars. Yet I believe you share my feeling that we're less secure than ever.

JESSE JACKSON '88   900 BRENTWOOD ROAD N.E.   P.O. BOX 90900   WASHINGTON, D.C. 20090-0900

- 2 -

Not so long ago we were the world's largest creditor nation. Today we're the largest debtor. And you and I both know our economy is shakier than ever.

I believe that, like me, you care about our painfully slow progress towards nuclear disarmament ... towards peace in Central America ... towards ending apartheid ... towards solving the trade deficit.

Everywhere I go in this beautiful country of ours, I meet people with similar concerns. Concern not only for the future of our children, but for the children of Nicaragua and Israel and Soweto. Concern not only for the loss of jobs at home, but for the loss of respect from other nations.

According to President Reagan, progress depends on fighting communism and promoting the growth of American corporations around the world.

Ronald Reagan views the world as a conflict between East and West. He tells us that change in the Third World comes from communist upheaval, rather than from poverty and repression.

The Reagan Doctrine is a program based on fear and mistrust and greed.

I think America deserves better.

The Reagan Administration feels it isn't bound by international law. But President Reagan was wrong when he illegally mined the harbors of Nicaragua and defied the World Court. He was wrong when he traded arms for hostages and misled Congress and the public. He has lost the moral authority to challenge the Ayatollah for Iran's mining of Persian Gulf waters.

The Reagan Administration thinks it can determine the outcome of upheaval and revolution -- but that is an impossible task.

Our tax dollars go to support the Contras' senseless violence in Central America. How does that help our national security?

- 3 -

Over 50,000 nuclear warheads exist today, poised to destroy the world at the touch of a button. And how does that help our national security?

America deserves better.

In 1988 we can offer a new vision -- a vision based on meeting the needs of our own people, and of people around the world.

We can bring hope, not fear, into the world.

We can ground our foreign policy in a more sensible view of the world, one which reflects the humanity in our values and serves our national interests.

That's why I hope you'll join my "Kitchen Cabinet." I want you to compare your own views with mine on some of today's major foreign policy issues.

Do you believe, as I do, that building a more secure America means adopting national policies that keep us strong, and international policies that keep us respected?

Do you agree with me that allying ourselves with dictators who will be overthrown by their own people does not build national security?

Do you share my conviction that putting more than half of our scientists to work developing new weapons does not build national security? When Japan beats us in the world economy because three out of four Japanese scientists are researching industrial and commercial innovations?

To me, building a more secure America means:

o aggressive negotiations with the Soviet Union ... mutual, verifiable reductions in nuclear stockpiles ... diplomatic pressure to ease the oppression against Soviet Jews.

o expanded diplomacy reaching out to all parties in the Middle East ... a comprehensive political settlement that benefits both Israelis and Arabs ... an immediate arms embargo against both Iran and Iraq.

- 4 -

o withdrawal of all U.S. military aid to Central
America ... economic sanctions against South
Africa ... linking foreign aid and trade
benefits to guarantees of <u>human</u> <u>rights</u>.

And I believe that building a more secure America
means eliminating our trade deficit.

It's not the Taiwanese or the Japanese who are to
blame for America's trade wounds.

It's our two trillion dollar national debt.

It's the merger mania which has poured capital into
senseless acquisitions instead of into technological
innovation.

It's the greed of the corporations who close down
factories to avoid paying U.S. workers a decent wage and
move production overseas, where workers are not allowed
to organize.

I believe that our true national security lies in
getting our national priorities straight. Don't you
agree?

To me, national security means cutting the waste and
mismanagement out of our military budget. It means keeping our dollars at home so that we can rebuild America.

We're often reminded that we live in a great nation
-- and we do. But it can be greater still if we follow a
new definition of greatness.

Our nation's greatness is not based on military
might. I believe it's based on how we value and care
for people -- on our achievements in education, health,
culture, housing and employment.

o If we care for our young and educate them to
work in tomorrow's world, we'll have national
security.

o If we provide decent, safe and sanitary housing
and food for the poor, then we'll have national
security.

- 5 -

o   If we provide meaningful employment for all
    capable Americans and demand that workers in
    other countries have similar rights, we'll
    have national security.

o   If we allow other nations to determine their
    own destiny and gain respect in the world for
    our concern for human rights and economic
    justice, we'll have national security.

I hope you'll join with me in forging this new
definition of national security. I want you to help me
build a foreign policy that isn't foreign to our values
as a nation.

The poll I mentioned early in this letter covers six
of the major foreign policy issues of the 1988 Presidential campaign. I call it my "Kitchen Cabinet" foreign
policy poll -- because it's important to me to know your
views on these issues.

I ask you to take a moment right now -- wherever you
may be -- to complete this questionnaire. I'd like for
you to send it back to me this week.

As you can see from the survey, I don't evade the
issues. I think it's important to let the world know
where Jesse Jackson stands on these urgent problems that
affect America's security.

Obviously, there are many other issues I couldn't
include in my brief listing in the "Kitchen Cabinet"
poll: the global environmental crisis, foreign aid and
development, immigration, hunger and famine, the defense
of Western Europe and Japan, and many, many more. I've
chosen just six issues because of intense public concern.

If you agree with me on most of these six issues,
then I ask you stand with me and support my campaign for
the Democratic nomination for President in 1988.

I'm asking for your financial support as well as
your political support -- to help build a more secure
America.

Our message of integrity and hope speaks to the

- 6 -

concerns of most Americans, but we can reach them only with your help.

And I ask that you join me this week.

At this critical time in the campaign, just before some of the major primaries, your gift will go especially far. And because of Federal "matching funds," the power of your money will double for us.

The Federal Election Commission will match every dollar you contribute up to a maximum of $250. So your gift of $25, $35, $50, $100, or $250 will mean twice as much for the campaign.

We're running a lean, cost-effective campaign with the support of thousands of keenly committed volunteers. We don't need as much as some of the other candidates to get out our message of hope -- but we do need your help to stay competitive.

With your financial support, we'll be able to transform the 1988 Presidential campaign into a call for the rebuilding of America.

It's time for a new direction for America ... for a foreign policy based on more than military strength. It's time for a foreign policy based on American values.

I ask you to join with me to make America once again a symbol of hope throughout the world ... and a shining example of hope at home.

Sincerely,

Jesse L. Jackson

P.S.   Please take a moment now to complete the informal "Kitchen Cabinet" foreign policy poll I've enclosed with this letter.

P.P.S. Your gift of $25, $35, $50, $100, or $250 will be matched, dollar for dollar, by the Federal Election Committee.

Authorized and paid for by Jesse Jackson for President '88, Howard Renzi, Treasurer

99301B

Jesse
Jackson
'88
FOR PRESIDENT

T
O

Jesse Jackson

F
R
O
M

Deborah Sample Agre
P.O. Box 1282
Berkeley, CA 94701

Dear Jesse:
    I'm glad to join your "Kitchen Cabinet." I've
compared my views on foreign policy with yours on the
survey below. Like you, I want a foreign policy that
promotes <u>real security</u>, not false security -- and puts
more of our resources into meeting America's urgent
human needs.
    Here's my contribution to help you reach voters in
the crucial upcoming primaries. I understand the
federal government will match my gift -- dollar for
dollar -- up to $250.

    ( )$25   ( )$35   ( )$50   ( )$100

    ( )$250   ( )$1,000   ( )$_____

The Federal Election Commission requires that we ask for the   3001C
following information and we need it to qualify for matching funds:

_____   _____
YOUR OCCUPATION   YOUR EMPLOYER

JESSE JACKSON 1988 KITCHEN CABINET FOREIGN POLICY POLL

PREPARED FOR

Deborah Sample Agre
Berkeley, CA

NUCLEAR DISARMAMENT: Star Wars runs up our budget deficit and robs our nation of the resources we need to meet urgent human needs. For the sake of our survival and the survival of our children, we must *reduce* nuclear weapons, and convert our nation's war economy to a *peace* economy.

☐ AGREE   ☐ DISAGREE   ☐ NO OPINION

CENTRAL AMERICA: In the name of "anti-communism," the Reagan Administration funds a war that has killed 150,000 people and made millions refugees. But paying mercenaries to carry out senseless violence in Central America does *not* make us more secure. Our true national interest lies in promoting *peace*.

☐ AGREE   ☐ DISAGREE   ☐ NO OPINION

Continued on back

900 BRENTWOOD ROAD, N.E.   P.O. BOX 90970   WASHINGTON, D.C. 20090-0970

Continued from front

TRADE DEFICIT: America's trade wounds are self-inflicted. GM, GE and other giant multinational corporations are exporting some of our best jobs overseas. It's time to stop merger mania and come to grips with our nation's *real* economic problem: the need to meet human needs for jobs, health, housing and education.

☐ AGREE   ☐ DISAGREE   ☐ NO OPINION

MIDDLE EAST: After seven years of Reagan's confused policies, scores of Americans are dead, Israelis and Palestinians are still killing each other, and we're stuck in an undeclared war in the Persian Gulf. It's time to bring all parties together to hammer out a *comprehensive* peace plan for the region, guaranteeing security for Israel and justice for the Palestinians.

☐ AGREE   ☐ DISAGREE   ☐ NO OPINION

RELATIONS WITH THE SOVIET UNION: Nuclear and conventional disarmament is essential. But during this period of *glasnost*, our negotiations with the Soviet Union must put human rights and the plight of Soviet Jews high on the agenda. Promoting the right of *all* people to choose their destiny will further enhance our ability to bring moral pressure on behalf of the oppressed.

☐ AGREE   ☐ DISAGREE   ☐ NO OPINION

SOUTH AFRICA: Apartheid shocks our humanity and offends our sense of justice. Yet the Reagan Administration still supports the South African regime. To ally ourselves with a tiny minority while alienating South Africa's majority is not only morally wrong, but self-destructive. We must end this horror peacefully—by imposing full economic sanctions against South Africa immediately.

☐ AGREE   ☐ DISAGREE   ☐ NO OPINION

POLITICAL CONTRIBUTION INFORMATION

(1) Any individual may contribute up to $1,000 to JESSE JACKSON FOR PRESIDENT '88. Members of a family, or partners in an unincorporated business, may each contribute up to $1,000.

(2) The JESSE JACKSON FOR PRESIDENT '88 Campaign cannot accept contributions from any corporation, labor union, or church.

(3) Individual contributions to JESSE JACKSON FOR PRESIDENT '88 can be matched, dollar for dollar, up to a maximum of $250 by the Federal Election Commission.

(4) Personal checks or money orders of up to $250 qualify for federal matching if they are accompanied by the contributor's name, full address, occupation, and employer's name.

 99302B

99304

BUSINESS REPLY MAIL
FIRST CLASS PERMIT NO. 16724 WASHINGTON, DC

POSTAGE WILL BE PAID BY ADDRESSEE

JESSE JACKSON '88
900 Brentwood Road, N.E.
P.O. Box 96400
Washington, D.C. 20077-7327

NO POSTAGE
NECESSARY IF
MAILED IN THE
UNITED STATES

Bill Cosby Acquisition Package

If anyone in America could defy the unwritten rule that the candidate is the best letter-signer any campaign can find, it would have been Bill Cosby, whose weekly television series consistently topped the ratings in 1988. But it didn't work. By comparison with almost any other direct mail fundraising program, the results of the following appeal by Bill Cosby might seem spectacular. It was mailed via first class at a cost of about forty-three cents per package and produced a substantial profit for the Jackson campaign. However, all three letters signed by Jesse Jackson "outpulled" the Cosby package.

BILL COSBY

Friday morning

Dear Friend,

This is about what you and I can do so we can be proud of the world we'll pass on to the next generation.

I play a father on The Cosby Show. We look at the natural conflicts that are part of raising kids. All families have them -- and they're relieved to see our show turn them into laughter.

I'm also a father in real life. But in raising my kids, there are some problems that are no laughing matter.

When I take my youngest daughter to the city, she wants to know why there are people taking drugs or sleeping in the streets. She wants to know why kids her age go hungry.

What does a father say? That's the kind of question we look to our nation's leaders to answer. And the callous answers we've gotten these past seven years make your blood run cold.

Right now, there's only one Presidential candidate with an answer I can be proud of.

There's only one candidate who says America can and must house the homeless, stop the drug epidemic and feed the hungry. There's only one candidate with a creative plan to make this a country we can be proud to pass on to our kids.

That candidate is my friend Jesse Jackson.

Look what this guy is saying: If America makes good its promise of quality education for all, then we'll be proud of the America we pass on to our children.

99321

Page 2

If America helps farmers who want to keep their farms -- instead of sending money to a war that kills farmers in Central America -- then we'll be proud of the America we pass on to our children.

If America renews its commitment to equal opportunity for all, then we'll be proud of the America we pass on to our children.

Jesse Jackson is the only candidate who can get all of us to roll up our sleeves and solve the problems our kids ask us about.

I'm thankful that I'm able to provide a more than comfortable living for my kids. But I understand too well the anguish of parents who can't.

I remember the look in my own mother's eyes when I was growing up in Philadelphia. Sometimes, she didn't know where she could find the next meal to feed her hungry sons.

That's why I'm supporting Jesse Jackson. He has a sound plan for full employment. And Jesse means jobs at wages that will allow America's parents to support their kids.

Jesse means jobs that will make our country a better one to leave to the next generation. Jobs repairing our highways and bridges ... making our water fit to drink and our air fit to breathe ... caring for our children and our aged.

What's more, Jesse Jackson has the kind of moral character that's a model for our kids (unlike the image presented by the present Administration).

I believe in Jesse Jackson. I believe America is ready to support Jesse Jackson, too -- but only if enough Americans get to hear his message.

You see, three and a half years ago, TV experts were saying The Cosby Show would only last a few weeks.

Page 3

They said the American viewing audience wouldn't
watch a show about the funny, everyday problems of a
middle-class black family.

The American public proved they have a mind of
their own. They showed those experts they were wrong!

I believe that all kinds of people like my show
because it's about the ways our American families are
alike, not the ways they're different.

Jesse Jackson's Presidential campaign, too, is
about the common ground we share as Americans. Jesse
Jackson's message is one of healing, and of hope.

My show would never have hit Number One if
America hadn't had a chance to see it.

And the only way to elect Jesse Jackson President
is to be sure America gets a chance to see him. And
to hear his message -- that we can make this country
one we'll be proud to pass on to our kids.

That's how the Jackson campaign has gone the
amazing distance it's gone so far. Not by endorsements from powerful politicians. Not with funds from
rich power brokers.

Jesse Jackson's campaign has been built on
ordinary folks hearing what he has to say. And
realizing that it matches their own hopes and dreams.

But not having fat cats in his campaign, Jesse
needs you now more than ever. You and people like
you, people who want to leave our kids a better world
to grow up in.

I ask you to join me by making a contribution to
"Jesse Jackson '88" in the next ten days. The sooner
the better.

Your $25, $35, $50, $100, or $250 will help Jesse
Jackson get his message out to the voters.

You've shown in the past that you're a person

Page 4

concerned with justice. And that you don't need
gimmicks to lend your support. So I'm not offering you
any gimmicks.

I'm just asking you plain -- please dig deep into
your checkbook and send as large a contribution as you
can to "Jesse Jackson '88." And please, send your
check right away.

When my daughter asks me about the hungry, about
the homeless, I look into her eyes. I ask myself,
what about when she's older? Will she feel my
generation did everything we could to leave hers
a nation she could be proud of?

Please join me in doing everything you and I can
do, today. Let's give America a President that will
make this a nation we can be proud to pass on to our
kids. Join me in supporting my good friend -- Jesse
Jackson.

Sincerely,

Bill Cosby

P.S. I don't know a whole lot about politics, but I
know $2 is better than $1. And Jesse tells me
that your gift of $25, $35, $50, $100, or $250 to
his Presidential campaign will be matched, dollar
for dollar, by the federal government. Please
send your check today!

Authorized and paid for by Jesse Jackson '88, Howard Renzi, Treasurer

3215E

To:

Bill Cosby

Jesse Jackson '88

FOR PRESIDENT

From:

Deborah Sample Agre
P.O. Box 1282
Berkeley, CA 94701

Dear Bill:

Yes, I'll join you in supporting the one Presidential candidate who will make this a country we can be proud to pass on to the next generation. Here's my contribution to "JESSE JACKSON '88." I understand that the federal government will match my gift, dollar for dollar, up to $250.

( )$25   ( )$35   ( )$50   ( )$100

( )$250   ( )$1,000   ( )$_____

Important: Please read the reverse side. The Federal Election Commission requires that we ask for the following information and **we need it to qualify for matching funds:**

_____   _____
YOUR OCCUPATION   YOUR EMPLOYER

POLITICAL CONTRIBUTION INFORMATION

(1) Any individual may contribute up to $1,000 to JESSE JACKSON FOR PRESIDENT '88. Members of a family, or partners in an unincorporated business, may each contribute up to $1,000.

(2) The JESSE JACKSON FOR PRESIDENT '88 Campaign cannot accept contributions from any corporation, labor union, or church. Contributions and gifts are not deductible as charitable contributions for Federal income tax purposes.

(3) Individual contributions to JESSE JACKSON FOR PRESIDENT '88 can be matched, dollar for dollar, up to a maximum of $250 by the Federal Election Commission.

(4) Personal checks or money orders of up to $250 qualify for federal matching **if** they are accompanied by the contributor's name, full address, occupation, and employer's name.

900 BRENTWOOD ROAD, N.E.   P.O. BOX 90970   WASHINGTON, D.C. 20090-0970

99304

 99322

BUSINESS REPLY MAIL
FIRST CLASS PERMIT NO. 16724 WASHINGTON, DC

POSTAGE WILL BE PAID BY ADDRESSEE

JESSE JACKSON '88
900 Brentwood Road, N.E.
P.O. Box 96400
Washington, D.C. 20077-7327

NO POSTAGE
NECESSARY IF
MAILED IN THE
UNITED STATES

Jesse Jackson

FIRST CLASS MAIL

Your free stamps enclosed.

"HOPE Stamp" Resolicitation Package

More than 94,000 contributors to Jesse Jackson's 1984 and 1988 campaigns were mailed a special version of the "HOPE Stamp" donor acquisition package. While expensive as a prospecting vehicle because of the cost of laser-printing and the stamps enclosed, this was an *inexpensive* donor resolicitation at only forty-four cents each with first class postage. The mailing produced a net profit of $220,000, fulfilling everyone's hopes.

Please read this <u>important</u> <u>notice</u> <u>before</u> you use your JESSE JACKSON STAMPS.

HO PE

Jesse Jackson
for President

We're sending you these stamps because we need your help to broadcast Jesse Jackson's message of hope across the land. Please use these stamps on your letters or bills—or put them on the back to seal the envelopes. But please **don't use them as postage stamps.** They're produced by the Jesse Jackson campaign, not the U.S. Postal Service.

99307A

HO HO HO HO
PE PE PE PE
Jesse Jackson for President (×4)

HO HO HO HO
PE PE PE PE
Jesse Jackson for President (×4)

99304

NO POSTAGE
NECESSARY IF
MAILED IN THE
UNITED STATES

BUSINESS REPLY MAIL
FIRST CLASS PERMIT NO. 16724 WASHINGTON, DC

POSTAGE WILL BE PAID BY ADDRESSEE

JESSE JACKSON '88

900 Brentwood Road, N.E.
P.O. Box 96400
Washington, D.C. 20077-7327

Jesse Jackson

Thursday afternoon

Dear Friend and Caring Citizen,

I'm sending you these stamps because you've shown your commitment to justice and your support for me -- and because I know you're one of those Americans who haven't lost hope.

Like me, you don't believe 20 million Americans must go hungry.

Like me, you don't believe we have to sit by and watch more Americans become homeless.

Like me, you don't believe that a growing number of America's children should have to settle for a second-class education.

And like me, and the thousands of people who have already joined my campaign, you haven't given in to the politics of despair.

And so I'd like to ask you to help my 1988 Presidential campaign in a very special way by using the stamps I'm sending. I'll tell you how in a moment -- but first let me explain to you as clearly as I can why I need your help again today.

I want and need your renewed support now because too many of our citizens are losing hope.

I hear it from young people who know they'll never do any better than a dead-end job. From senior citizens who see their meager incomes threatened. From locked-out workers, sold-out farmers, and bought-out middle managers.

But at the same time, from citizens and friends such as yourself, I hear renewed determination. I hear that we can, we will, we must confront these troubled times and rise above them.

There is a way up -- and out. But we must be smart enough to forge it and strong enough to take it.

JESSE JACKSON '88   900 BRENTWOOD ROAD N.E.   P.O. BOX 90900   WASHINGTON, D.C. 20090-0900

Page 2

We hear about the crisis of the American family.
Well, as you know, I'm not a person who just reads up on
problems facing poor families, or a candidate who gets
briefed on the statistics. I lived it. I am the child
of a teenage mother who was the child of a teenage
mother.

My family was helped by getting a good home in a
public housing project. By my daddy (who only went to
the third grade) getting the "veteran's 10 points" to
boost him into a job at the post office. Momma worked
too, and together they created a stable home that
allowed me to get a high school education and earn a
college scholarship.

I am living proof that government policies can make
a difference in the crisis facing today's families.

We must put America back to work, so America's
parents can support their children.

Raise the minimum wage, to lift up America's nine
million working poor.

Ensure quality child care and dependent care for
all families.

Provide a uniform, national allowance to all needy
families -- single-parent and two-parent alike.

But what will help our families most is giving our
children a vision and hope for the future. So they
don't turn to suicide, or dope, or to uncaring sex that
leads to babies having babies.

Protecting America's families is not simply a problem of the poor. It's a challenge to our entire society.
We will either raise up the poorest of us, or gradually
lower the standard of living for all of us.

I'm sure you agree with me that this nation is too
great to go backward.

But we can become an even greater nation, if we
follow a new definition of greatness.

Our nation's greatness is not in the size of our
GNP, our military might, our technological achievements
-- necessary as these may be.

Page 3

If we provide decent homes for the homeless ... and better homes for working families doubled up in substandard housing, then we'll be a great nation.

If we make good the promise of quality public education for all our children ... renew our commitment to equal opportunity for all, then we will be a great nation.

If we guarantee the right to food ... provide quality health care for all, then we'll be a great nation.

Greatness lies in how we value and care for our people.

For too long, America has let Ronald Reagan tell us there's no money to stop hunger, solve homelessness, help our families in crisis.

But America can solve these problems. It will take better leadership. And it will take citizens like you, people willing to roll up their sleeves and get involved.

To do it, we must put the human race ahead of the arms race. That is what I hope the American people are learning from my second campaign for the presidency.

Because of your past support, and your long commitment to human justice and dignity, I want to ask you to do three things today.

First, please stand up with me again. Show you believe America still has hope by signing the enclosed "Declaration of Independence from the Politics of Despair." I want to get these Declarations from thousands of thoughtful Americans like you -- so I can show the news media and the politicians that people really do care.

Second, please use the stamps I've enclosed. Put them on your letters and also on your bills. (There's always a person on the other end who opens the bills -- someone who may well be one of the working poor).

I'm asking you to use these stamps because my campaign is not a campaign of fat cats. We're a campaign of the grass roots. With your renewed help, these

Page 4

stamps can broadcast the message of new hope across this land.

    Third, I ask you to make a special gift to "JESSE JACKSON '88" in the next 10 days.

    Your $25, $35, $50, $100, $250, or $1,000 will help me reach voters in the crucial primaries coming up in New York, Pennsylvania, Ohio, and California.

    And, up to $250, the impact of your contribution will be twice as great because of Federal Matching Funds.

    During the years I marched at the side of the Rev. Dr. Martin Luther King, many people tried to make us lose hope. They said Jim Crow would never fall.

    Those same people broadcast their message of despair to you and me today. But we can take strength from the message of Martin's life:

    There may be storm clouds of despair over our national life ... But don't surrender ... to darkness, fear, hatred. Don't let them break your spirit. Hold out till morning comes.

    I know morning will come.

    Together, we will save the children ... protect our families ... house the homeless ... feed the hungry ... achieve peace in our time ... and we will do it now.

    From the bottom of my heart, my deepest thanks to you for your continuing support and involvement.

                        With highest hopes,

                        Jesse Jackson
                        Jesse L. Jackson

P.S.   The stamps I've enclosed take the place of high-priced campaign ads. When you send them, they carry your personal endorsement -- a priceless campaign asset that money can't buy.

P.P.S. Your gift of $25, $35, $50, $100, or $250 will be matched, dollar for dollar, by the Federal Election Commission.

                                                        99291

Authorized and paid for by Jesse Jackson for President '88, Howard Renzi, Treasurer

Declaration of Independence from the Politics of Despair

YES, JESSE, you can count on me again! I refuse to give in to the politics of despair. Real patriotism means putting our minds, hearts and bodies to work for the best interests of our country.

With renewed determination, I'll stand up with you to confront these troubled times and rise above them. I'll help you give America new leadership to:

- Put the human race above the arms race, with a comprehensive program to end poverty: full employment, a higher minimum wage, a welfare system with built-in respect and dignity.

- Keep the promise of equal opportunity in education for every child.

- Guarantee the right to food for America's 20 million hungry citizens.

- Protect America's families—put America back to work and guarantee national allowances to needy families, quality childcare and dependent care, and access to health care for all.

- Provide homes to the homeless—and a national housing policy to give a better future to working families doubled up in substandard apartments.

- Truly guarantee to all citizens equal access to housing, employment, education, health care and political participation.

Signature _____

Jesse Jackson '88

FOR PRESIDENT

900 BRENTWOOD ROAD, N.E.
P.O. BOX 90970
WASHINGTON, D.C. 20090-0970

☐ I'll help broadcast your message of new hope for America by using "Jesse Jackson for President" stamps.

☐ Here's my special new gift to help you reach voters in crucial upcoming primaries. I understand the federal government will match my gift—dollar for dollar—up to $250.

☐ $25   ☐ $35   ☐ $50   ☐ $100
☐ $250   ☐ $1,000   ☐ $_____

IMPORTANT: Please read and complete this information.

(1) Any individual may contribute up to $1,000 to JESSE JACKSON FOR PRESIDENT '88. Members of a family, or partners in an unincorporated business, may each contribute up to $1,000.

(2) The JESSE JACKSON FOR PRESIDENT '88 Campaign cannot accept contributions from any corporation, labor union, or church.

(3) Individual contributions to JESSE JACKSON FOR PRESIDENT '88 can be matched, dollar for dollar, up to a maximum of $250 by the Federal Election Commission.

(4) Personal checks or money orders of up to $250 qualify for federal matching if they are accompanied by the contributor's name, full address, occupation, and employer's name.

The Federal Election Commission requires that we ask for the following information and **we need it to qualify for matching funds:**

_____
YOUR OCCUPATION

_____
YOUR EMPLOYER

99292

TELEPOST. *ACTION ALERT*®

Action Alert

On the heels of Jesse Jackson's spectacular showing in the "Super Tuesday" states — those twenty-seven states in which Democrats voted on March 8th — the Jackson campaign mailed a brief, tele-gram-like appeal to some 16,000 of its Maxi-Donors. The quantity was limited because of the rela-tively high cost of the mailing — eighty-two cents per package — and because returns were still coming in strong not only from the "HOPE Stamp" resolicitation but also from the *three* donor resolicitation mailings dropped in February. Still, the "Action Alert" netted the campaign more than $95,000.

Jesse Jackson
900 Brentwood Road, N.E.
P.O. Box 96400
Washington, D.C. 20077-7327

TELEPOST.
ACTION ALERT.

March 11, 1988

MR. JOHN SAMPLE
TELEPOST
1951 KIDWELL DRIVE
VIENNA VA 22180

Dear MR SAMPLE,

We did it.

With your generous support, we won a spectacular victory on Super Tuesday.

We won the popular vote -- over 2-1/2 million voters chose Jesse Jackson -- proving that I am the candidate of all the people.

We finished first or second in 20 of the 27 states, with surprisingly strong showings in the two biggest, Texas and Florida. These major victories followed big breakthroughs in Iowa, Minnesota, Maine and Vermont.

Without broad popular support -- and an effective grassroots organization -- these victories would not have been possible.

Our campaign has won just under 400 delegates -- already more than we brought to the 1984 Democratic Convention, and only 30 delegates behind the frontrunner.

Our great success comes not just from Black voters but from an expanding base of whites, Hispanics and Asians -- women and men of all ages, occupations and faiths.

It's clear that: with your ongoing support, I can continue to expand my base, and Jesse Jackson can, indeed, be President of all the people. This is an exciting moment in history and you made it possible.

I couldn't have done any of this without you.

Because of your generous support, my message of new hope and new leadership is being heard in millions of living rooms all across the country. I am the only candidate presenting a positive message. My message is a message that reflects the hopes and dreams of all Americans.

Now, for the first time, millions are hearing me speak of the need for economic justice and of an end to economic violence. Economic violence committed by multinational corporations that close plants on workers without notice and move jobs to slave-wage countries. Economic justice for workers left without jobs, health care or hope.

Now, your concerns are on the national political agenda.

But, to take advantage of this historic opportunity -- to be the candidate of all Americans -- I urgently need your help again today.

My own home state of Illinois holds it primary next week, followed by Michigan, New York, Pennsylvania and Ohio. Nearly a thousand delegates are at stake.

MR. JOHN SAMPLE, Page 2

I can do well in these big urban states -- but only if I can get my message out to the people. And to get that message out, I need your help.

Our goal is within reach.

Please send your maximum extra contribution of $1.5HPC or more to JESSE JACKSON '88 today. Together, we'll change the face of American politics.

Your friend,

Jesse Jackson

Jesse L. Jackson

URGENT REPLY MEMO TO JESSE JACKSON

(Please tear off and return this part *with your check in the postage-paid envelope provided.)*

To: Jesse Jackson

From: MR. JOHN SAMPLE
TELEPOST
1951 KIDWELL DRIVE
VIENNA VA 22180

KEYCODE

YES, JESSE, YOU CAN COUNT ON ME AGAIN!

Your big victory on "Super Tuesday" proves that Jesse Jackson is the candidate of <u>all</u> the people. I'm enclosing my maximum extra gift to JESSE JACKSON '88 to help you go <u>all the way</u> -- so you can carry your message of new hope and new leadership to voters in the big urban states in the weeks ahead.

( ) $1.5HPC   ( ) $_____

IMPORTANT: *Please complete the Contributor Information below, and be sure your name and address above are spelled correctly.*

We need this information so we can obtain Federal Matching Funds for your contribution:

_____   _____
Occupation   Employer

##########
##########   *Please <u>refold</u> this part in thirds and insert
##########   it in the postage-paid reply envelope so that
               the address below shows through the window.*

First Class Permit #16724 Wash DC
Postage Will Be Paid By Addressee

Jesse Jackson
900 BRENTWOOD ROAD, N.E.
P.O. Box 96400
Washington, D.C. 20077-7327

1STCLASS:LNGCAI:PPBRE:2ND PAGE CHAAM-SENDCAI-SENDCAIOO1:3

NO POSTAGE
NECESSARY
IF MAILED
IN THE
UNITED STATES

BUSINESS   REPLY   MAIL

Jesse Jackson '88

FOR PRESIDENT

900 BRENTWOOD ROAD, N.E.　　P.O. BOX 90970
WASHINGTON, D.C. 20090-0970

FIRST CLASS MAIL

Mr. John Doe
123 Main Street
Anytown, AS 00000

High-Dollar "Kitchen Cabinet" Acquisition Package

Nearly 9,000 affluent prospective first-time donors to the 1988 Jesse Jackson campaign were mailed a high-quality, "oversized" version of the "Kitchen Cabinet" donor acquisition package. More than six hundred responded with gifts averaging $93. Included were a great many who sent the $250 requested.

Jesse Jackson '88

FOR PRESIDENT

900 BRENTWOOD ROAD NE
PO BOX 90070
WASHINGTON DC 20090-0070

Mr. John Doe   March 2, 1988
123 Main Street
Anytown, AS 00000

Dear Mr. Doe,

Ronald Reagan has his "Kitchen Cabinet." It's a tiny group of rich men from Southern California who are about the same age as he.

When President Reagan wants advice, he doesn't turn to the Congress, or to those who've devoted their lives to studying the issues. He turns to his friends.

Well, I want <u>you</u> to join <u>my</u> "Kitchen Cabinet"!

Along with this letter, I'm sending you an informal "Kitchen Cabinet" poll on foreign policy issues. I want you to complete it and return it to me this week.

I need your commitment to humanity, justice and peace to help shape the foreign policy agenda of the 1988 Presidential campaign.

I'm writing you because I know you've taken a stand for these basic American values -- and because I believe you share my grave concerns about America's role in the world. Because your concern springs from the deep vein of caring and goodness that represents the best of America, I want and need your support.

I will be proud and pleased to have you join the widening circle of my advisers.

My Presidential candidacy is a chance to turn America around in 1988. It's a chance to get beyond the bankruptcy of the Reagan Era and to form a new vision based on our common hopes and values.

For me, the starting point is this inescapable fact:

Never before has our fate as a nation depended so much on the state of the rest of the world.

- 2 -

The Reagan Administration has spent billions of dollars on Star Wars. Yet I believe you share my feeling that we're less secure than ever.

Not so long ago we were the world's largest creditor nation. Today we're the largest debtor. And you and I both know our economy is shakier than ever.

I believe that, like me, you care about our painfully slow progress towards nuclear disarmament ... towards peace in Central America ... towards ending apartheid ... towards solving the trade deficit.

Everywhere I go in this beautiful country of ours, I meet people with similar concerns. Concern not only for the future of our children, but for the children of Nicaragua and Israel and Soweto. Concern not only for the loss of jobs at home, but for the loss of respect from other nations.

According to President Reagan, progress depends on fighting communism and promoting the growth of American corporations around the world.

Ronald Reagan views the world as a conflict between East and West. He tells us that change in the Third World comes from communist upheaval, rather than from poverty and repression.

The Reagan Doctrine is a program based on fear and mistrust and greed.

I think <u>America</u> <u>deserves</u> <u>better</u>.

The Reagan Administration feels it isn't bound by international law. But President Reagan was wrong when he illegally mined the harbors of Nicaragua and defied the World Court. He was wrong when he traded arms for hostages and misled Congress and the public. He has lost the moral authority to challenge the Ayatollah for Iran's mining of Persian Gulf waters.

The Reagan Administration thinks it can determine the outcome of upheaval and revolution -- but that is an impossible task.

Millions of our tax dollars have gone to support the Contras' senseless violence in Central America. How does that help our national security?

Over 50,000 nuclear warheads exist today, poised to

- 3 -

destroy the world at the touch of a button. And how does that help our national security?

America deserves better.

In 1988 we can offer a new vision -- a vision based on meeting the needs of our own people, and of people around the world.

We can bring hope, not fear, into the world.

We can ground our foreign policy in a more sensible view of the world, one which reflects the humanity in our values and serves our national interests.

That's why I hope you'll join my "Kitchen Cabinet." I want you to compare your own views with mine on some of today's major foreign policy issues.

Do you believe, as I do, that building a more secure America means adopting national policies that keep us strong, and international policies that keep us respected?

Do you agree with me that allying ourselves with dictators who will be overthrown by their own people does not build national security?

Do you share my conviction that putting more than half of our scientists to work developing new weapons does not build national security? When Japan beats us in the world economy because three out of four Japanese scientists are researching industrial and commercial innovations?

To me, building a more secure America means:

o aggressive negotiations with the Soviet Union ... mutual, verifiable reductions in nuclear stockpiles ... diplomatic pressure to ease the oppression against Soviet Jews.

o expanded diplomacy reaching out to all parties in the Middle East ... a comprehensive political settlement that benefits both Israelis and Arabs ... an immediate arms embargo against both Iran and Iraq.

o withdrawal of all U.S. military aid to Central America ... economic sanctions against South Africa ... linking foreign aid and trade benefits to guarantees of human rights.

- 4 -

And I believe that building a more secure America means eliminating our trade deficit.

It's not the Taiwanese or the Japanese who are to blame for America's trade wounds.

It's our two trillion dollar national debt.

It's the merger mania which has poured capital into senseless acquisitions instead of into technological innovation.

It's the greed of the corporations who close down factories to avoid paying U.S. workers a decent wage and move production overseas, where workers are not allowed to organize.

I believe that our true national security lies in getting our national priorities straight. Do you agree?

To me, national security means cutting the waste and mismanagement out of our military budget. It means keeping our dollars at home so that we can rebuild America.

We're often reminded that we live in a great nation -- and we do. But it can be greater still if we follow a new definition of greatness.

Our nation's greatness is not based on military might. I believe it's based on how we value and care for people -- on our achievements in education, health, culture, housing, and employment.

o If we care for our young and educate them to work in tomorrow's world, we'll have national security.

o If we provide decent, safe and sanitary housing and food for the poor, then we'll have national security.

o If we provide meaningful employment for all capable Americans and demand that workers in other countries have similar rights, we'll have national security.

o If we allow other nations to determine their own destiny and gain respect in the world for our concern for human rights and economic justice, we'll have national security.

- 5 -

I hope you'll join with me in forging this new definition of national security. I want you to help me build a foreign policy that isn't foreign to our values as a nation.

The poll I mentioned early in this letter covers six of the major foreign policy issues of the 1988 Presidential campaign. I call it my "Kitchen Cabinet" foreign policy poll -- because it's important to me to know your views on these issues.

I ask you to take a moment right now -- wherever you may be -- to complete this questionnaire. I'd like you to send it back to me this week.

As you can see from the survey, I don't evade the issues. I think it's important to let the world know where Jesse Jackson stands on these urgent problems that affect America's security.

Obviously, there are many other foreign policy issues I couldn't include in my brief listing in the "Kitchen Cabinet" poll: the global environmental crisis, foreign aid and development, immigration, hunger and famine, the defense of Western Europe and Japan, and many, many more. I've chosen just six issues because there's such intense public concern about them.

If you agree with me on most of these six issues, then I ask you to stand with me and support my campaign for the Democratic nomination for President in 1988.

I'm asking for your financial support as well as your political support -- to help build a more secure America.

Politics isn't cheap. It takes money to run a Presidential campaign -- lots of it. And my campaign has too little.

That's why I am asking you today for your most generous contribution -- a gift of $250 or more.

The federal government will match every dollar of your $250 contribution, so your gift will go twice as far.

Please send more if you can. With a gift of $1,000 -- the maximum permitted under the law -- you will be entitled to receive a "Jesse Jackson Gold Card."

- 6 -

The Gold Card will entitle you to free admission to any Jesse Jackson campaign events in your area -- and to special Jackson receptions at the Democratic National Convention in Atlanta in July.

Our message of integrity and hope speaks to the concerns of most Americans, but we can reach them only with your most generous help.

And I ask that you join me this week.

At this critical time in the campaign, just before some of the major primaries, your gift will go especially far.

We're running a lean, cost-effective campaign with the support of thousands of keenly committed volunteers. We don't need as much as some of the other candidates to get out our message of hope -- but we do need your generous help to stay competitive.

With your contribution of $250 or more, we'll be able to transform the 1988 Presidential campaign into a call for the rebuilding of America.

It's time for a new direction for America ... for a foreign policy based on more than military strength. It's time for a foreign policy based on American values.

I ask you to join with me to make America once again a symbol of hope throughout the world ... and a shining example of hope at home.

Sincerely,

Jesse Jackson

Jesse L. Jackson

P.S. Please take a moment now to complete the informal "Kitchen Cabinet" foreign policy poll I've enclosed with this letter and return it to me with your maximum contribution. I'd like to have both of them in my hands this week.

Authorized and paid for by Jesse Jackson '88, Howard Renzi, Treasurer

Jesse Jackson '88

FOR PRESIDENT

900 BRENTWOOD ROAD, N.E. P.O. BOX 90970
WASHINGTON, D.C. 20090-0970

To Jesse Jackson:

Yes, I'm pleased to join your "Kitchen Cabinet." I've compared my views on foreign policy with yours on the survey below. Like you, I want a foreign policy that promotes *real security*, not false security—and puts more of our resources into meeting America's urgent human needs.

Here's my contribution to help you reach voters in the important upcoming primaries with your message of new hope and new leadership. I understand the federal government will match the first $250 of my gift. My check (payable to JESSE JACKSON '88) is in the amount of:

☐ **$250**   ☐ **$**_____

☐ My check is enclosed for the maximum $1000 contribution permitted under the law. I understand I will receive a JESSE JACKSON GOLD CARD entitling me to free admission to all Jackson campaign fundraising events for the rest of the year.

JESSE JACKSON KITCHEN CABINET FOREIGN POLICY POLL

NUCLEAR DISARMAMENT: Star Wars runs up our budget deficit and robs our nation of the resources we need to meet urgent human needs. For the sake of our survival and the survival of our children, we must *reduce* nuclear weapons, and convert our nation's war economy to a *peace* economy.

☐ AGREE   ☐ DISAGREE   ☐ NO OPINION

CENTRAL AMERICA: In the name of "anti-communism," the Reagan Administration funds a war that has killed 150,000 people and made millions refugees. But paying mercenaries to carry out senseless violence in Central America does *not* make us more secure. Our true national interest lies in promoting *peace*.

☐ AGREE   ☐ DISAGREE   ☐ NO OPINION

continued on next page

Prepared expressly for:

Mr. John Doe
123 Main Street
Anytown, AS 00000

IMPORTANT: Please complete the Contributor Information on the next page, and be sure your name and address above is spelled correctly.

continued from first page

TRADE DEFICIT: America's trade wounds are self-inflicted. GM, GE and other giant multinational corporations are exporting some of our best jobs overseas. It's time to stop merger mania and come to grips with our nation's *real* economic problem: the need to meet human needs for jobs, health, housing and education.

☐ AGREE   ☐ DISAGREE   ☐ NO OPINION

MIDDLE EAST: After seven years of Reagan's confused policies, scores of Americans are dead, Israelis and Palestinians are still killing each other, and we're stuck in an undeclared war in the Persian Gulf. It's time to bring all parties together to hammer out a *comprehensive* peace plan for the region, guaranteeing security for Israel and justice for the Palestinians.

☐ AGREE   ☐ DISAGREE   ☐ NO OPINION

RELATIONS WITH THE SOVIET UNION: Nuclear and conventional disarmament is essential. But during this period of *glasnost,* our negotiations with the Soviet Union must put human rights and the plight of Soviet Jews high on the agenda. Promoting the right of *all* people to choose their destiny will further enhance our ability to bring moral pressure on behalf of the oppressed.

☐ AGREE   ☐ DISAGREE   ☐ NO OPINION

SOUTH AFRICA: Apartheid shocks our humanity and offends our sense of justice. Yet the Reagan Administration still supports the South African regime. To ally ourselves with a tiny minority while alienating South Africa's majority is not only morally wrong, but self-destructive. We must end this horror peacefully—by imposing full economic sanctions against South Africa immediately.

☐ AGREE   ☐ DISAGREE   ☐ NO OPINION

POLITICAL CONTRIBUTION INFORMATION

(1) Any individual may contribute up to $1,000 to JESSE JACKSON FOR PRESIDENT '88. Members of a family, or partners in an unincorporated business, may each contribute up to $1,000.

(2) The JESSE JACKSON FOR PRESIDENT '88 Campaign cannot accept contributions from any corporation, labor union, or church.

(3) Individual contributions to JESSE JACKSON FOR PRESIDENT '88 can be matched, dollar for dollar, up to a maximum of $250 by the Federal Election Commission.

(4) Personal checks or money orders of up to $250 qualify for federal matching if they are accompanied by the contributor's name, full address, occupation, and employer's name.

The Federal Election Commission requires that we ask for the following information and **we need it to qualify for matching funds:**

YOUR OCCUPATION

YOUR EMPLOYER

Jesse
Jackson
'88
FOR PRESIDENT

900 BRENTWOOD ROAD N.E.
P.O. BOX 90970
WASHINGTON, D.C. 20090-0970

USA 22

Jesse Jackson
900 Brentwood Rd N.E.
P.O. Box 90970
Washington, DC 20090-0970

Jesse Jackson '88
FOR PRESIDENT
900 BRENTWOOD ROAD, N.E.
P.O. BOX 90900
WASHINGTON, D.C. 20090-0900

Telephone Fundraising Pledge Card

During the month of March 1988, The Progressive Group, Inc. undertook to call 6,755 selected previous donors to Jesse Jackson's presidential campaign. The program cost about $3.70 per name called. Over nine hundred sent gifts in response; the average was $66. Pledge card packages like the one reproduced here were sent to all those who promised gifts on the phone.

Jesse Jackson
'88
FOR PRESIDENT

900 BRENTWOOD ROAD, N.E.
P.O. BOX 90900
WASHINGTON, D.C. 20090-0900

I'm glad someone from my staff was able to reach you the other night on the telephone. I asked them to call to tell you that I'm running for President of the United States and I need your help to do it.

I'm running again because -- like you -- I know that <u>America deserves better leadership</u>.

When the President of the United States vetoes a bill imposing sanctions on a government that jails and kills South African children, what value does he place on children's lives?

America deserves better leadership.

When the government of the United States denies help to students who want to go to college, and farmers who want to save their farms ... yet gives money to kill students and farmers in Central America ... what does that say about our values as a nation and as a people?

America deserves better leadership.

I want your help because I feel this nation must reject the distorted values of the Reagan Administration ... which places private greed over public need and service ... and emphasizes military posturing over peaceful negotiations.

We're often reminded that we live in a great nation -- and we do. But it can be greater still if we follow a new definition of greatness.

Our nation's greatness is not in the size of our GNP. It's not our military might.

More fundamental to national greatness, by my definition, is how we treat children, the poor, and the elderly.

* If we care for our young, insuring their proper nutrition and educate them to work in tomorrow's world, we'll be a great nation.

* If we provide decent, safe and sanitary housing and food for the poor, then we'll be a great nation.

* If we provide health care and food and show respect for our elderly, then we'll be a great nation.

<u>Greatness is in how we value and care for our people</u>.

That is the persective I want to lay before the American people in my second campaign for the Presidency.

If, as I believe, you <u>do</u> share many of my views, I invite you to help my campaign for the Democratic nomination for President in 1988 -- to put <u>our</u> views at the top of the nation's political agenda.

And to demonstrate to skeptical reporters and the general public that there is deep, continued support for my candidacy, I want to get off to a rapid and dramatic start.

In 1984, we won five states, finished second in four others, and ended a strong third in eight more. We raised $9.1 million. We got 3.5 million primary and caucus votes -- over one of every five votes cast for <u>all</u> Democratic candidates in 1984! And we got 465-1/2 delegate votes at the Democratic National Convention.

To accomplish all this, my support came exclusively from committed individual citizens like you.

Now, in this 1988 campaign, I need <u>your</u> support.

And I ask that you join me <u>within the next 10 days</u>.

Your contribution of $250, $100, $50, $30 or whatever you can afford to "Jesse Jackson `88" will assist my campaign in Iowa, New Hampshire, and the "Super Tuesday" states. And every penny of your gift will be matched by the Federal Election Commission, so you'll be getting double the bang for your buck.

With your early help, and the support and encouragement of other friends throughout the country, I'll be able to demonstrate dramatically and concretely that the necessary resources are available to me for the Presidential race.

With your support, I will use my campaign for the Presidency to restore the <u>hope</u> of our young people.

Together, we <u>will</u> save the children . . . strengthen the cities . . . heal the land . . . invest in America . . . and achieve peace in our time . . . and we will do it now.

From the bottom of my heart, my deepest thanks to you for your support and encouragement.

                              With high hopes,

                              Jesse Jackson, Sr.

                              Jesse L. Jackson

P.S. With a contribution of $250, you'll be a Founding Member of my 1988 campaign, and I promise that I'll keep you fully informed of all important developments. Also, my staff will notify you of any special opportunities to meet with me in the course of my travels.

Jesse Jackson '88
FOR PRESIDENT

900 BRENTWOOD ROAD, N.E.
P.O. BOX 96400
WASHINGTON, D.C. 20077-7327

I want to help your 1988 Presidential Campaign immediately and help you receive the maximum in Federal "Matching Funds" so you can take your message of hope to the American public. I filled in the important information on the back, and I'm sending my check today so that every dollar will be matched by the Federal Election Commission.

Leadership Circle

Please return this card along with your check payable to "Jesse Jackson '88 for President". (over, please)

POLITICAL CONTRIBUTOR INFORMATION

(1) Any individual may contribute up to $1,000 to JESSE JACKSON '88. Members of a family, or partners in an unincorporated business, may each contribute up to $1,000.

(2) The JESSE JACKSON '88 Presidential Campaign cannot accept contributions from any corporation or labor union.

(3) Contributions to JESSE JACKSON '88 can be matched, dollar for dollar, up to a maximum of $250 by the Federal Election Commission.

(4) Personal checks or money orders of up to $250 qualify for Federal matching if they are accompanied by the contributor's name, full address, occupation and employer's name.

(5) Matching funds provided by the Federal Election Commission will be disbursed soon after January 1, 1988, when they can be used to help finance campaign activities in Iowa, New Hampshire, and other important primary and caucus states.

The Federal Election Commission requires that we ask for the following information and we need it to qualify for matching funds:

Your occupation

Your employer

Your employer's city and state

JESSE JACKSON '88   900 BRENTWOOD ROAD, N.E.   P.O. BOX 96400   WASHINGTON, D.C. 20090

NO POSTAGE
NECESSARY IF
MAILED IN THE
UNITED STATES

BUSINESS REPLY MAIL
FIRST CLASS PERMIT NO. 16724 WASHINGTON, DC

POSTAGE WILL BE PAID BY ADDRESSEE

JESSE JACKSON '88
900 Brentwood Road, N.E.
P.O. Box 96400
Washington, D.C. 20077-7327

■ ■ ■ ■ ■

There may be no better example than Jesse Jackson of what it takes
for a political candidate to raise large amounts of money by mail. Most
people in politics believe that few candidates can do so, and except for
presidential candidates, who can benefit from federal matching funds,
they're probably right.

Successful direct mail fundraising is about gut-level *issues* — not
legislation, or programs, or abstractions, but the things people talk
about in bars and at the dinner table. Direct mail fundraising is about
ideas — not intellectualisms, but concepts that cast new light on the
world.

It wasn't just Jesse Jackson's popularity and high name recognition
that made his direct mail success possible. Other politicians are famous
and popular. Jackson's eloquence, his ability to translate complicated
problems into dramatic ideas, and his fearlessness in addressing American society's fundamental issues contributed even more.

And by the way: his consultants think they, too, had a little something to do with Jesse Jackson's success in the mails.

Working With a Direct Mail Consultant

8

In-House Versus Outside Management

I admit it: I'm biased. As a direct mail fundraising consultant, both self-interest and experience lead me to believe that you'd probably be well advised to hire a consultant to help you launch — and manage — your direct mail fundraising program.

I've made every effort in this book to explain clearly how our business is conducted. Nonetheless, you can see that it's very complicated and makes lots of demands on your time and managerial expertise. Chances are, you'll need help — a great deal of it.

Too often, I've seen direct mail fundraising programs that are managed in-house by nonprofit organizations or political campaigns fail to realize their full potential for the following reasons:

❐ because staff was distracted by other priorities;

❐ because they lacked the time or resources to meet maildates on a consistent basis, month after month;

❐ because the attitudes they conveyed in their mailings were parochial, overly self-serving or simply uninteresting;

❐ because they didn't have the depth and scope of experience to know how to respond quickly when creative challenges arose;

❐ or because they just didn't have the breadth of experience to see opportunities for what they were, or to know what to do about them when they surfaced.

Frequently, these organizations chose to manage their programs in-house either because they wanted to save money or because they felt they knew better than anyone else how best to present themselves to the world. In most circumstances, neither reason holds water.

The "savings" from in-house management are often illusory: even if returns on individual mailings are as good as any consultant might obtain, an in-house organization rarely can achieve the consistency and frequency of a mailing schedule managed by outside professionals.

A public interest group rarely has the full range of skills and resources necessary to survive in the Darwinian marketplace of public interest fundraising. Public interest marketing demands a lot more than an intimate understanding of your organization and its work. It's not enough to tell the world what you need. You have to convey your message — cost-effectively — in a way that connects on a visceral level with your constituents and *motivates* them to act, generously and immediately. This calls for a special set of marketing and communications skills that are not common in managers — nonprofit, political or otherwise. It also calls for an ability to work with specialized suppliers or vendors: a network of list brokers, printers, lettershops and other vendors that will enable you to produce your mailings on time, and cost-effectively.

Moreover, nowadays, the difference between success or failure in a mailing can result from very subtle changes in list selection, copy, design, packaging or other factors. *An organization's competitive advantage in direct mail fundraising lies on the margins* — in very small numbers. For example:

❏ Lowering the cost of printing by two cents per package could allow you to mail a million donor acquisition letters — and recruit ten or twenty thousand new members — instead of mailing 100,000 and generating only a couple of thousand gifts. A consultant's clout with printers could make this much difference in the price.

❏ Mailing eight donor resolicitation letters next year instead of six could increase your organization's net direct mail revenue by twelve or fifteen percent. If your staff is stretched thin, a consultant's attention to the mailing schedule could make the difference.

❏ Enhancements in copy and design derived from experience with many other public interest groups could lift the response rate in each of your donor resolicitations from five percent to eight or ten percent. When the year's at an end, you could find yourself with an active donor base that is twenty or thirty percent larger.

Differences of this magnitude could make or break your strategic plan.

With all this said, however, *some* organizations are better off managing their programs in-house. This may be the case for your group under the following circumstances:

❏ If your annual budget is less than $100,000, you're unlikely to be able to afford professional help on a continuing basis.

❏ If your constituency or market is too small to permit aggressive donor acquisition by mail, you're unlikely to gain enough benefit from an ongoing relationship with a consultant.

❏ If you've been in the mails for years and your strategy calls for a modest, continuing program along well-established lines that your staff is competent to handle, chances are slim that you'll need anything more than copywriting, technical assistance or an occasional bit of advice.

❐   If — on the other end of the spectrum — your direct mail fundraising program is so large and lucrative that you can afford to hire a staff of full-time, top-flight fundraising professionals, you're probably right to handle the job in-house. With several hundred thousand donors and a budget in excess of $20 million, that might be the case. However, if you've gotten that far, you've probably long since figured out that you benefit from hiring not just one but perhaps several outside consultants to provide a steady stream of new ideas and to keep your staff on their toes.

While neither the very biggest nor the smallest organizations may need outside consultants to manage their direct mail fundraising programs, most of the rest probably do. Chances are, that includes you.

Here, then, are a few guidelines to observe as you look around in search of a direct mail fundraising firm that's right for you.

Selecting the Right Consultant

There's no license required to hang out a shingle as a direct mail fundraising consultant. There's no test to pass, no certification procedure. And you won't find many of us in the yellow pages.

While there is a national organization that has established a code of ethics for the profession and a mechanism to enforce it — the Association of Direct Response Fundraising Counsel (ADRFCO) — in mid-1989 its members did not yet include a majority of the public interest direct mail consulting firms at work around the country. (For a listing of members and other information, write ADRFCO, 1501 Broadway, Suite 610, New York, New York 10036, or phone 212/354-7150.)

A great many of the companies that offer direct mail management, creative or consulting services to public interest organizations are engaged in some *other* business — as printers, computer service bureaus, advertising agencies, list brokers, public relations consultants, or design firms. By and large, with some very notable exceptions, the quality of service offered by these groups is low. Often it's "free" — and in some cases that's exactly what it's worth.

There is also an uncounted number of solo consultants serving one or a few clients, with little or no staff. In a few cases, they're refugees from the constraints imposed by their earlier jobs at larger firms and may offer a *range* of previous experience. Most, however, gained their principal experience in *one* direct mail fundraising program, typically as staff for a nonprofit organization or political campaign, or in commercial direct response marketing. These consultants may offer services ranging from copywriting alone, to full-service management and consulting, to data entry. Some are brilliant fundraisers, but skill levels vary widely among the solo consultants.

Among the dozens of established consulting firms — only a handful of which are more than ten years old — the level of skill and breadth of experience also vary. These firms are often highly specialized — geographically, politically and by issue. Some work exclusively for nonprofit or political clients; many pay the bills by taking commercial assignments (for which fees are typically much higher). Some work with a broad range of clients, while others emphasize one or a few special markets or issues. Most serve fewer than a dozen organizations at any one time. In most cases, the total staff numbers twenty persons or less.

With such a variety of choices, then, how can you select the consultant that's right for *your* organization?

As you start the process, you're likely to rely heavily on what you can learn of the firms' reputation and experience. Some may clearly be unsuitable because their track record is unimpressive or is based on issues and organizations that seem irrelevant, while others may clearly be inadequate to the task of meeting your diverse needs. That will help you narrow the field down to a manageable number of three or four prospects. But then the choice is likely to get tougher.

You might start by requesting sample mailing packages from each of the finalists — and then *read* them. You'll learn a lot. (If they won't send samples, you'll learn something from that, too.)

Naturally, you should also ask for references, or a client list, or both. If you follow up with phone calls to the consultants' references, you'll learn a lot from that, too.

But, even after all that, you may still face a difficult choice. Here are the *real* issues to consider at that point:

❐ *Understanding*: Do you and the consultant speak the same language? Regardless of whether the firm has direct experience with the issues your organization addresses, do you believe the consulting staff understands what you're about and the values that motivate your constituents? Will they be able to present your programs in fundraising appeals that are honest, accurate and effective?

❐ *Range of services*: Does the consultant have the experience and the resources to do the *whole* job, and do it right? If a firm doesn't itself offer all the services you need, does it have well-established relationships with other vendors who do?

❑ *Contract terms*: Is the consultant offering you attractive financial incentives — such as capital to finance your program or a "guarantee" that you'll make a profit — or offering to accept only a percentage of the returns in compensation? Any or all of these incentive arrangements *may* be legitimate, but they bear an extra-careful look because they're also commonly used by crooks. And there are a few of those in the direct mail field, as there are in any other.

❑ *Creativity*: Will the consultant create specially tailored packages for your direct mail fundraising program — or apply formulas (and recycle packages) that have proven successful for other organizations? Winning formulas on which successful agencies have been built include such things as sweepstakes offers and extremely inexpensive prospect package formats. There's no such thing as a "right" or a "wrong" way to look at this question, but it's important stylistically and it may have financial implications. To launch a sweepstakes or use some other tested but controversial formula may be cost-effective, but it may also undermine your support from your board or major funders — or even risk the ire of regulatory authorities. Just be sure you know what you're getting into.

❑ *Decision-making*: Who will make the key creative and financial decisions — you or the consultant? Does the firm want you to write a check and leave them alone? Or will you be entering into what is effectively a partnership, with the firm making recommendations and you or your staff making the real decisions at every crucial point along the way?

❑ *Accessibility*: Just because a firm is located in your city doesn't mean you'll get the attention you deserve. Regardless of geographic location, are you convinced that the consultant will be available to answer your questions and address your concerns in a timely fashion? Will you get service — or a runaround? Will your telephone calls be answered? Will you have opportunities for periodic strategy and creative meetings?

❑ *Compensation*: Aside from the management or consulting fees the firm will charge you, what other fees will you be paying? Will the consultant mark up printing and other vendor bills, receive all the list rental revenue, or even receive title to your donor or membership list? The proposed "fees" may look a whole lot lower than they really are. Look at the whole compensation package before you conclude that one firm is less expensive than another.

If these considerations don't do the trick, there's one more that may decide the question once and for all:

Which of the consultants you're considering is likely to best understand your strategy, and to design — then implement — the most effective direct mail fundraising program to help you reach your goals?

If you find the right firm, you may be squarely on track toward your strategic goals. Now all you have to do is figure out how to work with the consultant you've selected.

Making the Relationship Work: Managing a Consultant

As a client of a direct mail fundraising firm, you can exert considerable control in four ways:

❏ *Creative responsibility* — You have to expect — and you should insist on — being involved in the fundamental creative decisions. It's your responsibility as much as the consultant's to develop a marketing plan that meets your organization's long-term strategic needs, and to devise marketing concepts for individual mailings that fairly reflect the overall strategy. No matter how much you may rely on your consultant for solid advice on both creative and technical matters, you (or a key staff member) must maintain an overview of the program on a continuing basis.

❏ *Management style* — If you've hired a firm to manage your direct mail fundraising program, let them do the job. Ask questions, insist on signing off on all major decisions — but don't micro-manage their work, as though you don't need their help except as messengers between you and the printshop. You've got better things to do than to second-guess their segmentations or argue constantly about type sizes or ink colors. If over an extended period they haven't produced acceptable results — or you just don't like the way they represent you to the world — fire them and find another firm.

❏ *Planning and scheduling* — If direct mail is going to work for you, you'll have to mail again and again on a reliable, consistent schedule. This means you'll have to resist the perfectionist temptation to rewrite or redesign every appeal or to insist on waiting an extra few weeks before the last trickle of test results confirm a decision to roll out a new package. Occasionally, caution and extra attention to detail are important enough to delay a mailing — *but not very often.* One of the most important things your direct mail consultant can do for you is to help you work out a long-term mailing schedule —

and stick to it. If they're missing maildates right and left — and it's not your fault — then it's time to reexamine the relationship.

☐ *Trust* — Your consultant is not the enemy. While it's important that financial aspects of the relationship be conducted at arm's length and with all due consideration for what is legal and proper, it's counter-productive to nit-pick every bill and question every minor departure from the mailing budget. If the company is taking advantage of you, or consistently overspending by significant amounts, by all means talk to them. It may be time to look for an alternative. As a response to such situations, distrust isn't a constructive alternative. It can be demoralizing for a consultant to face the third degree about every minor decision — and ultimately *you'll* pay the price.

The relationship between you and your direct mail consultant is a two-way proposition, and you're responsible for making the most of it — because you're footing the bill. But, in many ways, the burden will be on the company you hire. Not only will your consultant be managing the work they've contracted to do for you; they'll also have to manage their relationship with *you*.

Managing a Client

Whether called a "client consultant," "account executive," "program coordinator," or something else entirely, the person within your consultant's firm who is in charge of the overall management of your account should be responsible for the following items, as drawn from the Client Consultants' job description at Mal Warwick & Associates, Inc.:

1. Strategic planning and analysis

☐ Be familiar with the terms of the client's contract and with the provisions of any proposal or marketing plan.

☐ Review the long-term direct mail schedule on a monthly basis, updating it at least quarterly, and obtain the client's approval for each update.

☐ Analyze and review the results of each mailing, with particular attention to testing data, so you're sure they're reflected in the design of future mailings.

☐ Take the fullest possible advantage of your clients' donor lists with frequent and varied donor renewal and special appeal programs specially tailored to the client's program.

❒ Prepare timely statistical reports for the client, and help interpret the data.

2. Copywriting and package design

❒ Initiate creative meetings or focus groups to determine marketing strategy.

❒ Develop a marketing concept for each mailing and work with the copywriter and designer to ensure that the concept is properly executed and that the resulting package adequately reflects the client's program as well as budgetary limitations.

❒ Take full advantage of potential marketing opportunities through aggressive package and price testing.

3. Management and coordination

❒ Stay in close contact with the client and discuss plans and program performance as often as needed, but at least monthly.

❒ Obtain and keep on file timely client approvals for budget, copy, art and donor file segmentations.

❒ Be aware at all times of the status of production work and list acquisition on every project in order to certify that schedules are being met (or to notify the client in advance if they're not).

❒ Seek to ensure that the client's mailing list is properly maintained and managed, that caging, cashiering and donor acknowledgment services are adequately performed, and that useful and accurate reports to track each mailing are generated and delivered.

❒ Maintain close communication with the telephone fundraising firm, computer service bureau or other major program vendor.

4. Financial oversight

❒ Draft, monitor and update the budget for each mailing.

❒ Monitor each client's payments to head off financial problems before they develop.

5. Overall marketing and management

❒ *Take advantage of new opportunities* for the client — whether they result from changing events reported on the evening news, changing circumstances in clients' organizations, or changing patterns in the returns from direct mail campaigns. (I tell our Client Consultants that they're not obligated to come up with brilliant ideas three

times a week but that I do expect them to gain enough of a feel for
their clients' work that they can sense when it's important to talk
about making major changes.)

❑ *Pay close attention to clients' mailing programs*: identify and avoid
major errors or problems, even if that means stopping work on a
mailing that might lose the client money, delaying a maildate to
head off significant design or production problems, or testing a
new package because the old one isn't meeting the program's goals.

*If you're lucky enough to find a consultant who'll do all
this for you — and you cooperate fully — you'll be well
on the way to getting the most from your direct mail
fundraising program.*

With skill, patience, adequate investment, and a little luck, you'll be
able to derive full value from your organization's resources and multiply your impact. By making the right strategic choices — and using
state-of-the-art direct mail techniques to further your strategic goals —
you'll become part of a revolution that has already started to change the
face of American society.

Fundraising for the 21st Century

9

Direct mail fundraising as it was conducted in its infancy following World War II bears little resemblance to the intensely competitive and complex industry it's become in recent years. Like other technology-driven industries, direct mail fundraising has experienced accelerating change as one innovation after another multiplied the possibilities in what has often seemed a geometric progression.

In this chapter, we'll take a look at what direct mail fundraising has wrought in the crucial twenty-year period since the ZIP code entered American life as well as what changes have occurred in the direct mail field along the way. Then we'll consider some of the new technologies and new techniques just now coming into common usage by direct mail fundraisers, and we'll examine their implications for the future. In the chapter's final section, we'll venture into science fiction and take a look at a few of the seemingly limitless possibilities for fundraising in the 21st Century.

Revolution in the Mailbox

The American political system has changed dramatically since the 1960s because a handful of visionary direct mail specialists largely unknown to the general public successfully applied the techniques of direct response marketing to the challenge of creating social change.

Writing in the April 1989 issue of *Fund Raising Management*, Roger Craver, a pioneer in direct mail fundraising, contended that "The climate of frustration and alienation of the late 1960's and early 1970's was particularly suited for direct mail." Craver wrote,

> It all seemed to happen at once, one of those accidents of history when a given technology proves so unusually suited for its times that it goes beyond merely filling a need ... and begins to effect actual societal change. [In 1969], Richard Viguerie had just launched his pioneering efforts to build the mailing lists and devise the techniques that would give voice to the new conservatives. Morris Dees, a young Alabama lawyer and commercial direct-mail entrepreneur, was plotting the then unconventional use of direct mail to help the anti-war presidential candidate George McGovern. And my partners and I were testing the unheard of concept of recruiting hundreds of thousands of small gift contributors as members of the 'citizens lobby' that became Common Cause.

These early experiments in political direct mail fundraising paid off quickly and dramatically. Craver continued:

The political pundits laughed, but they didn't laugh long. Within two years, George McGovern had amassed more than 350,000 donors — giving him enough financial support to bypass the Democratic bosses, go directly to rank-and-file Democrats and secure his party's nomination for the presidency. Common Cause reached the 250,000-member mark and succeeded in its lobbying efforts to end both the outmoded seniority system and the process of secret votes in Congress. And Viguerie stunned conventional politicians with his capacity to raise millions of dollars for conservative candidates.

The revolution led by Craver, Viguerie, Dees, Tom Mathews, Peter Tagger and others has left an indelible imprint on American society. Through direct mail, popular but unconventional candidates without access to established funding sources have financed some of the most fateful political campaigns in recent American history. Among them were George McGovern in 1972, George Wallace and Ronald Reagan in 1976, Reagan again in 1980, John Anderson in 1980, Gary Hart in 1984 and Jesse Jackson in 1988 — the candidates and the campaigns that have changed their parties' politics for many years to come. Against the odds, both conservatives and progressives have gained footholds at all levels of government because of funds raised by mail.

Through direct mail, private citizens by the millions have become personally — sometimes intensely — involved in national politics. Millions have become donors to the Republican and Democratic parties and have helped shape their agendas by the sheer force of their numbers. Check-writing activists have also underwritten campaigns for a great many candidates for the U. S. Senate, House of Representatives, governorships and other public offices. Direct mail has accelerated the country's political realignment as a strategic tool in the hands of leaders of the New Politics, both of the Left and of the Right. Membership-based, non-party political committees have become fixtures on the political landscape. Election after election, they selectively direct their resources toward compatible candidates, helping to shape the future destinies of their parties — and of the country.

But politics is more than candidates and political parties, and the impact of direct mail fundraising extends beyond the boundaries of the formal political process, as Craver pointed out in his *Fund Raising Management* article:

Had it done nothing more than contribute to the breaking up of the concentrated, centralized power of the political parties — enabling more unconventional candidates to have their day in the sun — direct mail would have made a significant contribution to American political history. But perhaps even more significant has been its

contribution to the building of a massive political force in this
country — the citizen action organization.

Direct mail fundraising has given birth to some of this nation's
most innovative and effective nongovernmental institutions and given
new life to many others. Direct mail-based public interest organizations
have successfully pushed for legal and political reform, protection of
the environment and of animal life, safeguards for civil liberties and
women's rights, and support for human rights both at home and
abroad. Groups on the other end of the political spectrum — similarly
spawned by direct mail — have also had great impact by ending the
political careers of many leading liberals and blocking gun control and
other reforms.

In an age of increasing distrust for politics and policymakers, and
of decreasing voter participation, direct mail fundraising has provided
many Americans with a simple and effective channel for political
expression. Sending a political contribution via direct mail is not a
substitute for voting, of course; in fact, the overwhelming majority of
political direct mail donors are also voters whom direct mail affords
extra opportunities for political participation. Direct mail has come to
play so large a role for a number of reasons:

❑   It's an important source of *information*. Unlike much of what passes
    for political communication through television, radio, or other
    means, messages delivered by mail are typically packed with infor-
    mation. Information, in its truest sense, is that which is new and
    surprising, and direct mail is full of surprises. Only outspoken
    candidates or nonprofit organizations with clear messages can
    successfully raise significant amounts of money by mail. *Direct mail
    doesn't work well unless it's based on ideas*. Double-talk, compromise
    and obfuscation don't sell: only clarity works.

❑   It's *involving*. By targeting only the best prospects through careful
    list selection and sophisticated data processing techniques, direct
    mail fundraising reaches *individuals* with messages they're likely to
    be interested in receiving. And, by definition, direct mail asks for
    action. In the article I've cited, Craver called direct mail "the best
    antidote ever invented for political alienation." In a much more
    focused way than voting, contributing by mail provides a ready-
    made means to "do something" about today's headlines. As Craver
    wrote, "Direct mail — with its small checks, its surveys, its angry
    postcards to the politicians — provides genuine recourse, along
    with a safety valve for steaming political emotions."

❑   It's *inexpensive*. Compared to television or newspaper advertising
    — or to most any other form of mass communication — direct mail

can be an economical way to get a message across. This is true simply because, properly managed, direct mail can *make* money, possibly lots of it. At the same time, the price paid by individual donors is small. Nearly everyone with a mailbox can afford an occasional $15 or $25 contribution to make a political statement. Millions take advantage of this bargain.

The non-fundraising applications of direct mail techniques have also been widespread and effective. Elections have been won or lost because voters were swayed by "persuasion mail," typically delivered shortly before Election Day. Candidates have assembled long lists of critical endorsements, recruited thousands of volunteers or affected public opinion through the resourceful use of direct mail techniques. Single-issue interests such as labor, environmental, "pro-Choice" and anti-abortion organizations have used direct mail to mobilize volunteers and deliver their messages to targeted voters, sometimes with decisive effect. Increasingly, too, citizens are *voting* by mail, as local jurisdictions more and more often find absentee balloting popular, convenient and cost-effective.

Whether you're seeking to change laws or meet individual human needs, to educate the general public or teach the next generation, your use of direct mail fundraising will move you squarely into the middle of a technological revolution that is changing the character of American democracy.

New Frontiers in Fundraising

While Roger Craver, Richard Viguerie and other direct mail pioneers were launching their early efforts to crash the gates of the political world, others were applying new direct mail techniques to broaden the base of charitable and religious causes. Large charities which had raised money by mail for two decades were learning from the experience, refining old techniques and trying new ones; they were joined by a growing number of newcomers. Meanwhile, a boom in commercial direct response marketing was starting, making available to fundraisers a fast-growing body of tested marketing methods. Through the combined influence of all these new players, and the accumulated impact of new technology and economic trends, direct mail fundraising has changed profoundly since the 1960s. Among the many changes are these:

(1) *The advent of the ZIP code.* ZIP codes weren't in widespread use until the early 1970s, although they'd been introduced a decade earlier.

The ZIP code made computerization practical. (Just imagine sorting a quarter-million-name statewide list into alphabetical order!)

(2) *Computerization*. The computer has become indispensable in direct mail fundraising. In everything we do — from list maintenance and printing names and addresses, to management, analysis, and even copywriting and design — our work today would be impossible without computers. Direct mail fundraising is an information-based activity. It's been many years since the three-by-five card and the Addressograph were up to the task of managing the information our business requires.

(3) *Donor file segmentation*. In the 1970s, with computers becoming more widely available, fundraisers began learning the value of storing and using extensive giving histories for individual donors. Speedy and precise data processing made it possible for direct mail fundraisers to slice their lists of donors and prospects into ever-smaller pieces. Today, mailings may consist of more than one hundred segments or "cells" individually identified so as to measure differences in response and engineer cost savings in future mailings. Just twenty years ago, nonprofits commonly mailed the same resolicitation package to everyone on their donor files. Today, the rule is to classify donors in terms of "recency, frequency and dollar amount" and to mail many different packages simultaneously to different segments of the same list, as I've described in detail in this book. With this technique, direct mail fundraisers have dramatically increased the net income from nonprofit donor lists. By recognizing donors' varying levels and types of interest, we've also made vast improvements in communications between donors and the organizations they support. Many nonprofits have derived large, added dividends from their direct mail programs by contributing to the strategically important process of cultivating prospective donors of major gifts.

(4) *Personalization*. Before the advent of the computer and computer-driven printers, direct mail fundraisers almost invariably addressed prospects — and even their donors — in the impersonal idiom of the "Dear Friend" letter. Personalization enables us to include in our appeals not only donors' titles, names, and addresses but also anything else a computer may keep on file about them, from facts embedded in a giving history to personal preferences. Once very expensive, personalization has become cost-effective in many applications and is now widely used even in donor acquisition programs. While it is normally driven by computer formulas that define classes and categories of donors, personalization allows direct mail fundraisers to come surprisingly close to genuinely

personal, one-to-one communications — and it's getting better every year.

(5) *Merge-purge*. This basic tool of direct mail donor acquisition was not introduced until 1968. Without merge-purge, and the efficiency with which it reduces duplicate appeals and allows mailers to eliminate previous donors from their prospect mailings, the multi-million-piece prospect mailings of the past two decades might easily have provoked much more intense and widespread anger than they have. In addition, merge-purge has helped keep the lid on the rising cost of prospecting. Today, in part because the merge-purge process brings invaluable information to light about the overlap and relationships among mailing lists, it helps us target prospective contributors with ever-greater precision, which results in reduced costs, higher response rates and less frequent donor complaints.

(6) *Testing*. The conceptual backbone of today's direct mail fundraising was anathema to most fundraisers twenty years ago. On those infrequent occasions when it was proposed, testing was typically rejected out of hand as undignified or unnecessarily expensive. It could be thought insulting to suggest, for example, that donors' actual behavior should determine which of two alternative fund-raising letters ought to be used. The prevailing assumption was that any competent nonprofit manager knew far better than his donors how to promote his own organization. By now, most have awakened to the reality that donors make their own decisions. Our own guesses and preconceptions must be tested in the fundraising marketplace.

(7) *Growing competition*. One of the leading charitable fundraising specialists in 1969 was Jerry Huntsinger. Writing in the retrospective twentieth anniversary issue of *Fund Raising Management* (April 1989), Huntsinger contended that increasingly poor response makes it unrealistic for most charities to mail 10 million or more prospect packages annually. A great many did so in what he termed the "golden age" of direct mail prospecting in the 1970s and 1980s, but that's becoming less common with every passing year. In fact, Huntsinger claimed, "Some organizations were shocked to discover they could no longer mail enough pieces to prospective donors to even keep up with the inevitable attrition on their house file!" In other words, some charities were discovering the harsh reality of free market economics: they'd built huge donor files on the cheap in a wide-open market, but increasing competition was now preventing them from maintaining their "market share." Huntsinger attributed the problem, in part, to the public's "loss of

faith in the integrity of nonprofits." I think that's nonsense. But I agree that *very* few causes and candidates can succeed with the old "mass-mailing" techniques. During the past five years, my colleagues and I haven't even *tried* to mail 10 million pieces annually for any one client. These days, *selective targeting, not "mass marketing," is the key to successful direct mail fundraising for most public interest groups.*

(8) *Inflation.* In 1969, the typical cost of mailing one thousand prospect packages was about $85, including list rental, production and nonprofit postage (which was then $18 per thousand, or less than two cents per piece). The returns were usually $125 to $175 per thousand, turning a nice profit. During the past twenty years, however, mailing costs have risen two to three hundred percent — and because of growing competition, returns have not kept pace. The average charitable gift has risen, and well-run resolicitation programs have continued to yield handsome profits, but donor acquisition efforts are generally much less cost-effective than they were twenty years ago.

(9) *Changing standards of success.* Gone are the days when you wouldn't use a mailing list that didn't promise to break even. As Huntsinger noted, "Now, there is a new word on the street: 'Investment.'. . . [Today] many charities are pleased if they can enroll a new donor for an investment of $5 to $10." Because their donor resolicitation programs are so very profitable, some nonprofits will gladly invest far more, as I've explained in this book. The standard of success in direct mail fundraising is no longer a single number expressed in dollars and cents. Like the U. S. private sector, which is waking up to the fact that obsession with short-term profits can undermine a company's long-term health, the independent sector today is looking on direct mail fundraising from a longer perspective. The ultimate standard of success in direct mail is the extent to which it helps an organization achieve its strategic goals.

(10) *The spread of telephone fundraising.* Commercial telemarketing has its roots in telephone sales efforts first undertaken many decades ago, but the systematic use of telephone technology to raise money for public interest organizations is a phenomenon of the 1980s. Few current telephone fundraising firms were in existence before 1980. Their success in obtaining sometimes spectacular results has persuaded most nonprofit organizations to use telephone fundraising techniques in a wide range of applications despite resistance from many donors. Today, telephone fundraising is an integral part of every successful, large-scale direct mail fundraising program.

Before these profound changes seized hold of the direct mail fundraising field, the world somehow managed to get along without computers, ZIP codes, laser printers or WATS lines. The challenge for charitable fundraisers then was to print, address and mail the largest possible number of letters at the lowest possible cost.

Today, decades after the eclipse of the one-penny stamp, many of the fundamentals are the same. But seemingly daily changes in technology pose new challenges — and new possibilities — that are constantly widening the boundaries of the direct mail fundraising field. The following are among the newer techniques now in use — many of them borrowed from the multi-billion-dollar business of catalog sales and other forms of direct marketing. (In their commercial applications, some of these methods are anything but new. Fundraisers seem to learn slowly.)

Geodemographics and Psychographics

Fast computers with vast storage capacity make it possible to improve prospect targeting by identifying those of the country's 36,000 ZIP codes (or the smaller "census block groups" defined by the Census Bureau) in which the prevailing demographic characteristics suggest that residents will have a greater tendency to contribute to your organization. The assumption is that people who share personal characteristics with many of your donors are good prospects for you. This method is called "geodemographics" because it weds geographic targeting with demographic criteria. "Psychographics" — classifying individuals on the basis of their lifestyle, behavior, personal preferences and purchasing habits — is another method often used to target prospective individual supporters.

In both geodemographics and psychographics, complex computer programs are used to analyze your donor file, principally in order to help you conduct donor prospecting in a more cost-effective manner. They determine the geographic distribution of your donors, or their predominant psychographic characteristics as defined by the patterns that emerge when they are matched against a huge commercial database of American families about whom lifestyle and behavioral data are on file. (Much of this data is gathered from the survey cards packaged with product warranties by many consumer goods manufacturers.)

Geodemographics is typically used to *limit* the number of names selected from large lists of non-donors, such as voter-registration or automobile registration files. The computer will identify in which ZIP codes or "census block groups" your donors are clustered — and, by extension, which seem the best places to go hunting for new donors. Some commercial targeting services classify every one of the nation's

254,000 census blocks into one or another of several dozen types that share demographic, political and lifestyle characteristics determined by a minute analysis of census data.

With these services, an analysis of your file will determine which types, or "clusters," of census block groups seem the best bets for your organization. Other services (typically less expensive) produce a simpler ZIP code or census block "overlay" — a matrix or pattern of ZIP codes or the smaller block groups. Either way, the computer-determined pattern is then used to refine your lists, by allowing you to include only those neighborhoods that are most likely to support your cause, or to drop those that seem least promising.

Psychographic criteria are often applied to large databases — containing names, addresses and other information for as many as 80 million households — in order to select relatively small segments for targeted marketing efforts. As with geodemographics, the principal purpose is normally to make prospecting more cost-effective.

Generally, both processes require that your donor file consist of at least 50,000 names (100,000 would be better). These are expensive procedures and are rarely used except by the largest direct mail fund-raising programs — generally, those that are desperate to expand their prospect universe and are willing to pay to do so.

If this discussion suggests to you that Big Brother is about to take over the fundraising field too, don't worry. Charitable behavior is different from other forms of consumer behavior. I haven't heard a single spectacular success story about either technique: both geode-mographics and psychographics are used to gain small advantages on the margin. Unless they become far more refined than anyone in the industry can currently predict, these sophisticated targeting methods will continue to have limited applications.

A similar but more accessible and more widely used geodemographic procedure subjects your list to computer analysis, grouping your donors by ZIP code and determining what commercial mailers call "market penetration." The computer simply compares the number of donors you have in each ZIP code with the population of that area, and ranks all the ZIP codes represented from top to bottom according to the percentage of population that supports you. The ZIP codes in which your supporters live are then typically grouped into five categories, with the top quintile including the "best" twenty percent and the bottom quintile representing the "worst." As in geodemographic targeting, you're then able to target names from prospect lists by confining your mailing as selectively as you wish to the ZIP codes in one, two, three or four quintiles. To use this method, too, the vendors of most such services say your donor list must consist of 50,000 names or more — the bigger the better — or their computer analysis is likely to be faulty. Even in the best of cases, however, this method is also short on miracles.

Geodemographics and psychographics are by no means the last word in targeted marketing. For example, a newer approach pioneered by the J. Walter Thompson agency takes note of the reality that people with the same demographic and psychographic characteristics may be at dramatically different stages in their lives and thus respond in totally different ways to appeals directed at them. This "Lifestage" approach subdivides the three major segments — singles, couples and parents — into groups such as "starting-out singles," "mature parents" and "left-alone singles." According to this analysis, each of nine such groups requires a different marketing approach because each is, in fact, a separate target market. Commercial advertisers now actively take these differences into account, and fundraisers are hot on their trail.

Focus Groups

Fundraisers have borrowed the focus group technique from the world of advertising and marketing research. In a focus group, a carefully selected group of up to twelve individuals — usually volunteers, either donors or prospects, depending upon the circumstances — is methodically quizzed about their attitudes and reactions to your organization, your program or your fundraising materials. A trained facilitator leads the discussion, following a predetermined script or format. Often, but not always, program managers and copywriters may observe the discussion — hidden from view behind mirrored glass or on videotape shot from a concealed camera. The focus group's objective is to gain insight that you may use to improve your operations. In direct mail, focus groups are a form of "pre-testing" to narrow testing options down to those that appear most promising.

Focus groups provide *qualitative*, not quantitative, information, and the results are less than scientific. Often two, three or more focus groups are conducted before any conclusions are drawn.

Donor Surveys

A donor survey is a small-scale application of *quantitative* survey research or public opinion polling techniques, with the "public" generally limited to your own list of donors. Normally, a sample of a few hundred donors will suffice (just as valid national opinion polls may consist of interviews with as few as 400 persons). Donor surveys are often conducted in conjunction with focus groups, which are used to refine the questions to be asked. A donor survey can help you learn about the demographics and the basic attitudes of your supporters — and help you devise fundraising programs to tailor your appeals to them.

Unfortunately, most public interest groups resist spending money on donor surveys and focus groups. To me, their advantages are obvious: both techniques make it easier to target fundraising appeals and to devise effective marketing concepts, by providing facts in place of speculation or wishful thinking. But, just as many American businesses once rejected advertising as foolish and wasteful, nonprofit executives and board members tend to spurn market research. As fundraising becomes more complex and competitive, however, focus groups and donor surveys will inevitably come into wider use.

"On-line Packaging"

Printing, personalization and bundling for the post office can now be integrated into one continuous process on an assembly line. A single line may simultaneously use several different computer-driven addressing technologies, including "laser printers," "ink-jet" and high-speed "line printers," each of which produces a distinctive appearance on the page.

On-line packaging allows direct mailers to design ever larger and more complex personalized packages — full of such goodies as petitions and postcards and even laminated items such as bumperstrips, stickers and membership cards, with the addressee's name appearing half a dozen or a dozen times throughout the package, in different sizes, typestyles and colors.

In one end go the raw materials: paper, ink, glue; names, addresses and other data, stored magnetically; words and images engraved on printing plates or stored as digital data. Out the other end come finished, multiply personalized packages. It's Henry Ford's dream carried to an extreme.

These complicated assembly-line processes are labor-intensive, so on-line packages are often prohibitively expensive in small quantities. However, producing several hundred thousand may cost little or nothing more than printing, addressing and mailing a comparable quantity of more conventional packages in business envelopes. In multi-million-piece runs they *may* be even cheaper.

Currently, on-line methods are used primarily to produce fundraising packages with a distinctive and dramatic appearance and to print the donor's name and address in many different places and in several different typestyles. By contrast, commercial mailers sometimes use these methods to produce dozens of different "editions" of their packages, varying copy, graphics and other elements to match individuals' predicted purchasing preferences. This theoretically unlimited segmentation capability represents the greatest long-term potential of on-line packaging.

"Electronic Mail"

So-called electronic mail is a computerized system to print, personalize and distribute written fundraising appeals with unusual speed. The form of electronic mail used in fundraising is different from purely electronic messaging systems known by the same name, which are used on many computer networks.

With a copy of your donor list and the text of your appeal in hand, a company specializing in this service will use laser printers (or some other, high-speed, computer-driven method) to reproduce personalized messages on pre-printed forms, often resembling telegrams. Some electronic mail services actually use electronic means to transmit both lists and messages to regional centers around the country, where the packages are printed, assembled and mailed. Electronic mail services can often achieve one- or two-day delivery nationwide. Other vendors print everything in one place and then ship to regional centers for distribution through the Postal Service.

Fundraising by Fax

In 1989 there were more than 3.2 million fax machines in operation in the United States, including 22,000 in private homes. The total was projected to reach 5 million by 1991. A few venturesome fundraisers have already tried this new-wave communications medium, and their numbers will surely grow, too.

With legislative controls in the works around the country, fundraising by fax is not likely to prove a popular donor acquisition method. (Personally, I find the very idea of prospecting by fax to be repulsive. It makes my blood boil to think that some jerk would tie up precious time on my fax line by sending me a prospect appeal — a long one, no doubt!) However, as an efficient means to contact proven supporters who *want* to hear from you from time to time, fax holds considerable promise. You may want to ask your best donors to supply you with fax numbers.

Eventually — perhaps not many years from now — fax may become as widely used a means of person-to-person communications as is the telephone today. Then, many organizations may distribute fundraising appeals to their supporters via fax in favor of mail.

Direct Response TV

Television commercials can be produced either to appeal directly for contributions or to ask viewers to call toll-free numbers for more information or free premiums. The purpose of the exercise is generally to acquire names and addresses of donors, or of qualified *prospects* who ask for information and may later be solicited for gifts *by mail*.

Typically, acquiring donors in this fashion is more costly than it is by mail, and the names acquired are almost never profitable in the near term. While broadcasting a message by television is much cheaper if you measure the cost of reaching one prospective donor, direct response TV is much more costly in terms of expenditures per *respondent*. The "response rate" is far, far lower in direct response TV than in direct mail — typically, a minute fraction of one percent as opposed to response rates of one to fifteen percent experienced by most mailers.

Only a rare nonprofit organization with the broadest humanitarian appeal can make direct response television work cost-effectively today. But cable television, with its specialized programming and finely tuned audience segmentation, offers long-term possibilities.

Audio and Videocassettes

Home video was a $6 billion industry in 1989, already outstripping the box office receipts of the U.S. film industry. Two-thirds of all American households had one or more videocassette players. Fundraising appeals are now sometimes packaged in living sound and color on videocassettes and distributed to an organization's donors. Large institutions may even use video technology for donor acquisition.

Much cheaper audio cassettes are also occasionally used with success in fundraising. (When hundreds are reproduced at a time, audio cassettes may cost about $1 apiece, while videocassettes run approximately $4.) At additional cost, tape cassettes of either type can even be *personalized* if the narrator is extremely patient (or paid enough) to record every addressee's name.

Interactive 900-numbers

Here's an interesting and important variant on the more familiar toll-free 800-numbers. With 900-numbers, the caller pays a fee of from fifty cents to fifteen dollars to make the call, and the sponsoring organization later receives any net revenue that may be realized after the costs of the phone call are deducted. In current public interest applications, the typical charge to the caller is $3 while the cost to the organization of receiving and processing a call averages $2.35, including initial set-up costs, thus permitting a tidy profit.

900-numbers are potentially a low-cost (or even profitable) way to acquire names of qualified donor prospects. More important, they're also a means to provide services to donors or members at no net cost to your organization. You might offer a "legislative hotline," "calendar updates" or up-to-date information about several specific issues through one or more 900-numbers — and possibly turn a profit in the process.

The most interesting aspect of 900-numbers is their *interactive* capacity. With nothing more complicated than a Touch-Tone telephone — a tool now found in eighty-five percent of American homes — your donors can talk back to you. They can vote, order products or publications, pledge their support and participate in myriad other ways.

900-numbers have been used by the Natural Resources Defense Council, the National Rifle Association and the Better World Society, among others. One organization gathered hundreds of thousands of names and netted more than $500,000 from book sales through a 900-number early in 1989.

In mid-1989, however, 900-numbers were not yet in wide use. Long-distance carriers had only recently broadened access to the service, and service bureaus capable of meeting the many technical challenges were just gaining a foothold.

Electronic Funds Transfer (EFT)

EFT is a banking procedure most extensively used in Japan, where it is used in place of personal checking accounts. It's becoming increasingly widespread as a way to streamline business transactions and cash management in the United States. Already, some two billion transactions are made in the U. S. every year. Today, only a few consumers use EFT services to pay their bills, but twenty or thirty years from now we may all be doing so.

Applied to fundraising, EFT allows individual donors to authorize their banks to deduct fixed sums on a weekly, monthly, quarterly or annual basis and transfer them electronically to their charities' bank accounts. This is a little like asking your bank to pay the gas and electric bill every month — and, for the charity, it may look as good as a fat dividend from stock in the local utility company. Donors who typically contribute $30 to $50 a year may be willing to give $10 or $15 per month, or $120 to $180 per year, through EFT — a three- or four-fold increase. In some EFT fundraising programs, as many as one-third of the donors even authorize the bank to upgrade their contributions each year by ten percent or more — to help "fight inflation."

EFT is widely used in fundraising in Canada, where it's called "Pre-Authorized Chequing ("PAC"). In the United States, the EFT Corporation (La Jolla, Calif.) and a few similar specialized vendors have been working for years with a surprisingly small number of charities. Greenpeace and the National Rifle Association raise huge sums through EFT. Too few other nonprofits have had the foresight to adopt this ideal fundraising system.

With its 89 percent renewal rate, 97 percent pledge fulfillment, low collection cost (there are no reminders to send), and often dramatic donor upgrading, a monthly EFT pledge or sustainer program can be enormously profitable for a public interest group, even if only a tiny percentage of the donor file agrees to join. EFT's predictable cash flow is an important bonus to a nonprofit organization, and donors like its convenience.

However, most donors resist pre-authorized donations because they don't want to contribute every month and because they may distrust the electronic technology. Only your most dedicated supporters are likely to join if you offer them the choice — and even they may not jump at the chance. The result is that both money and time are required to convert even a small number of donors to EFT. And the catch is that such programs are normally cost-effective only after several hundred people have joined.

If you have 20,000 or more active donors, chances are a sufficient number will respond to a skillful appeal, enabling your organization to establish a cost-effective EFT system; eventually, you'll raise substantial funds through EFT, but it may take awhile to reap the rewards.

■ ■ ■ ■ ■

Many of the larger and more sophisticated direct mail fundraising programs make such extensive use of these new techniques and technologies that they could hardly get along without them. While some of these methods work only on a large scale and may require large investments, most are within reach of small and medium-sized organizations as well. If you turn up your nose at such things because they seem newfangled or slick, you may be making a big mistake. Fundraising today is a whole lot different from what it used to be — and it won't ever look the same again.

Inventing the Future of Fundraising

There is only a hint of the potential shape of fundraising in the 21st Century in today's video and telefax technology, survey research, on-line packaging and other methods to refine our targeting and zero in on finer and finer segments of the population with ever more precisely crafted appeals.

"Fiber optics" could change all our lives as dramatically as has the microchip. This cutting-edge technology, which transmits pulses of laser light through minute strands of transparent cable, was beginning to dominate long-distance telephone communications by 1989. But fiber optics holds much greater promise than making your cross-country calls clear as a bell and increasing the phone company's profits. Fiber optics may some day be the technological key to a nationwide communications system that is literally "the next best thing to being there."

The fiber optic network envisioned by the long-term planners at Bell Labs and in universities and think tanks has awesome potential. As Stewart Brand explained in his fascinating book, *The Media Lab*: *Inventing the Future at M.I.T.* (Penguin Books, New York, 1988), fiber optic cable has practically unlimited capacity to convey information in digital form. Unlike copper telephone wires and satellite dishes, a nationwide fiber optic cable network could simultaneously transmit *uniquely tailored messages* from millions of transmitters to millions of receivers. Virtually *all* information can be transmitted digitally via fiber optics — not just computer output and telephone conversations but high-definition television broadcasts, photographs, movies, magazine articles, newspapers, even money — and fundraising appeals.

Wired into a nationwide fiber optic cable network, your home communication system three or four decades down the road may be performing a great many seemingly unrelated functions. Such a system could take the place of today's television, cable TV hookup, telephone, answering machine, fax, home computer, security alarm system and bank ATM — as well as the carrier who delivers the newspaper to your door, the gas and electric meter-readers, and your friendly lettercarrier from the United States Postal Service. If current trends toward work at home continue, you may also be receiving and transmitting business correspondence through your home communication system. Here are just a few of the other products a fiber optic network is capable of delivering directly to you:

❏ a personalized daily newspaper printed in your home and containing news and features only about the subjects *you* want to read about;

❒ personalized magazines produced on your home communications system and specifically tailored to *your* interests;

❒ news and entertainment (including recently released "films") selected from among almost limitless broadcasters and scheduled according to *your* specifications;

❒ both voice and visual messages ("letters" or "tapes") replayed in sequence according to *your* priorities, many of them having been answered (or screened out) in accord with your wishes;

❒ advertising from local stores, direct marketers, publishers, entertainment companies and others to match *your* buying preferences, age, lifestyle, as well as any requests you may register on the system; and

❒ a bank statement delivered with the frequency *you* specify, detailing how much money has been transferred from your account to pay utilities plus any other bills *you* have approved.

In such a flexible system, *individually tailored* newsletters and fund appeals could be the order of the day. The most sophisticated nonprofit organizations and political campaigns may no longer think about "segmentation" but about *individual* donors' behavior and their *individual* preferences. The best fundraisers will make maximum use of a database that contains all the pertinent details about every donor's giving history. The copy, the graphics, the offer and the means of transmission of next month's appeal may be combined in nearly as many configurations as there are donors on the file. "Segments" may be purely coincidental.

The picture I've painted of a "wired" nation and its potential to turn technology toward meeting individual preferences is *not* farfetched. Consider these facts:

❒ Telephone companies all across the country have begun installing fiber optic cable in new housing and office developments and are beginning to replace the old twisted copper cables that still transmit most telephone calls. The day is not far off when fiber optics will be the dominant communications technology.

❒ Newspapers, supermarkets, banks and on-line database vendors, plus computer, telephone and cable television companies have all begun nibbling away at the technological edges of this fantasy. Most of them are hungry for more. Lawyers, too, have gotten into the act, as turf battles have erupted among phone and cable TV companies and other players in this unmapped territory. Business alliances are forming and shifting. As time goes on, the legal and financial issues will sort themselves out. Technology tends to make its way into our lives no matter who profits.

❐ In *Maxi-Marketing* (McGraw Hill, New York, 1987), Stan Rapp and Tom Collins described how direct marketers are already using ultra-sophisticated database systems to tailor their appeals to individual consumer preferences. Instead of identical "catalogs" mailed in large quantities to consumers in the mass, merchandisers are offering goods to *individuals* based on their recorded buying preferences and characteristics. And they're making more money that way.

❐ As long ago as 1984, an issue of a 900,000-circulation magazine, *Farm Journal*, was delivered in 8,896 different versions. Each was a specially tailored publication with its own unique editorial contents and advertising, assembled and bound in accordance with subscribers' preferences as well as with geographical differences. Other magazines have since adopted similar approaches.

❐ Political consultants have been targeting voters in this complex and flexible fashion for many years. They know that voting behavior is much more than a matter of party preferences, race or gender. Voters are *individuals*. Well-run political campaigns recognize that individual characteristics — including age, proclivity to vote, income level, home ownership and lifestyle — may individually or in combination have greater influence on a voter's decision at the polls than any of the more obvious and traditional characteristics. Political messages — especially those delivered by mail — may be segmented with seemingly infinite care to take individual differences into account.

Stewart Brand reports that if the visionaries at Bell have their way, fiber optics may be wired into ninety percent of American homes before a quarter of the 21st Century has gone by — just a moment away in historical terms. Before you know it, the whole fantasy could become real.

As that day draws nearer, there will be many new, sweeping changes that will profoundly change the character of fundraising. Among the trends whose beginnings are discernible today are the following:

❐ *The lines among advertising, public relations and fundraising will blur.* All organizations, whether or not they're operated for profit, will be forced to take a holistic view of the ways they communicate with their constituents. Nonprofit organizations and political campaigns, faced with demands from donors for information presented more selectively, will need to invest more in *communications*. Direct mail and telephone fundraising will come to be seen as primitive forms of two-way communication, which will become an intrinsic part of most advertising, PR and fundraising efforts. Alliances will form among specialists in all these fields, and new sub-specialties will emerge as use of the new technology becomes more widespread.

❐ The cashless society is slower in coming than predicted by futurists and trend-mongers, but it will eventually arrive because cash and checks are antiquated instruments that are slow and costly to process. The implications for fundraisers are significant. Larger, more easily adaptable charities and campaigns will gain added advantage over those that are too small to profit from EFT's economies of scale, or too slow to adopt new procedures. And as pre-authorized periodic giving through EFT becomes more widely accepted, taking bigger bites out of individual contributors' pocketbooks than the occasional gifts that are now the norm, donors may be willing to give to fewer causes and candidates.

❐   In the new, demand-driven environment, donor acquisition programs will become ever more expensive. Any lingering illusions that prospecting ought to be profitable will disappear. Most causes and candidates will invest in market research, and they'll spend more money acknowledging, surveying, informing, resoliciting, cultivating and upgrading their donors. In perception and in reality, donors' value will grow, placing a premium on researching individual donors as well. All but the newest and most action-oriented causes will wake up to the central importance of such sources of major gifts as bequests, planned giving and capital campaigns. The distinction between direct mail and major donor fundraising, already imprecise in many nonprofits, will eventually dissolve. As the challenges of public interest fundraising become more sophisticated, specialized education and higher salaries for fundraisers are also likely to become more common.

❐   In the face of these trends, donors in increasing numbers will become pro-active. On-line information or donor counseling services will come into existence to lead donors through the maze of organizations' conflicting claims. The latter-day equivalent of newsletters or consumer guides will provide reports or directories about organizations active in addressing particular issues in response to donor requests. The associations of nonprofit organizations and so-called charitable "watchdog" agencies will either learn to provide these needed services or wither in the face of competitive groups established by private foundations, state government or for-profit corporations. Such agencies will promote the *habit* of giving, allowing donors to make up their own minds about where to invest their charitable dollars. Some, such as regional United Way organizations or community foundations supporting many causes and institutions, may have no choice but to offer donors direct opportunities to earmark their contributions.

If fiber optics and allied technologies may eventually change much of what we take for granted in fundraising today, a great deal will remain fundamentally unchanged. Short of environmental collapse, nuclear war or massive dislocations in the American economy, the years ahead promise more of the same:

❐ *The lion's share of public interest funding will continue to come from individuals, not institutions.* Despite unfavorable changes in tax legislation, the generosity of American donors has set records every year. That trend is likely to continue for years to come, favored by lengthening lifespans and other demographic patterns that concentrate more and more of our society's disposable income in the hands of those over the age of fifty, who give most charitable contributions. Also, with Americans making more frequent career changes and increasing their leisure time, they are more likely to serve as volunteers for public interest causes and institutions, thus further increasing the chances they'll become active donors (since studies show volunteers support their charities more generously than do non-volunteers). Barring major tax changes or social upheavals, neither charitable foundations nor profit-making corporations — sources of institutional support favored in the United States — are likely to increase their support for public interest activities as quickly as are individuals.

❐ *Donors will become increasingly sophisticated.* Technical or legal hurdles may prevent us from realizing the type of one-on-one fundraising I've described above. But fundraisers will continually be forced to become ever more selective, using greater personalization and digging more and more deeply into their databases in search of buried treasure. "Mass-mail," now on its death bed, will soon writhe its last. Those cheap, generic direct mail packages used to attract donors' attention will become uneconomic for all but the few best-known causes and candidates; other organizations will have to work a lot harder to get their messages across.

❐ *Regulations to prevent charitable fraud will multiply.* State, and soon federal, officials will bow to public pressures and extend the reach of regulations limiting the freedom of action of nonprofit organizations and the consultants who serve them. Small or poor nonprofits, and small consulting firms, will find full compliance increasingly expensive — and, perhaps, eventually impossible. Without standardized forms and procedures — plus "grandfather" clauses that waive fees for small existing groups or some other device to cushion the blow on the vast majority of the nearly one million nonprofits in the United States — most will be forced to choose between complying with the law and closing their doors. Inevitably, like endangered species in an ecology whose balance has been suddenly upset, a great many will disappear. Small consulting firms may opt to seek non-regulated business in public relations, advertising or political consulting.

❑ *The need for public interest funding will, if anything, increase.* The cost of activities that attract many of the largest charitable gifts — health, education, human services, the arts — continue on a steeply rising curve. Political trends suggest that, for years to come, government under either party is more likely to encourage private initiatives to meet social needs than to legislate expensive new programs. Even after the United States finally joins the real world and institutes a national health care delivery system, the need for massive private support for health programs will remain virtually limitless, and the need for other social benefit programs will continue apace. Spurred by these developments, the "Third Sector" will continue to grow.

❑ *Fundraising will become increasingly internationalized.* There is growing recognition worldwide that environmental problems, the arms race, drug trafficking and terrorism are truly global problems. This recognition, spurred by the decrease in tensions between the superpowers, has dramatically broadened the outlook of many leading nonprofit organizations in the United States. After modest first steps in recent years, U. S. public interest groups — and their fundraising consultants — will expand their reach overseas, recognizing that international cooperation is essential if we are to solve the world's most pressing problems. Donors' dollars — and yen, marks, pounds and rubles — will cross borders more and more frequently as the independent sector in Europe, Australia, Japan, the Eastern Bloc and the Third World takes strength from better established voluntary associations in North America. With governments virtually everywhere slimming down in the face of budgetary limitations, the growth rates of nonprofit organizations overseas are likely to exceed those of groups within the United States as the ethic of voluntary private action simultaneously spreads across the globe.

In the new, more complicated world of public interest fundraising, what we know today as "direct mail fundraising" may no longer be recognizable to us after the turn of the 21st Century. Within our lifetime, the character of "mail" and the manner in which it is is delivered will surely be transformed. The mechanisms by which money is transferred from donors to public interest groups may eventually bear little resemblance to current methods, either. But some close analogue of direct mail fundraising will flourish.

Today, despite occasional complaints from many donors, despite the clumsiness of our efforts to target and personalize our appeals, direct mail remains the easiest and least intrusive means for people to learn about and respond to the needs of public interest organizations. To play a part in saving lives and making history, donors needn't suffer through rote appeals delivered on their doorsteps by scruffy canvassers, or eat rubber chicken and listen to boring speeches, or view documentaries in damp church basements. Direct mail fundraising is ideal for today's *busy* people. It's ideal, too, for elderly people, whose proportion in the U. S. population is rapidly increasing. Millions of Americans have come to rely upon direct mail as an easy and accessible way to participate in public life — even to vote.

Thirty years and more from now — in whatever direction new technology may take it — direct mail fundraising in some form will still be helping nonprofit organizations and political committees acquire, resolicit, and cultivate donors in large numbers.

Direct mail will continue to serve as the flexible tool it is. It will help public interest groups implement strategies of growth, involvement, efficiency, stability or visibility. Direct mail will continue playing a *strategic* role for the Third Sector for many decades to come, helping voluntary associations serve the public interest in ever more creative and responsive ways.

Glossary of Direct Mail Fundraising Terms

ACCOUNT EXECUTIVE. The individual who manages a client's direct mail fundraising activities on behalf of a consulting firm. (Also known as CLIENT CONSULTANT.)

ACQUISITION MAILING. A mailing to prospects to "acquire" new donors, members, or subscribers (also called PROSPECT MAILING).

ACTIVE DONOR. A DONOR whose last gift to an organization was received within the past twelve months (in some organizations, within thirteen, eighteen or twenty-four months).

ANNUAL APPEAL. For organizations with inactive direct mail fundraising programs, the year's single or principal fundraising appeal, typically mailed at the end or the beginning of the calendar year.

ASK, or ASK AMOUNT. Generally, the minimum (or most heavily emphasized) individual gift suggested in a fundraising PACKAGE. Not the total amount asked of all DONORS.

ATTRITION. The loss of donors due to death, illness, address changes, changing fortunes or changing priorities.

BACK-END PREMIUM. A free gift offered in exchange for a donation (generally, a donation above a certain minimum amount).

BACK-END SERVICES. The part of the direct mail campaign concerned with CAGING, CASHIERING, tabulating the results, sending DONOR ACKNOWLEDGMENTS or fulfilling promises made in the mailing, as well as with storing and updating the list of respondents.

BUCKSLIP. A small slip of paper — 3-1/2 x 8-1/2 inches is a common size — that fits into the PACKAGE and dramatically illustrates some particular feature of the OFFER, such as a free calendar or book (usually promised for gifts above a certain minimum amount).

BULK MAIL. Third class mail, which requires a minimum of 200 identical pieces per mailing. Qualifying nonprofit organizations pay discounted rates, currently about half those paid by business mailers.

BUSINESS REPLY ENVELOPE (BRE). A self-addressed envelope that guarantees payment of postage on receipt by the organization that prints it. (Also called POSTAGE-PAID ENVELOPE).

CAGING. Recording and tallying the raw information from direct mail, telephone fundraising or other DIRECT RESPONSE campaigns so that the responses may be analyzed and decisions made about future campaigns. Information tallied includes the identity of each donor, the date and amount of each gift and its source. Called "caging" after 19th

Century "post office desks," with their multiple cubbyholes or "cages" into which mail was sorted and classified.

CARRIER ENVELOPE. The outside envelope that contains the appeal letter and other components of the direct mail PACKAGE; also known as an "outer" or "carrier."

CASHIERING. Processing and depositing contributions mailed in response to a direct mail, TELEPHONE FUNDRAISING or other DIRECT RESPONSE campaign.

CHESHIRE LABEL. A strip of plain paper on which the addressee's name and address are imprinted by computer. Usually printed four across a sheet. Named after the machine that addresses, cuts and glues the labels onto envelopes or RESPONSE DEVICES. Currently, the most common form of addressing in direct mail fundraising.

CLIENT CONSULTANT. (Also known as ACCOUNT EXECUTIVE.) An employee of a consulting agency who manages a client's direct mail fundraising activities on the firm's behalf.

CLOSED-FACE ENVELOPE. An envelope that does not have a window. (See also WINDOW ENVELOPE.)

COMPILED LIST. A mailing list derived from publicly accessible sources such as directories, telephone books, or city and county records. Contrast with DONOR LIST.

CONTINUATION MAILING. A mailing to larger quantities of prospective donors on lists that have been tested first in modest quantities. (See also ROLL-OUT).

CONTROL PACKAGE. A direct mail acquisition PACKAGE that has performed successfully and against which any new acquisition package is tested.

COPY PLATFORM. A concept on the basis of which a direct mail PACKAGE is to be written. Usually spells out the ASK, the OFFER, the opening lines of the appeal letter and the envelope TEASER language, if any.

COPYWRITING. The creative process involved in conceiving, designing and writing a fundraising PACKAGE. Alternatively, the actual wording of the fundraising appeal.

DATABASE. A LIST of names, addresses and other information (in fund-raising, especially the giving history) maintained on a computer in such a way that selections may be made or the list ordered on the basis of numerous criteria. Sometimes, a database combines several lists on the basis of some common factor, such as source, into one merged, master list from which duplicates are eliminated.

DEMOGRAPHICS. The study of statistical data about groups of people, especially such characteristics as age, income, gender, religious affiliation and educational level.

DIRECT RESPONSE. A form of advertising that elicits a direct action by the recipient of the message. The advertising may be a letter, telephone call, newspaper or magazine ad, or radio or television spot; normally asks for response by mail or telephone.

DONOR. An individual who has contributed money to a nonprofit organization or political committee.

DONOR ACKNOWLEDGMENT. Acknowledges a DONOR'S contribution with a receipt and/or a thank-you letter or note, possibly with other inserts.

DONOR ACQUISITION COST. The difference between the cost of the mailing and the amount it generated in contributions, divided by the number of DONORS acquired. Expressed as dollars and cents per donor acquired.

DONOR BASE. The list of an organization's contributors.

DONOR CONVERSION. The process of persuading DONORS who have responded to an organization's PROSPECT MAILINGS with an initial gift to become active, regular or frequent donors to the organization.

DONOR CULTIVATION. A long-term process through which a nonprofit organization or political committee acquaints selected DONORS with its work and becomes better acquainted with the donors' needs and preferences, in hopes of eventually securing large donations.

DONOR FILE. Also donor list. A computer listing, or DATABASE, of the names, addresses, sources and contribution history of an organization's donors. Sometimes contains additional information, if available.

DONOR RECOGNITION. Any means by which a nonprofit organization or political committee publicly acknowledges a DONOR'S support. Examples are plaques and certificates, listings in newsletters or annual reports, screen credit in films and video presentations and mention at public events.

DONOR RESEARCH. Generally refers to the process of searching through information available to the general public (from such sources as newspapers, magazines and directories) to unearth facts about an organization's best specific, individual prospective DONORS of MAJOR GIFTS. Contrast with MARKET RESEARCH, which aims at *groups* of donors rather than individuals.

DONOR RESOLICITATION. An organization's letter or phone call requesting additional support from individuals who have previously supported its work. (Also called SPECIAL APPEAL or, sometimes, RENEWAL).

DONOR RETENTION. The ability to maintain individuals as active and continuing DONORS to an organization; also, the process of seeking that end.

DONOR SURVEY. An in-depth, quantitative study of the beliefs, attitudes, DEMOGRAPHIC and PSYCHOGRAPHIC characteristics of an organization's DONORS by means of statistically valid survey research techniques applied to a small sample of the DONOR BASE.

DUPE RATE. The percentage of names identified as duplicates or invalid addresses; also known as the MERGE FACTOR.

80-20 RULE. The maxim that the top twenty percent of an organization's DONORS contribute approximately eighty percent of its revenue, while the bottom eighty percent of the donors contribute just twenty percent.

ELECTRONIC FUNDS TRANSFER (EFT). A method whereby individual DONORS may instruct their banks to make automatic monthly or quarterly deductions from their accounts, which are transferred electronically to the accounts of the charitable organizations of their choice.

ELECTRONIC MAIL. A computerized system that prints, personalizes and distributes written fundraising appeals with great speed; usually used for urgent appeals.

FIBER OPTICS. A telecommunications medium that transmits digital information in the form of pulses of laser light through minute strands of transparent cable. Now coming into wide use across the United States, fiber optics is expected to be the predominant form of transmitting both voice and data over long distances in the 21st Century.

FILE. A computerized LIST.

FLASHCOUNT. A periodic statistical report of the results of an individual mailing that summarizes the returns for each list or KEYCODE by percent response, average contribution and other measures during a particular period of time, usually no more than a few months.

FOCUS GROUP. A method of qualitative research in which groups of up to twelve DONORS or DONOR PROSPECTS are methodically interviewed about their attitudes and reactions toward an organization or the materials it produces.

FORMAT. The size, shape and color of the envelope, the character of the inserts, and the extent (or lack) of PERSONALIZATION of a direct mail PACKAGE.

FORMER DONORS. Donors who have not contributed to an organization in two or more years (three or more years, for some organizations).

FREQUENCY. The number of times an individual has contributed to an organization, either cumulatively or within a specific period of time.

FRONT-END PREMIUM. An item included in a direct mail PACKAGE as an up-front "free" gift in order to encourage response. Typical front-end premiums are membership cards, stickers, decals, stamps, keychains, address labels, letter-openers.

FULFILLMENT RATE. The percentage of DONORS who actually send in checks in response to a TELEPHONE FUNDRAISING campaign or other fundraising effort which elicits PLEDGES rather than immediate cash gifts.

FUNDRAISING RATIO. The ratio of cost to revenue, expressed as a percentage; the cost of a dollar raised expressed in dollars and cents. A traditional method used to evaluate the efficiency of fundraising programs.

GEODEMOGRAPHICS. In fundraising, a method of targeting PROSPECTIVE DONORS based on the demographic characteristics revealed in Census data for residents of specific geographic areas, selected on the basis that their demographic profile closely matches that of an organization's previous DONORS. See also PSYCHOGRAPHICS.

GIFT CLUB or GIVING CLUB. An association or category established by a nonprofit organization or political committee that is limited to DONORS who contribute frequent or generous gifts, often receiving special benefits and/or DONOR RECOGNITION.

GIFT LEVEL. Generally, a measure of an individual DONOR'S capacity for future gifts based on the size of her past contributions. Such measurements may include the amount of the highest previous contribution, the total cumulative amount of all gifts received to date, or the amount of the most recent contribution.

HIGH-DOLLAR MAILING. Direct mail fundraising PACKAGES specifically designed to elicit above-average gifts, by using larger envelopes, extensive personalization and a high ASK, and mailed to very selective lists.

HOUSE FILE or HOUSE LIST. The names and addresses of an organization's active and recently lapsed DONORS, members, supporters and subscribers.

IMPACT PRINTER. A computer-driven printing mechanism in which metal or plastic characters directly strike the paper. Impact printers include "daisy-wheel" machines that make a typewriter-like impression, and "line-printers" that operate at very high speed and leave an often sketchy impression on the page, commonly associated with computer printers.

INDEPENDENT SECTOR. The term denoting the nonprofit world — that is, organizations that are neither governmental nor profit-making businesses. (A coalition of nonprofit organizations also operates under this name.) Also THIRD SECTOR.

INK-JET PRINTING. Printing (generally of a name, address and KEYCODE) executed by a high-speed printer that produces an image by spraying ink through small jets to imitate typewriter print.

INQUIRIES. In fundraising, individuals who have responded to an advertisement or a direct mail package with a request for information or a response to a survey but have not sent contributions.

INVOLVEMENT DEVICE. An element in a direct mail PACKAGE used to heighten interest in the package and to provide recipients with opportunities to use their hands or to participate in some way to assist the mailer. Common examples are petitions, "surveys," post cards addressed to decision-makers, stamps and stickers.

KEYCODE. A code consisting of letters and/or numbers assigned to a specific LIST or segment of a list for the purpose of tracking responses so the list's effectiveness relative to other lists may be evaluated. Usually printed on the mailing label or RESPONSE DEVICE. See also SOURCE CODE.

LAPSED DONORS. DONORS whose last gift arrived at least a year to eighteen months ago but no longer than two to three years ago. In some organizations, they're called LYBUNTS ("Last Year But Unfortunately Not This Year").

LASER PRINTING. In direct mail fundraising, a PERSONALIZED process of reproducing printed material that combines photocopier technology with computerized LIST MAINTENANCE techniques, permitting each sheet or printed impression to include information unique to one individual on a DONOR FILE.

LETTERSHOP. Sometimes called a "mailhouse." The shop in which the individual components of a mailing are collated, inserted and packaged for delivery to the post office. Lettershops also frequently address and affix postage to the mailing PACKAGES.

LIFETIME VALUE. Refers to the long-term value of a DONOR, member, subscriber or buyer from an organization's perspective. Calculated by one of several methods, this value provides guidance when setting investment levels in ACQUISITION MAIL.

LIFT LETTER. A second or supplementary letter included in a fund-raising PACKAGE to reinforce the message of the main letter or present an argument for a contribution from a different point of view. Often signed by a celebrity or other influential individual.

LIST. In direct mail, a DATABASE of names and addresses of individuals who share one or more characteristics, such as membership in or support of a given organization.

LIST BROKER. An agent who brings together LIST OWNERS and mailers to arrange the rental or exchange of mailing LISTS (in whole or part). Although the principal parties are the actual list owner and list user, the list broker acts on behalf of the mailer to make all necessary arrangements with the LIST MANAGER, who acts as the agent for the list user.

LIST EXCHANGE. An exchange of donor, member or subscriber LISTS between two organizations, generally on a name-for-name basis, with the two organizations usually mailing at different times.

LIST MAINTENANCE. The ongoing process of updating and correcting a DONOR FILE or other computerized mailing LIST.

LIST MANAGER. The organization or individual, often a LIST BROKER or direct mail consultant, who is responsible for the promotion and record-keeping necessary for the regular exchange or rental of a mailing list.

LIST OWNER. The organization or individual that owns rental or exchange rights to a mailing LIST.

LIST RENTAL. The arrangement through which a LIST OWNER furnishes names for one-time use only to a mailer.

LIST TEST. A random sampling of a LIST used to determine the cost-effectiveness of mailing to the entire list. In most fundraising applications, list tests are based on samples of between 3,000 and 10,000 names.

LIVE STAMP. An actual postage stamp affixed by hand or machine, usually either to a CARRIER ENVELOPE or to a reply envelope.

MAGNETIC TAPE. An early but now universally accepted electronic storage medium favored in the direct mail industry to record and reproduce via computer the data on a mailing LIST.

MAIL-RESPONSIVENESS. The propensity for an individual to respond to a sales offer or funding appeal sent by mail.

MAJOR GIFT. A significant and out-of-the-ordinary gift, which may be as little as $100 for some organizations or upwards of $1,000,000 for others.

MARKET. The intended audience of an appeal; the likely or potential supporters of an organization; the prospect LISTS that together comprise an organization's UNIVERSE.

MARKET RESEARCH. In fundraising, refers to DONOR SURVEYS, FOCUS GROUPS and other methods used to study the beliefs, attitudes, DEMOGRAPHIC and PSYCHOGRAPHIC characteristics of previous or potential donors, in order to understand how to devise and deliver more effective appeals for support.

MARKETING CONCEPT. The concept on which a fundraising PACKAGE is based. A capsule statement of the connection between the OFFER, the MARKET and the signer of the appeal letter.

MAXI-DONORS. Those DONORS who have recently and/or frequently given generous contributions.

MEMBERSHIP RENEWAL. A RESOLICITATION, used by organizations with formal membership structures, requesting payment of an individual's annual dues. Alternatively, a response to a dues notice, or a system to collect dues from the membership as a whole.

MERGE/PURGE. A computer operation that combines two or more mailing LISTS in a matching process to produce one FILE that is relatively free of duplicates and to measure the degree to which the component lists overlap with each other.

MERGE DUPES. Also MULTI-DONORS. DONORS, members or subscribers found on more than one PROSPECT LIST. In commercial direct mail, called MULTI-BUYERS.

MERGE FACTOR. The percentage of names identified as duplicates or bad addresses; also known as the DUPE RATE.

MULTI-BUYERS. See MULTI-DONORS.

MULTI-DONORS. Also MERGE DUPES. DONORS, members or subscribers found on more than one PROSPECT LIST. In commercial direct mail, called MULTI-BUYERS.

OFFER. In fundraising, the programmatic action and/or individual benefits promised by an organization to those who send contributions, dues or subscription payments; also known as the "pitch." Commercially, the terms under which a specific product or service is promoted by a mailer. In fundraising, the offer is the set of needs, promises, or assurances that justifies the ASK.

ON-LINE PACKAGING. A production method that integrates printing, PERSONALIZATION and bundling for the post office into one continuous process on an assembly line.

PACKAGE. A direct mail appeal, its wrapping and all its contents. Commonly consists of a CARRIER ENVELOPE, a letter, a RESPONSE DEVICE, a BUSINESS REPLY ENVELOPE (BRE) and may include other items, such as a brochure, news clipping, or a FRONT-END PREMIUM.

PACKAGE TEST. Testing one direct mail PACKAGE (or one of its features or characteristics) against those of another by mailing both to statistically equivalent groups of individuals chosen at random from the same LIST or lists.

PERSONALIZATION. The reproduction of a message on individualized materials that bear the recipient's name and (often) other unique, personal information as well; methods include LASER PRINTING, INK-JET PRINTING and other computer-driven technologies.

PLANNED GIVING. Using estate planning methods to formulate and schedule contributions by an individual DONOR, generally involving large or long-term gifts or bequests.

PLEDGE. In fundraising, a promise made by a DONOR or PROSPECT to contribute money at a later time. Both the amount and the date when the gift will be made may be either specified or unspecified. Used as either noun or verb.

PLEDGE CARD. Also called pledge reminder. In TELEPHONE FUNDRAISING, a notice sent to remind those who PLEDGE to contribute to an organization. A REPLY ENVELOPE is almost always enclosed.

PLEDGE PROGRAM. A system, often a GIFT CLUB, through which ardent supporters of a nonprofit organization or political committee may give regular, generally monthly, donations and often receive special benefits in return. Can be implemented through ELECTRONIC FUNDS TRANSFER. (Sometimes called SUSTAINER PROGRAM.**)**

POSTAGE-PAID ENVELOPE. A self-addressed envelope that guarantees payment of postage on receipt by the organization that prints it. (Also called BUSINESS REPLY ENVELOPE (BRE).)

PREMIUM. A product offered or given to a prospective DONOR, member or subscriber as an incentive to respond to a direct mail PACKAGE. See BACK-END PREMIUM and FRONT-END PREMIUM.

PRESSURE-SENSITIVE LABELS. Mailing labels, generally affixed by hand, that do not require water. Colloquially called "peel-off" or "peel-and-stick" labels.

PROSPECT. In direct mail fundraising, a prospective new DONOR. In MAJOR GIFT fundraising, any prospective donor, including an organization's previous contributors.

PROSPECT MAILING. A mailing to prospective new DONORS, members or subscribers to ask for their support; also called ACQUISITION MAILING or "cold mail."

PSYCHOGRAPHICS. In fundraising, a method of targeting prospective DONORS based on their demonstrated (or predicted) lifestyle choices or behavioral traits. See also GEODEMOGRAPHICS.

RECENCY. The date (or time period) during which a DONOR'S latest contribution was received.

RESOLICITATION or RENEWAL MAILING. An organization's letter or phone call requesting additional support from individuals who have previously supported its work. (Also called SPECIAL APPEAL or DONOR RESOLICITATION.)

RESPONSE or REPLY DEVICE. A form, generally restating the OFFER and bearing the addressee's name and address and a KEY-CODE, on which the recipient is asked to indicate the size of her gift and sometimes other information as well.

ROLL-OUT. Generally, a mailing to larger quantities of prospective DONORS on LISTS that have been tested first in modest quantities. More precisely, using all available names remaining on one or more pre-tested lists in a CONTINUATION MAILING.

SALTING or SEEDING LISTS. A practice employed by LIST OWN-ERS and LIST BROKERS for protection against misuse or theft. Names and addresses, usually fictitious, are inserted on the LIST so that the owner or broker receives copies of all mailings sent to the list.

SEGMENTATION. The process of subdividing a LIST into subdivisions or "segments" usually defined by such variables as RECENCY, FREQUENCY or GIFT LEVEL.

SELF-MAILER. A direct mail PACKAGE that requires no separate CARRIER ENVELOPE, usually either a piece of paper with multiple folds or a booklet format.

SERVICE BUREAU. A company that offers BACK-END SERVICES, typically including a variety of data processing services.

SOURCE CODE. A KEYCODE denoting the specific LIST or segment of a list from which a DONOR's name and address were originally derived.

SPECIAL APPEAL. An appeal for funds from previous DONORS or members that is not a MEMBERSHIP RENEWAL notice. Many organizations send special appeals several times per year.

SPLIT TEST. A test of any variable in a mailing (such as PACKAGE variations, the ASK or different postage rates) by splitting one or more LISTS or segments into equal numbers of statistically identical names and addresses to determine which approach works better than others. Also called an "A/B split."

SUSTAINER PROGRAM. A GIFT CLUB through which ardent supporters of a nonprofit organization or political committee may give regular, generally monthly, donations and often receive special benefits and/or DONOR RECOGNITION. Can be implemented through ELECTRONIC FUNDS TRANSFER. Also known as PLEDGE PROGRAM.

TEASER. A brief message on the CARRIER ENVELOPE used to pique the reader's interest or curiosity — and thus increase the likelihood that the envelope will be opened.

TELEPHONE FUNDRAISING. Sometimes (to the author's annoyance) called telemarketing. Calling previous DONORS or prospective donors by phone to ask for donations.

TESTING. The process of comparing results for dissimilar items by simultaneously mailing each item to an equal number of statistically identical names. For statistical validity, changes in only one variable may be tested in any one test, such as, for example, different rates of postage, different suggested minimum gift amounts, different TEAS-ERS, different colored envelopes, or the like.

TEST MAILING. An organization's initial effort to gauge its potential to mount a cost-effective direct mail fundraising program.

THIRD SECTOR. The term denoting the nonprofit world — that is, organizations that are neither governmental nor profit-making businesses. Also INDEPENDENT SECTOR.

UNIQUE NAMES. Those names and addresses remaining on a merged or combined mailing LIST for a PROSPECT MAILING after a MERGE/PURGE has identified and eliminated duplicates and invalid addresses.

UNIVERSE. The total number of names and addresses that comprise a mailing LIST. Also, the total number of names and addresses judged to be good prospects to support a nonprofit organization or political committee.

UPDATING. Adding, changing, or deleting information on a DONOR LIST to increase its accuracy.

UPGRADING. The process of inducing previous DONORS to increase the amount or FREQUENCY of their gifts.

WINDOW ENVELOPE. An envelope that reveals the name and address through a die-cut hole, or window. An envelope may have more than one window to show other features of the enclosed material.

WORD-PROCESSING. In direct mail, generally refers to PERSONALIZATION that employs IMPACT PRINTERS to mimic individually typed letters.

Reading List

The Fifteen Most Useful Books

The following is a list of fifteen books about direct mail fundraising, fundraising in general, and direct marketing. I've found them to be the most helpful books for understanding and applying the principles of direct mail fundraising in the public interest. They're listed in descending order, more or less matching the degree to which my coworkers and I have personally found them to be useful. The first two books stand out above the rest.

1. Lautman, Kay and Henry Goldstein, *Dear Friend*: *Mastering the Art of Direct Mail Fund Raising*, Second Edition. Washington, D.C.: The Taft Group, 1990.

2. Trenbeth, Richard, *The Membership Mystique*. Fund-Raising Institute, 1986. (Box 365, Ambler PA 19002.)

3. Kuniholm, Roland, *Maximum Gifts by Return Mail*. Fund-Raising Institute, 1986.

4. Huntsinger, Jerry, *Fundraising Letters*, Second Edition. Emerson Publishers, 1985. (Box 15274, Richmond VA 23227.)

5. Seymour, Harold J., *Designs for Fund-Raising: Principles, Patterns, Techniques*. New York: McGraw-Hill, 1966.

6. Klein, Kim, *Fundraising for Social Change*, Second Edition. Chardon Press, 1988. (P. O. Box 101, Inverness, CA 94927.)

7. Kobs, James, *Profitable Direct Marketing*, Second Edition. Chicago: Crain Books, 1979.

8. Ogilvy, David, *Ogilvy on Advertising*. New York: Crown Publishers, 1983.

9. Benson, Richard V., *Secrets of Successful Direct Mail*. The Benson Organization, 1987. (4 Baywood Lane, Savannah GA 31411.)

10. Brakeley, George A., Jr., *Tested Ways to Successful Fund Raising*. New York: American Management Association, 1980.

11. Flanagan, Joan, *The Grass Roots Fundraising Book*. Chicago: Swallow Press, 1977.

12. Rapp, Stan and Tom Collins, *Maxi Marketing*. New York: McGraw Hill, 1987.

13. Kotler, Philip, *Strategic Marketing for Non-Profit Organizations*. New Jersey: Prentice-Hall, Inc., 1975.

14. Maas, Jane, *Better Brochures, Catalogues, and Mailing Pieces*. New York: St. Martin's Press, 1981.

15. Gurin, Maurice G., *What Volunteers Should Know for Successful Fund Raising*. New York: Stein & Day, 1980.

The Nine Most Useful Periodicals

Among the many periodicals published for fundraisers, nonprofit executives, direct marketers, and political campaign managers, these nine have proven themselves consistently the most helpful in my work in direct mail fundraising for public interest organizations.

1. *Nonprofit Times*, P.O. Box 408, Hopewell, New Jersey 08525. Monthly, $39 annual subscription (but free to nonprofit executives and fundraisers).

2. *The Chronicle of Philanthropy*, 1255 Twenty-third Street, N.W., Washington, D.C. 20037. Bi-weekly, $57.50 annual subscription.

3. *Direct*, Box 4949, Stamford, CT 06907-0949. Monthly, $64 annual subscription (but free to "senior executives in the direct marketing industry.")

4. *FRI Monthly*, Fund-Raising Institute, Box 365, Ambler, PA 19002. Monthly, $48.00 annual subscription.

5. *Who's Mailing What!* P.O. Box 8180, Stamford, CT 06905. $168.00 annual subscription.

6. *Fund Raising Management*, 224 Seventh Street, Garden City, New York 11530. Monthly, $43.00 annual subscription.

7. *DM News*, 19 West 21st Street, New York, NY 10010. Monthly, $36.00 annual subscription.

8. *Grassroots Fundraising Journal*, 517 Union Avenue, Knoxville, TN 37902. Bi-monthly, $20 annual subscription.

9. *Campaigns & Elections*, 1835 "K" Street, N.W., Suite 403, Washington, D.C. 20006. Bi-monthly, $29.95 annual subscription.

Index

E

About the author

In 1979, Mal Warwick founded the direct mail fundraising agency that bears his name. **Mal Warwick & Associates, Inc.** (Berkeley, Calif.) is now a full-service direct mail fundraising firm offering management, consulting and production services to nonprofit public interest organizations and progressive political campaigns. Mal Warwick serves as President and Creative Director.

Warwick is co-founder and board chair of **The Progressive Group, Inc.** (Northampton, Mass.), which furnishes telephone fundraising services to nonprofit organizations and political committees.

Warwick is also founder and President of **Response Management Technologies, Inc.** (Berkeley, Calif.), a firm that provides "back-end" donor management services — caging, cashiering, list maintenance and data processing — to nonprofit organizations and political committees.

Clients of these three companies have included Jesse Jackson for President '88, The Environmental Defense Fund, Special Olympics International, The National Abortion Rights Action League, Bread for the World and more than one hundred other national public interest organizations. In 1989, the three affiliated companies employed a staff of more than 150.

Warwick is Vice-Chair of the Association of Direct Response Fundraising Counsel and is a member of the Direct Mail Fundraisers Association, the National Society of Fund Raising Executives, the American Association of Political Consultants, the Nonprofit Mailers Federation, and the Direct Marketing Association of Washington, D.C. He is a frequent speaker at gatherings of direct mail or fundraising professionals and has contributed to many fundraising and direct mail trade journals.

For nearly twenty years before founding his direct mail fundraising agency, Warwick was involved in grassroots politics and other public interest activities. He was a 1963 graduate of the University of Michigan and studied Latin American Affairs at Columbia University from 1963 to 1965. He served as a Peace Corps Volunteer in Ecuador from 1965 to 1969 and has traveled in more than forty other countries.

For two years, he served as Executive Editor of Alternative Features Service, a weekly news and graphics service for alternative newspapers which he co-founded in 1971. From 1976 to 1980, he was the community organizer and campaign manager for the 2,000-member Berkeley Citizens Action.

Warwick lives a bi-coastal life but maintains his home in Berkeley, California.